The Chilcotin War

MEL ROTHENBURGER

MR. PAPERBACK
LANGLEY, B.C.

MR. PAPERBACK
P.O. Box 3399,
Langley, B.C. V3A 4R7

First printing — May 1978

Canadian Cataloguing in Publication Data

Rothenburger, Mel, 1944-
  The Chilcotin War

  Bibliography: p.
  ISBN 0-88983-011-8 pa.

  1. Tsilkotin Indians - Wars. 2. Tsilkotin
Indians - Land tenure. 3. Indians of North
America - British Columbia. I. Title.
E99.T78R6   971.1'004'97   C78-002066-9

COVER: The painting depicting Klatassine and his followers attacking the work camp, was commissioned specifically for this book and painted by Manitoba artist Terry McLean.

Contents

Introduction

Modern Indian-White confrontations like Kenora and Two Springs, though widely separated geographically, have served to focus new attention on a problem that has existed since the two cultures first met and which continues to exist across the country.

It has often been said that Canada did not suffer the tremendous upheavals experienced by our neighbors in the United States in settling the West. We did it without tragic wars against the native tribes that tarnish American history.

This may be true, but the fact that Canada escaped this high degree of bloodshed does not mean justice was always done. As the Hudson's Bay Company extended its empire west, it implemented a policy toward the Indians similar to that of the Victorian father—'spare the rod and spoil the child.' The fur trading base eventually gave way to the rush for gold, but the attitude remained substantially the same and in some ways intensified. What the Europeans did believe was that God put the resources of the country there for them to gather up, and that the natives were inferior savages who could not be allowed to stand in the way.

While the clash of these two cultures resulted in surprisingly little violence, it was there, usually involving brief and unspectacular confrontations. In B.C., the Indians became dependent on their White masters so that seldom were they inclined or able to resist.

7

Occasionally one of the more isolated tribes would make trouble. One of these groups lived on the Chilcotin plateau west of the Upper Fraser River. The Hudson's Bay Company had not been able to successfully induce them to enter the fur trade, and they were not in the direct path of the gold rush. Thus, when in the early 1860s Whites suddenly expressed interest in their land, the shock of this thrust was difficult to absorb, and the scene was set for violent conflict. The Chilcotin War, as it was called, is a relatively short page in the province's history which has largely been forgotten. But it was one of the most concerted efforts by B.C. Indians to fight back against the mysterious and destructive forces of European culture. It is representative of the injustices perpetrated upon the Indians of B.C. and of the misunderstandings which have continued to prevail.

By coincidence, it was the Chilcotins who became the accidental cause of the intensification of efforts by modern B.C. Indians to regain what they consider to be their rights.

On November 28, 1971, a Chilcotin Indian named Fred Quilt was driving home from Anahim Lake with some other members of his family after a party. Two RCMP officers came upon his stalled truck and Quilt was pulled from the cab. Two days later, Quilt was dead. His family, and the thousands of B.C. Indians who joined the cause, claimed that the death was caused by a savage kicking from one of the policemen.

A first inquest exonerating the RCMP was quashed after it was found that two of the jury members had police connections. In August 1972, Indians from around the province gathered in Kamloops for the second inquest. At their various meetings and in statements to the press, their leaders claimed the death of Quilt represented all that was corrupt about white society in its dealings with the Indians. Forty-six witnesses were called and over 50 exhibits were entered during 13 days of testimony—the most extensive inquest into a death ever, for an incident which lasted only a minute and a half.

The policemen were again cleared, much to the distress of the Indian activists. While it may have been clear that the two policemen did not, in fact, purposely inflict death-causing injury to Fred Quilt, the situation surrounding the incident grew out of improper or non-existing Indian policy perpetrated through the decades. The Chilcotin War of 1864 is an example of this insufficiency.

A large amount of written material about the Chilcotin uprising has fortunately been preserved in the form of newspaper articles, reports and correspondence. What was lacking was the compilation and co-ordination of this material. It is unfortunate that the written sources are not matched by photographic documentation of the actual conflict.

I offer particular thanks to the staff of the University of B.C.'s Special Collections Department and the Provincial Archives of B.C. for their assistance in helping me locate relevent information; to Cariboo College historian Chuck Bishop of Kamloops for reading the manuscript and suggesting changes; and to the Canada Council for providing a grant which made most of the research work on this book possible.

Mel Rothenburger

The sun was not yet up on the morning of October 26, 1864, when Rev. Robert Christopher Lundin Brown arose and hastened to the jail at Quesnellemouth on the upper Fraser River.

He shuddered as the cold penetrated his thick clothing. The sky was clear—it would be a bright frosty day.

The makeshift jail consisted of a dirty log cabin with one end partitioned for a cell. Inside, the jailer and three guards were warming their hands over a small pot-bellied heating stove.

The priest exchanged greetings with them and, without removing his coat, walked to the cell. Deep, lowing voices found his ears. Heat from the stove penetrated only a few feet and at the other end of the cabin the air remained extremely cold, which was just as well considering the stench radiating from the cell.

The jailer unlocked the heavy door and pulled it open. The lack of light inside contrasted even with the greyness of the early morning and Brown paused in the doorway to allow his eyes to become accustomed to it. But he could never get used to the foul, heavy air in this fetid place which had been the home of his five charges for the past two months.

The first time Brown entered this place weeks ago he had been frightened, despite the fact the five Chilcotin Indians were securely shackled to the walls and could do little but squat on the dirt floor in the dark all day long. They were fierce-looking creatures, their strange dress and appearance grotesque by white civilized standards. But the priest had soon uncovered an inherent innocence in these murderers to which he could not remain entirely unsympathetic.

This morning, they were already at their prayers, with the the voice of Klatassine, their war chief, rising above the others in icy breaths. They injected a sort of wailing into their prayers as they would have in their customary death chant, and the voices, now soft, now rising in pitch, presented an eerie sound.

In two hours they would be dead.

Lundin Brown entered and asked if they were ready to receive Holy Communion. They were, and he said the main parts of the service in their own language, of which he had learned enough for this purpose, and said the rest in English. The prisoners knew the service well enough to understand the meaning.

After they were finished, the Indians were given breakfast, then led outside by the jailer and guards to be pinioned. As they went out, Brown shook hands with each, saying a farewell. Piell (Klatassine's son) went first, then Chessus, then Tahpitt, Tellot and Klatassine.

As the big straps were fastened on them, pinning their arms to their sides, Piell wept, undoubtedly thinking of his wife and son. Chessus was as stern looking as he had always been, but he had gradually changed so that he was not as much the undisciplined savage. Tahpitt fidgeted slightly, but Tellot and Klatassine were stoical, resigned.

Before his arms were pinioned Klatassine grasped the hand of the priest once again and thanked him.

"You are my son and I will ever remember you, and we will meet again in a place where we will understand each other and need no interpreter," said Brown. "Keep a stout heart and think of Christ and lean on him."[2]

"Sotselne'tle," Klatassine replied quietly. "Take care."

Brown was talking to Piell when he heard one of the guards offer Klatassine a drink. The big Indian shook his head. It was offered again and he refused, but when the guards urged him again to drink, the priest interrupted.

"We must not press him. He doesn't need it."

It was time. The prisoners were lined up to be led to the scaffold which had been built nearby.

"Jesu Christ nerhunschita sincha coontesse—Jesus Christ be with thy spirits," the priest said to them.

Two hundred and fifty miners, merchants, and Indians watched as the condemned man walked toward the gallows a few minutes before 7 a.m.

Mrs. Lyette Allard Boucher, one of the audience, saw that Piell was visibly shaken. The other four appeared calm.

*   *   *

The circumstances which formed the backdrop to that day in the Fraser River gold rush district of British Columbia, were rooted in the very beginnings of the white man's invasion of Indian territory in the Pacific Northwest.

It was difficult for the native tribes to understand the Europeans' conviction that the whites had a God-given right to take the land, that the resources had been placed there to await the arrival of a superior society and culture.

Tragedy was almost inevitable.

When the Hudson's Bay Company was first making contact with the Chilcotin[3] Indians on their vast plateau west of the upper Fraser River in attempts to establish a fur trade with them, Alfred Waddington was a young man carving success for himself in industrial Europe. A native of London, he had received his education in England, France, and Germany. His business interests had included cotton-milling, steel manufacturing, and mining. He was 48 years old when he heard about the gold discoveries in California. Still a bachelor, he disposed of all his possessions and joined the stampede.

In San Francisco he held a partnership in the large wholesale grocery firm of Dulip and Waddington. But in 1858 the stories of a new gold strike in New Caledonia (proclaimed the colony of British Columbia later that year) sent hungry prospectors flocking north. That spring Waddington sailed for Victoria on Vancouver Island to establish a branch of the business. He found that "everybody was bound for Victoria" and he was not impressed with his fellow emigrants. "Victoria was assailed by an indescribable array of Polish Jews, Italian fishermen, French cooks, jobbers, speculators of every kind.... To the above lists may be added a fair seasoning of gamblers, swindlers, thieves, drunkards, and jail birds, let loose by the Governor of California for the benefit of mankind, besides the halt, lame, blind and mad."[4] Some 20,000 people made the trip that summer.

In this bustling centre of commerce which had started as a quiet Hudson's Bay Company fort, Waddington became a successful businessman and land-owner, served briefly in the legislative assembly of the colonial government and was considered for mayor.

Since 1843, when James Douglas began construction of Victoria as a Hudson's Bay Company fort, the island community had taken only a few years to gain an important position in business and commerce. After his own arrival, Waddington saw Victoria almost literally burst out of the walls of the fort and spread onto the surrounding land. Soon the fort itself was all but gone. There were houses and stores and public buildings, hotels and shanties and tents. Many offices and stores were simply branches of San Francisco businesses, as was the case with his own. Since the goldseekers wanted only supplies and temporary lodging in Victoria before heading for the new El Dorado, the town's population was largely transient, but the trade from the steady flow of Americans kept the boom going.

Meanwhile, this new British colony, formed out of New Caledonia and the Queen Charlotte Islands in 1858, also made progress. Queen Victoria had chosen for it the name British Columbia, but it took more than a name and lines on a map to fashion an economic entity.

The job of turning a fur-trading territory into a viable colony fell initially to the Royal Engineers, a prestigious corps first formed centuries before. Colonel Richard Clement Moody, a former governor of the Falkland Islands, brought 165 men to British Columbia and started building a town on the north bank of the Fraser River a few miles upstream. First called Queens-borough, it was quickly renamed New Westminster. The townsite was located in a dense evergreen forest which had to be cleared for streets and lots, but slowly a new capital emerged.

The engineers also acted as a police force, and became road-builders for the colony. Lieutenant Henry Spencer Palmer, a surveyor in his early twenties who had come from England with the second detachment of Royal Engineers in the autumn of 1858, mapped out a wagon road to replace a trail between Port Douglas (on the north end of Harrison Lake) to Lillooet. In 1860 the Dewdney Road from Hope to Similkameen opened, and in 1862 construction started on the famous Cariboo Road up the treacherous Fraser Canyon.

The gold rush, which had originally started in the Thompson River country, leapfrogged around until the discoveries at Williams Creek brought it to a climax. This early emphasis on road-building played a large part in getting miners from the B.C. capital to the Cariboo.

Old Waddy, as Waddington was popularly known, became intrigued with the idea of a route to the Cariboo gold fields shorter than those through the Fraser Canyon from New Westminster.

One day as he lay in bed swollen and sore from one of his frequent attacks of gout, he spread out a map of B.C. and looked at the ragged coastline. Of the dozens of fiords, two caught his eye as cutting deeper toward the Chilcotin plateau than the rest—Burke Channel and Bute Inlet. Either could provide access to the plateau if a road or trail could be built up out of its gorge. Waddington also found that of all the inlets, these two were the only ones whose heads did not terminate so abruptly as to make passage into the connecting river valleys impossible.

Taking out a ruler, the old entrepreneur marked in some lines from Burke Channel, Bute Inlet and the Fraser River routes to Alexandria. Besides being short, the Bute Inlet route had the advantage of fast water access from Victoria. Burke Channel looked to be more than twice the distance that Bute Inlet was from Victoria.

His business required a considerable amount of travel around the mainland and the island, and during one of his visits to Nanaimo, Waddington spoke with a Hudson's Bay Company agent named Mark Bate. The HBC man had been at Nanaimo since 1857. He and others had sent an expedition to Bute Inlet in 1860 to pre-empt land, but the land had not been held. Waddington listened with interest to Bate's descriptions of the inlet gleaned from the limited exploration that had been done.

Major William Downie, a respected explorer, had failed to discover a pass from Bute in the summer of 1861, but, nevertheless, Waddington's infatuation with the concept of punching a road through from the sea at Bute Inlet to the interior grew. He, Alfred Waddington, would break the back of the Cascade range and open the way like a floodgate to the wealth of the Inland plains and gold fields. Besides being a short, quick route to the William's Creek mines, a Bute Inlet road could open up hundreds of thousands of acres for ranching. It would be a profitable enterprise and it would also secure for Victoria the commercial supremacy which New Westminster threatened to take away.

As New Westminster became an established though somewhat crude centre, there developed an intense and extremely bitter rivalry between the B.C. capital and Victoria. Waddington was well aware of the benefits his proposed route would have for his city and he sent his own exploring parties to seek a way through. They were more successful than Downie had been.

The result was the formation, by Waddington and several

Victoria investors, of the Bute Inlet Wagon Road Company Ltd. When they applied to B.C. for the toll road charter, Douglas, as governor of both the colonies, felt compelled to allow it even though it would compete with his own prized road projects leading from New Westminster. Col. Moody, as land commissioner for B.C., was not in favor of a road that would benefit Victoria, but the charter was granted and construction started in 1862.

The first objective was to get a pack trail completed from Bute Inlet to Alexandria. That required cutting through evergreen forest, traversing innumerable streams and blasting through sheer canyons for a distance of 80 miles up the valley of the Homathko[5] River, finally emerging onto the plateau. Some 40 miles further north the route would join up with the old trail running west across the plain to Alexandria. In total, the new route would cover 158 miles by land and 83 by lakes and rivers, plus 222 miles by sea between Victoria and Bute.[6]

The scenery of the Bute Inlet fiord fascinated Waddington almost as much as the grandeur of his project. He had now made several trips to it, and each time he stood on the deck of a ship or sat in a canoe looking up at the mountains forming the inlet, he was awed by their power. To his romantic mind the snow-streaked walls of rock reached upward like gothic buttresses. Beyond their seemingly impenetrable ridge lay the giant washboard of the Cascades barring passage to the Chilcotin plateau. He had the means to conquer these magnificent obstacles of Nature.

This feeling of exhilaration must have surged through him once again as the Hudson's Bay Company steamer *Enterprise* moved up Bute Inlet on April 24, 1863. He was on his way to the head of the inlet with a hundred men to renew the work interrupted by the previous winter.

The 62-year-old Waddington stood slightly stooped, bracing his 5 ft. 7 inch frame against a rail, wind rushing through the greying sideburns which stretched under his throat, grey-blue eyes looking out from his homely face upon the panorama of the mountains.

An acquaintance who had reviewed the work on the trail shortly before the workmen had retired back to Victoria the previous winter had been amazed both at Waddington's energy and his optimism.

"Mr. Waddington feels the utmost confidence in the success of his enterprise, and I am inclined to think and to hope he will not be disappointed, for his energy and activity and the pluck of a game cock that he displays deserves to be rewarded. He is

16

too much disposed to view things through a rose-colored glass and to regard the conception and execution of a favorite project as synonamous (sic) for getting, that though it is not an easy matter to give intelligent orders, it is infinitely more difficult to have them carried out."[7]

As the *Enterprise* approached the head of the inlet, evening was closing in, but the sight was still impressive. Another traveller, George Grant, described the scene at a later time: "Here and there, rifts in the mist, as it was broken by projecting peaks, revealed mountain sides curtained with glaciers. The only sound which broke the awful stillness was the muffled thunder of cataracts...gleaming far up among the scanty pines, washing down the slippery rocks in broad white bands, or leaping from bluff to bluff an hundred feet at a time, for more than a thousand feet down to the sea. We were at the head of Bute Inlet. The salt sea water could cut no deeper into the range that guards the western side of our continent. The mountains stood firm except where the Homathko cuts its way through, in a deep gorge, sentinelled on each side by snow-clad warders."[8]

When the *Enterprise* entered the Homathko River and steamed up to the proposed townsite, Waddington was "not a little surprised"[9] to find a long row of huts stretching along the bank.

Alexander McDonald, a settler who had started a farm on Puntzi Lake at the junction of the Bute and Bentinck Arm trails, had come down Waddington's route in the dead of last winter and found that a number of Chilcotin Indians had erected their tent-like gabled houses of brush and bark in Homathko Indian territory.

But the Indians had never camped in this particular spot and Waddington had not expected to see 250 Chilcotins, Euclataws, Homathkos and Klayoosh Indians encamped on the very site he had chosen for the town that would be named after him.

The friendly Homathkos were quickly called on to prove their worth, however. In the failing light, the captain of the *Enterprise* drove her bow into a muddy bank near the townsite. The Homathkos, under their chief Nunimimum, came out with their canoes and willingly helped transfer some of the provisions to shore. It would take some doing to unload the 19 mules and grey bell mare that were to be used for packing.

Waddington determined to get the Indians off his property. Corporal P.J. Leech of the Royal Engineers was here to survey and lay out the streets of the town, and there were houses to be built. Lots would soon be going on the market.

Even a year before, the sharing of a campground by these tribes could never have taken place. The warlike Euclataws from Cape Mudge and the Homathkos co-existed well enough. The Euclataws now frequently occupied territory further up the Homathko which had been forsaken by the Homathkos and their Klayoosh cousins for the mouths of that river and the Memeya,[10] which entered the inlet three miles from its head. But the Chilcotins, who held all the territory from The Canyon (30 miles upriver) north and onto the plain, were deadly enemies of the Euclataws.

The Euclataws were wary of the work party of 80 men Waddington had sent up to start the trail the previous season and the whites, or King George men as the Indians called them in Chinook trade language, came close to getting embroiled in an Indian war. The Euclataws had stolen the 11-year-old daughter of a chief of the Ansanies, a band of Chilcotins. Waddington, however, was able to intervene and establish a shaky peace between the enemies, who now visited and traded with one another on a limited basis.

Since the Coast Indians did not speak Chinook, Waddington would have to parley with the Chilcotins. There was a marked contrast between the Coast Indians and those of the plateau. The Homathkos were comparatively well-dressed in old soldiers' uniforms and white men's suits, and most carried blankets. Some painted their faces black on one side and vermillion on the other.

The Chilcotins, in comparison, were a haggard-looking group. The situation seemed something of a paradox since the Homathkos had been introduced to white men considerably later. In addition, the Chilcotins were more willing to work; it was for that reason Waddington had encouraged them the year before to come down to the inlet.

Despite their impoverished state, the Chilcotins maintained a certain latent ferocity in their appearance. Generally stout and broad-chested, but sinewy, they wore bone rings through their noses and often smeared their faces and bodies with a sort of sooty grease this time of year for protection against wind and sun. The squaws had flattish foreheads purposely deformed in infancy to make it easier to bear the straps of heavy packs which they spent much of their adult lives carrying.

Most wore blankets and were in various states of nudity from the waist up or down, with buckskin breeches, shirts or robes. A few wealthier ones sported wolf-skin robes, and fringes of squirrel or marten fur on their tangled black hair, which was either worn short or braided by the men, long and braided by the women. Necklaces or earrings of shell or bear claw completed the dress.[11]

Waddington sought out Tellot,[12] a minor Chilcotin chief from near Tatla Lake on the plateau, and presented him with a traditional "cultus potlatch" of tobacco. The small, withered, middle-aged chief produced a small package wrapped in several pieces of flannel. It contained a piece of the Illustrated London News of 1847 with a picture of two ships leaving England—Sir John Franklin's party for the Arctic. On the margin was written: "Tellot, Chilcoaten (sic) chief, a good guide— faithful and trustworthy." It was signed by Capt. Thomas Price, a Royal Engineer who had headed an exploration party through the Chilcotin region.

It was found that the Chilcotins had been anxiously awaiting the arrival of the Waddington party and were highly disappointed upon being informed they would not be required for packing. They looked on the mules with some disgust.

The Euclataws, on the other hand, were positively hostile to the appearance of the whites. They had attacked and killed other white parties before. But the sight of a hundred strong men unloading the big sea-going ship, aided by the Homathkos, was enough to stop them from causing any real trouble.

After a few hours the entire lot of them—Euclataws, Chilcotins, Klayoosh and Homathkos—began gathering up their belongings and tearing down their lodges to move out of the way. They had a few gifts from Waddington to encourage them.

Waddington could now get on with organizing things. Two log houses had already been built the previous year on the swampy flat picked for the townsite on the east side of the river. More houses, a frame store and a wharf were needed in addition to work on the trail. Among the party of men he had brought up were three stowaways discovered during coaling at Nanaimo who had been taken on to work, and four settlers intending to pre-empt land for farming and ranching.

Before work had been stopped the previous winter, 23 miles of trail 10 feet wide on the east side of the Homathko had been completed with the exception of a couple of short sections. Above that a few more miles had been blazed.

The Enterprise was finally freed from the muddy bank after 26 hours and the unloading was completed. It took the entire weekend to get the mules, lumber, food, implements, drills and other equipment sorted out and the men organized.

Waddington however, had sent up the first road party the day after arrival.

Leaving the camp to fend for itself, the *Enterprise* set out for Victoria. Everything appeared to be going smoothly, but on the Sunday Waddington discovered quite a commotion taking place in the Indian village which had been transported half a mile or so downriver.

Investigating, he found several of the natives roaring drunk, screaming, stumbling around, and generally getting out of hand. A small plunger which had been seen at the head of the inlet the day before was undoubtedly the source of the problem.

Waddington angrily gathered up ten armed men, including his works foreman William Brewster, and went looking for the plunger in a big 35-ft. cedar canoe purchased from a Stikine Indian. He had brought up French voyageurs especially for handling this craft. The men had been paddling their flat-bottomed canoe less than half an hour before they came upon the plunger in the inlet not far from the mouth of the river.

But there was no liquor on board and Waddington suspected it had been hidden somewhere on shore as a precaution, "for nothing was found but an empty 20 gallon keg with about a glass of some infernal mixture in it."[13]

The whiskey trade was a curse which unfortunately had become big business on the B.C. coast and was increasing inland with the gold rush. The brew had little resemblance to real whiskey, containing various combinations of alcohol, nitric acid, chewing tobacco, soap, ink, molasses, pepper, blue vitriol, and just about anything else that could be found to give it body. What it lacked in alcholic content the stuff made up in strength, and it was enough to drive any poor Indian foolish enough to drink it mad for a few hours, or kill him.

The only people on the boat were a young white man and his squaw, and he was anything but cooperative. He was ordered to leave the area immediately or have his boat confiscated. After taking down Waddington's and Brewster's names and threatening to see them in court, he sailed away down the inlet.

Waddington could do without drunken Indians getting into fights. He was happy to learn later from a few of the Indians that some of those responsible for the murders of white men in the past few months on the coast had been apprehended by British naval gunboats. Reports of the outrages, some of them evidently brought about by the whiskey trade, had poured into

Victoria over the last year. A trading schooner had been boarded by Coast Indians and the crew members murdered, the goods plundered. Another party of whites barely escaped on a schooner after killing three Stikine Indians in self-defense. On the southern end of the Princess Royal Islands which hugged the coastline across from the Queen Charlottes, the head of a European had been found on the beach. The body was discovered, partially naked and badly mutilated, a short distance away.

Incidents such as these had prompted the *British Colonist* of Victoria to speculate about an Indian war. "The murders and robberies," stated the *Colonist* in an editorial, "go to show that the naturally lawless spirits of the Indians fired by the rotgut whiskey supplied to them by villainous whites are fast breaking through the bounds of moral restraint to which a wholesome dread of the law has confined them for some years, and are preparing to work great mischief to the whites. Some of the tribes told the plundered men that they wanted satisfaction for friends lost by smallpox and other diseases caught from the whites. Others said that they were determined that the whites should not settle on their lands or mine their rivers, or frighten away the game, while another class, inbred assassins and thieves, appeared to murder and rob from actual love of the avocation."[14]

Waddington, since his project involved an invasion of territory previously held virtually undisturbed by Indians, was therefore wary of things like rotgut, but he was confident he could get along with the natives. His accomplishment of the year before in establishing peace between tribes who had warred for decades was evidence of that.

As it turned out, there were no repetitions of the incident with the plunger, and Waddington's men began making good progress. Some of the bridges built across the many streams dropping into the Homathko had been damaged by the weight of the snow and there were delays while they were repaired. One 66-foot span had to be almost entirely rebuilt.

The trail itself was pushed on another seven miles to a point where the mountain suddenly closed in on the east side of the river. This was the approach to The Canyon, a mile and a quarter of sheer granite bluff. Here, the trail would have to skip over to the opposite bank to continue upstream. The men started building a scow which would be attached to a line running across the river, and which would be capable of transporting supplies and animals. A log cabin would be built for the ferryman, who would live there full-time during the season.

The lower part of the trail was beginning to look quite settled. About five miles from the townsite Waddington took up ten acres for the road company and built a house, calling it the Camp, or Slough, of Despond. The name was chosen due to an outbreak of dysentery among the workmen who built it. For the first few weeks the Camp of Despond served as a station for forwarding stores as the trail progressed. It was the highest point on the river that could so far be travelled comfortably by canoe. A settler took up 120 acres nearby and built a house. A workman took 30 acres a few miles away and put up a house with the help of friends on Sundays.

Parts of the trail required considerable corduroying where it ran over swampy ground, but as far as it extended, it was put in good condition.

Corporal Leech travelled up and down the trail and surveyed the Waddington townsite. By the latter part of May he had laid out a grid of three streets running roughly parallel to the river, and seven cross streets.

"It will be big enough to contain any number of inhabitants and the neighbouring flat which is being explored and surveyed contains the richest garden and meadow ground," Waddington stated proudly.[15]

Some of the settlers began burning and tilling part of the meadow, since they had brought up a horse. Feed was also available on the opposite side of the river in another large meadow luxuriant with peavine. Except for spring flood season, horses or mules could swim across the river at that point.

The weather, not too hot, was favorable for working. The frame store was put up and Waddington also had a large log house built. Settlers built two more, making six houses in all at the townsite, the layout of which still had to be formally approved by Lands Commissioner Col. Richard Clement Moody. A pile driver was made for construction of a 40-foot wharf.

Waddington was confident the trail through The Canyon would be finished by the end of June, and, as that was the only big obstacle, travellers could then start using the route. Fifty men were still working on the trail.

This promising beginning did not follow through to an easy and early completion, however. In the middle of June, Waddington came down with another attack of gout which laid him up for three weeks. That was only the beginning of the old man's problems.

Early one Sunday morning a few workmen from Canyon Camp at the ferry started out on a hike up a high mountain to get a view of the surrounding country, especially The Canyon. They were accompanied for a short distance on the trail by three workmen who were leaving the wagon-road company's employment to go to the Cariboo with seven others.

When those who were remaining left the trail to head up the mountain, they bade the other three goodbye. One of them, Frederick John Saunders, the crew's commissary, described the adventure: "After several hours hard travelling, we rested for the view, and the sight was worthy of the trip. Looking far into the distance coastwise, could be traced the deep, dark array of magnificent forest growth, fringing the bank of the winding river down the valley, hemmed in by innumerable peaks of many heights, and when turning towards the interior, was to be seen distinctly, through a wide gap in the mountainous range, a gradual depression of the mountains, terminating into wide stretches of apparently verdant prairie land, presenting a scene of some relief as it were to the rugged, broken and entangled mass of the surrounding country. Eager for a glimpse of the big canyon on the return, we descended in its direction, and the grandeur of the sight can hardly be forgotten by those who saw the deep, dark, stupendous walls of rock, from whence came the echo of that solemn noise of the impetuous torrent below, never ceasing in its vibration; or hushed into repose, till passed the gateways of the enormous chasm. Our curiousity was much satisfied with these peeps of Nature's works and being well scratched all over, and disgracefully ragged, we arrived in camp at nightfall, hungry and weary."[16]

Saunders and his companions had a clear picture of why The Canyon was going to be so difficult. But the men who attempted to reach Alexandria found that the rest of the route could be inhospitable as well.

New to the country, they had to depend entirely on their guide, one of Alexander McDonald's ranch hands. After taking the party up the east branch of the Homathko[17] instead of the west, as directed by Waddington, and getting everybody lost over a period of eight or ten days, the guide deserted with one of the men who had been employed by Waddington as a blacksmith for the mules.

That left the hapless party to its own resources. After 23 days in the mountains, they made it back to Bute Inlet, living skeletons. In the last few days before reaching safety, the only food they had had was a wood rat and an old leather purse which they cooked. One of the men was so weak he could barely stand, and had he not been packed on the back of a Chilcotin Indian the last several miles he probably would not have survived.

The fiasco was quite a blow to Waddington, for he had hoped to show that his route could be easily travelled, but he could at least blame it on the guide and not the trail.

By then, The Canyon was being temporarily abandoned as a route. It became obvious it would be impossible to blast through it by the end of the year let alone during the summer. Now it would be difficult even to detour around it in time for next spring, but Waddington maintained his optimism. It was discouraging to his men to have to abandon the direct route, after successfully getting through the first 500 yards. There, a rock bluff shut off further penetration. It would take a lot more work and money to get through that than Waddington had expected— perhaps six months and $30,000. The trail was re-routed over a steep mountain which Waddington named after himself.[18]

The next problem to present itself was the packing of provisions and equipment. Because of the unfinished state of parts of the trail, it became necessary to hire Indians to do packing where the mules were useless. The Chilcotins were the only ones willing to pack and they proved a frequent nuisance. Waddington did not appear to have strong feelings about them one way or another, but the men working out on the trail did.

Saunders, who found them to be "a dirty, thriftless lot," recounted one incident which set future policy: "It was necessary to employ four of the Chilcoaten Indians, to pack provisions, to start in the morning, with the calculation of each taking his 75 lbs; they breakfasted first, of course, before starting, and the eating of that breakfast took so long, and the quantity they ate was so much, that the colored cook got quite angry and refused more, and they were so gorged with the beans, the bacon, the dried apple, the rice, the bread, the sugar and the molasses, washed down with numerous cups of both tea and coffee, when they all squatted down by the fire to smoke the slate pipe of kinickanic and tobacco, and then dared even to laugh at the idea of doing anything that day; this condition of things, though, did not work again, and suggested an amendment, consequently there was no more such breakfasting with them until such time as a day's work was done.[19]

The problem was that the Chilcotins were always short of food themselves and the workmen had to be strict unless they wanted them constantly begging like dogs at the supper table. The Chilcotins thought they should be fed free while they were working, but Brewster would not allow it and the Chilcotins would not accept food as actual payment. Brewster would give them the guns or blankets they asked for, but not the free food and he made a strict rule against giving away food.

Cheddeki, known as George to the whites, was one of those employed to pack. He was one of the more trusted Chilcotins, since he had worked for Waddington's party the previous year and did not cause trouble. He stated: "When the whites would be eating, they would give a bit of food to the children and the man in charge (Brewster) would take it away and throw it into the fire. They always made me and my wife eat in the hut so that we could not give any away."[20]

Chartres Brew, Chief Inspector of Police for B.C. who was later to visit the valley, found: "All the time it was known that the Indians were little removed from a state of starvation yet not the slightest effort was made to obtain the good will of the Indians or to guard against their enmity. When they worked they complained that Brewster paid them badly and gave them nothing to eat. They ought to have been paid their wages in money, but as one of Mr. Waddington's men said to me they did not get a chance of it. They got orders for powder, balls, clothes or blankets as they pleased. Of course payment in this way was a loss to them. They never took provisions in payment; they thought they had a right to be fed, but they were not. They begged food or stole it and if those means failed then they hunted or fished."

Brew further stated: "The women, particularly the younger ones, were better fed than the men as the price of prostitution to the hungry wretches was enough to eat."

At any rate, the Chilcotins did not stick around after earning blankets and a musket each. They took their families and friends who had not worked and went up the Homathko and into the Tatla Lake area to fish for *sapai*, or lake trout.

That left Waddington without any packers. He couldn't replace the Chilcotins, and his own men had to pack the heavy equipment and provisions.

July saw a sudden and unseasonable rise in the Homathko water level brought on by nine days of heavy rain. It made crossings at the ferry site extremely dangerous. "I never expected that it could form such an impetuous mass of rolling waters, cutting off all communication with the other side for several days," Waddington penned in a letter to Victoria while sitting in Canyon Pass work camp a mile or so up from the ferry on the right bank of the Homathko. With him were 80 men, in effect marooned by the swollen river.

At the ferryman's cabin on the left, or east bank were Saunders, Frank Cote (the senior canoeman), two Portuguese laborers, the cook, two Homathko Indians and Henry McNeill, the son of a former Hudson's Bay Company employee.

McNeill was a hardy and capable young man who had explored the route from the inlet through to Alexandria with H.O. Tiedemann in the summer of 1862. On the return trip McNeill had found the west branch of the Homathko superior to the east taken on the way up.

These men remained watching the river for several days, hoping it would go down enough so that fresh provisions could be taken across to the workmen on the other side. The river gave no hint of calming down and the Homathkos were persuaded with liberal reward to try the crossing in a canoe.

They went upriver as far as they could, several hundred yards, and pushed off. The river took hold of the canoe and drove it onto a hidden snag. The craft capsized and the Indians fought for their lives in the turbulent waters, finally reaching shore.

Waddington came down with several men and shot an arrow over to the cabin with a message that food was very low. Saunders, McNeill, and the others on the trail side talked it over and decided to try the crossing in the ferry scow. With Cote at the helm, they shoved off from the same place the Indians had. As the crowd on the opposite bank shouted encouragement, they fought to steer the unwieldy scow. Swirling around and bouncing off snags, they went whipping past the landing. Two miles down river they got into slower water and beached on the same shore they'd started from, with only wet provisions for their trouble.

A few days later, though, the river abated and a rope was stretched across it to guide the ferry. Now stores could be taken across safely, and a log cabin was built on the other side for storage.

While the stranding of the workmen had been the cause for some concern and excitement, it wasn't the biggest worry from the high water. The Homathko's small tributaries tore out ten bridges, much delaying progress.

Through all this, Waddington remained optimistic. By the end of August, he felt sure, the trail would be open to Puntzi Lake. When the end of August came and it wasn't, he went back to Victoria for two weeks to take care of business matters. Since there was no ship stopping in at Bute at the time, he took his big canoe, which he'd named the Waddington Cote after himself and his French canoeman.

The canoe was used on frequent occasions for trips to Victoria. Considering the turbulence of the sea as it flowed between the mainland and the Coast islands, the big Indian canoes were remarkably seaworthy. They varied in size from one man boats to vessels of 50 ft. or more, but the average for ocean use was 30 to 35 ft. in length. They were easily convertible to small schooners by the addition of mast and sail, though the Indians propelled them by single-bladed paddles. Carved from logs, the flat-bottomed craft were stable and had a good cargo capacity.

On this particular trip, it took Waddington and his party three and a half days to reach Victoria.

The road-builder found himself having to launch into an immediate campaign defending his project. The root of the problem, as was to be expected, was New Westminster's jealousy of the Bute Inlet road-building scheme.

The Bute Inlet road had become a focal point for the feud between Victoria and New Westminster. To the people of Victoria, New Westminster was "a pimple on the face of creation" while New Westminsterites referred to Victoria as being located "on a frogpond."[22] In Victoria, the Bute Inlet road was looked upon as "a fine route" which "is another guarantee of our commercial supremacy."[23] But in New Westminster it was "not in the best interests of the country" and "a scheme hatched in Victoria for the express purpose of perpetrating their grip upon our commerce."[24]

It had to be admitted that the exploring expeditions sent through the Homathko Valley by Waddington had, after difficult journeys, resulted in reports that led him to believe the route was better than it was turning out to be. The opponents of the route were quick to grasp at anything unfavorable to it, and news of the difficulties experienced that summer quickly spread from Victoria to New Westminster. The result was some damaging publicity which Waddington had to combat.

He patiently explained away the difficulties not directly related to the route, and as for The Canyon, that problem would probably be solved by the time he returned. Waddington spoke in glowing terms of the new town being developed, and of the farms starting to appear along the route.

He got half a dozen men who had worked on the trail to sign a statement saying allegations that the route was impracticable were "entirely at variance with the truth."[25]

Waddington then chartered a sloop and sailed back to Bute

Inlet with more provisions for the workmen.

By the middle of September, the trail had still not got past The Canyon. While the detour was being completed, a bluff on the other side of The Canyon presented another barrier. Big 12-foot lever drills were being used for boring the dynamite holes, but progress was slow. A party was working down towards The Canyon from the inland side of the bluff. Waddington now set back his completion schedule to the end of November, and went inland on a reconnaisance trip.

There was still considerable exploring to be done. Taking the trail along the east branch would add about 15 miles of water travel via Tatlayoko Lake, but the west branch was more easily travelled by land.

Tellot and his Chilcotins returned to the inlet from the area Waddington was looking at for the big salmon run. They brought with them a few extra Indians and about 20 coyote-like dogs used for packing. When they appeared in one of the upper camps, everyone was out working on the trail except Saunders. While Saunders talked to Tellot, several of the Indians quietly went about stealing everything they could. Saunders saw it, but figured with the 8 to 1 odds against him he should wait for the other white men to return.

For a few hours he played along, sharing a laugh with them now and then and pretending he knew nothing. But as they squatted around the campfire he could see knives, forks, tobacco and other articles stuffed under their clothing and in their quivers.

About an hour before sunset the workmen returned and Saunders told them what had been happening. Saunders and McNeill complained to Tellot, who wasn't really a bad sort himself and the chief went about getting the stolen articles back.

McNeill, a tall and wiry man, rolled over a scar-faced Indian who had been slumbering by the fire. Two knives and some tobacco fell out of his quiver along with his arrows. The savage put up no resistance, turning over the stolen goods and pointing out where other things had been hidden by his comrades.

Tellot was told to move his band away from the camp so that there would be no further occurrences of that nature. The chief, though, was asked to guide a party to Alexandria, and he agreed. He was to be paid one musket, powder and shot, a pair of blankets, and food for his wife and three children during his absence. One of the workers also traded him a plug of tobacco for a wolf-dog pup.

There were five men in the party, including McNeill and one of the men who had been lost on the disastrous expedition that summer. One of them returned, sick, a few days later, but the rest made it through.

Brewster, meanwhile, made a trip to Victoria to hire new hands. "Willie" Brewster did not much like Victoria. A native Canadian, he missed the comforts of the family house he had left for the uncertainties of life in the west. This seasonal work with Waddington's road party was the steadiest he had found in his five years on the coast. Victoria was an expensive place to live, and despite the rigors of the labor, the uncivilized country and the nuisance of the Siwashes, he enjoyed working at Bute Inlet much more than languishing in Victoria. He had got on with Waddington as store keeper and had been promoted to work foreman when his predecessor suffered a broken leg.

While looking for new workers, Brewster took the opportunity presented by the visit to back up his employer's claims that the road was going well and that it would be finished by the end of the season.

A month and a half after Brewster's trip, Waddington was in Victoria again claiming the trail would be put through that year, except that now work would have to continue until Christmas. The 20 men he left with Brewster were still at the canyon bluff blasting and scaffolding.

* * *

On November 22, a "dull, dreary, wintery day," an English mining company employee named Francis Poole paddled into North Bentinck Arm in a canoe. He was en route from Victoria to the Queen Charlotte Islands where he was searching for copper, but the sloop on which he was travelling had a stop to make at New Aberdeen, or Bella Coola, at the end of this arm of the Burke Channel. As the ship neared its destination, Poole had gone on ahead in the canoe for an advance look.

He reached the tiny settlement three hours ahead of the sloop *Leonide*. A handful of whites inhabited Bella Coola, which would be the counterpart of Waddington's Bute Inlet townsite if the Bentinck Arm road to the Cariboo became a reality.

Poole had visited this area the year before when he had been employed in an exploring expedition across the Cascade Mountains from Bella Coola. Twenty days after departure, nine of the 40 men who had started on the expedition reached Alexandria.

Poole discovered on his second visit to The Arm that he had

been an unwitting party to the deaths of hundreds of native Indians. During the trip overland, some expedition members had come down with smallpox and had been left with Bella Coola and Chilcotin Indians to recover.

In April 1862 a miner with smallpox had arrived in Victoria from San Francisco. It very quickly reached Indian camps near the colonial capital and though it wasn't the first such epidemic to strike the Indians, this one became the most disastrous. The Vancouver Island natives who now traded in Victoria in great numbers took the disease back with them. The smallpox became a lethal fire, jumping from whites to Indians and from tribe to tribe.

Only a month after the smallpox had been introduced to Victoria, Poole and his party had begun their expedition from North Bentinck Arm. The first major Indian village come upon by the expedition after ascending the Bella Coola Valley onto the Chilcotin plateau was on Nancootlem, at Anahim Lake.[26] The band was led by the powerful old chief Anahim. It was there that two of the party became ill and were left in the care of the Chilcotins.

In July, the same Lieutenant Henry Palmer who had surveyed the routes to the goldfields via New Westminster was engaged in a formal survey of the North Bentinck Arm route to Alexandria, which continued past Nancootlem and joined the Bute Inlet trail at Puntzi Lake. He noted the fast spread of the disease: "Smallpox has this year contributed a sad quota of death. During my stay there this disease, which had only just broken out when I arrived, spread so rapidly that, in a week, nearly all the healthy had scattered from the lodges and gone to encamp by families in the woods, only, it is to be feared, to carry away the seeds of infection and death in the blankets and other articles they took with them. Numbers were dying each day; sick men and women were taken out into the woods and left with a blanket and two or three salmon to die by themselves and rot unburied; sick children were tied to trees, and naked, gray-haired medicine-men, hideously painted, howled and gesticulated night and day in front of the lodges in mad efforts to stay the progress of the disease."[27]

The observations Palmer wrote of were made in July of 1862. In October of that year, James Young, a newspaper correspondent from Ottawa travelling with two companions from Alexandria toward Bella Coola on Palmer's trail, discovered how extensively the disease had spread into Chilcotin territory. He had been told by Robert McLeod, a packer, of the devastation of the Chilcotin Indian village at

30

Nancootlem, but that was no preparation for seeing it:

"One afternoon we were skirting the edge of a lake, on the other side of which rose a wall of snow-clad mountains, when a nauseating smell assailed our nostrils. A breeze swept the offensive smell away, and then when it dropped, we again smelled it. Puzzled, we walked along the trail, and came upon a large Indian village, of some twenty or thirty houses. No dogs appeared to warn the occupants of our approach, nor came any of the inhabitants to greet or question us.

"We stopped at the sight of this silent village."

"We are approaching a village of the dead," said Mr. (A.L.) Fortune. "Look," and he pointed at two heaps of earth that looked much like a grave. But more demonstrative was a heap of brush piled over another Indian corpse, and beside this yet another partially wrapped in a blanket, his face turned to the sky and his shrunken eyes drawn into the skull. When I saw flies crawling over those sightless and decaying bodies I almost retched.

"Speechless, we realized that this was Nancootlem. Bob McLeod had told us about it, but we had not been able to picture it.

"The trail skirted the village, but as we moved on, Mr. Fortune said, 'I am going to look in some of these houses.'

"We followed, and saw in many of the houses corpses that had been deserted when their owners were still alive. We saw signs of a fight against a relentless enemy, a sudden conquering fear, and a flight by all those who could flee, leaving their dead unburied, and their sick to become dead, uncared for.

"Shortly we could stand no more, and departed as far as we could. The trail turned around the north end of the lake and pointed to the snowy mountains.

"At the north end of the lake the smell of wood-smoke caught our attention, and by a little stream a man sat by a fire in front of a brush hut. He was horribly pockmarked but there was no fever upon him. He had survived the tragic epidemic.

"When he saw us he rose to his feet. He had a knife in his hand, and from the look of anger and hatred in his face, I wondered if he would attack all four of us.

" 'Cultus whiteman,' he shouted. 'Cultus whiteman bring smallpox, kill all my people.'

"We tried to talk to him, but without avail. Finally Mr. Fortune left some food for him and we departed, rather hurriedly, for an arrow in one's back was not desired. But the Indian was busy with food and didn't use an arrow."[28]

Young and his companions were later confronted with similiar sickening scenes when they descended into the Bella Coola Valley. His diary relates the following incident which occurred while the three travellers were staying in Bella Coola under the roof of storekeeper Peter White:

"In the morning I was up a few minutes earlier than the rest, took the shutter off the window, and looking out, saw a horrible sight. An Indian lay on the ground twenty feet from the window, dead, very dead indeed. A blanket was lying nearby and in the strengthening light I could see that the man had been disembowelled and partly eaten.

" 'Peter,' I called, 'Look outside.'

"Peter was pulling on his breeches. He looked out the window.

" 'Yeah, we'll have to get some of the braves to bury him.'

" 'He probably died on my door-step last night. You heard some noises, didn't you?'

"Peter had heard them, too, and with his knowledge had interpreted the noises, and had kept on sleeping, or trying to.

" 'The Indians have the idea that they will go to their lushest paradise if they die on a whiteman's doorstep, or better still, right in his shack, and ever since this smallpox hit there has been an almost nightly seige of potential corpses crawling to my doorstep.'

"He sounded weary.

" 'The wolves do a pretty good job of cleaning up. Most of the time they leave just a few bones, maybe the skull. That poor buck out there didn't come early enough in the night to get properly disposed of.' "

"Poole was surprised at the decimation, though his immediate concern was with the practical problems involved.

"I learnt that the smallpox had carried off hundreds of Indians since my first visit there; and as the party I then headed was the unfortunate means of introducing the fell disease amongst them, I began to fear lest the natives should oppose my landing."[29]

The effects of the smallpox did hit closer to home than that once he got into Bella Coola, however. "Remarking a fine specimen of Young India (North Pacific section) gazing at me, not with eyes indicating intense hatred, as I had expected, but with an expression of sorrow, I sympathizingly inquired the cause. He was one of those whom the smallpox had spared, but had nonetheless so deeply marked that I did not recognize his face in the least. But the moment he spoke I knew him to be my old Indian friend Jim, our guide on the Bentinck Trail over the Blue Mountains. But for Jim none of that party of ours would be alive at this day."

Poole shared the hospitality of A.H. Wallace, the customs house officer and hotelier at Bella Coola, and then visited fur trader Jim Taylor at his small ranch three miles up the Bella Coola River. "On our way thither we passed by two Indian settlements, or bivouacs rather. They were almost deserted, the smallpox having the previous year reduced the tribes there from 4000 to a few dozens."

Poole enjoyed his short stay in Taylor's log house. His host presented him with a pup which Poole named Cato.

"The spirit that could induce an educated man to brave the loneliness and discomforts of a quasi-permanent residence in such a desert calls for admiration," wrote Poole. "At the same time, when the tremendous risk of life and the distant hope of profit are considered, it seems hardly possible to look upon isolated undertakings of this description as other than foolhardy."

Indeed, the past year had not been very profitable for Taylor. The last winter had been bad. The local Indians, dying from starvation and smallpox, provided few furs and bought little from the traders.

Taylor and another trader named Angus Macleod decided to go up to Nancootlem and see if they could do business, but they found the situation there little better. The Chilcotins were still feeling the effects of the epidemic.

The Indians had long ceased giving their dead a proper burial, simply dragging the bodies into the woods or walking there themselves before death claimed them. The worst of the epidemic was over, however, and those who still lived had a good chance to survive.

McLeod and Taylor saw here an excellent opportunity to make some profit. They gathered up the blankets from the corpses in the woods and sold them to the Chilcotins again.

The re-introduction of the infested blankets started a new outbreak among the Indians of Nancootlem, and it moved inland and killed many more. Taylor had been immunized; Macleod hadn't and the smallpox claimed him along with the Chilcotins.

By the time the epidemic burned itself out two years after the outbreak, it had killed 20,000 of British Columbia's 60,000 Indians. Of the 1,500 Chilcotins, barely half had survived.

The Chilcotins at Bute Inlet had seen their once proud people almost destroyed by the white man's disease. It should not have been surprising, therefore, that they were neither especially noble-looking creatures, nor very honest with or willing to work hard for white men.

* * *

With all the previous delays, it was not surprising that Alfred Waddington's men did not make it through the gallery of rock that year as he had hoped, even though they worked into December. Completion would have to wait until the following spring when weather permitted them to resume. Then, success was all but certain.

The handful of settlers who had built houses on the Homathko remained there during the rest of the winter. A few Indians also wintered there. Some of the road party's stores were left in buildings at the townsite under the care of settler John Clark. A good-looking Chilcotin Indian of about 25, Cusshen, was hired to look after another small quantity upstream, to make sure it was not stolen.

The band of Chilcotins remaining in Homathko territory that winter lived mostly off the fish they had caught the preceding fall. An occasional trip to one of the nearby small lakes might yield trout, Kokanee, whitefish or suckers through the ice, but their main subsistence was the dried salmon stored in pit caches. There were also bear, beaver, rabbits, and other smaller game in the valley, but these were tough to come by in the winter. Snares and traps were more successful at this time of year than muskets or bows and arrows.

Their gabled lodges, insulated with brush, tree bark and dirt, protected them from snow and cold. An opening running the length of the ridge pole allowed good ventilation and light, and fires were kept burning day and night. In extreme winters, houses were dug out of the ground. These were extremely warm, but uncomfortable and poorly ventilated.[30]

At one time the Chilcotins had been a prosperous and powerful people. Their territory covered the Chilcotin plateau from Alexandria on the Fraser River to the Coastal mountains, and north-south 150 miles.

Until recently they had remained largely unaffected by the invasion of the white man. The Hudson's Bay Company had built a trading post, Ft. Chilcotin, on the Chilko River south of Puntzi Lake. But the Chilcotin Indians didn't fit in with the fur trade. The post was closed, re-opened, and closed again.

Until the gold rush, the Chilcotins had received two main inheritances from their contact with the whites: the horse, and the Christian religion. The former provided them with swift transportation over their rolling territory. Their natural religion involved shamanism and the belief that each person had a soul, but there was no concept of heaven or life hereafter. Roman Catholic missionaries at Ft. Alexandria introduced the teachings of Christ, and self-appointed priests or prophets held some sway in the Chilcotin bands for a time. Christianity retained some influence among them despite the absence of concerted teaching.

Another facet of white civilization taken on by the Chilcotin directly from the whites or indirectly from neighboring tribes was the concept of established leadership. The main units had been bands and families, and leadership had been largely informal. Now, however, they had developed a loose chieftainship system and some powerful families had gained ascendency.

The Chilcotins, because their contact with the whites had been limited, were much less prepared for the dramatic changes brought about by the gold rush than were other tribes. The King George Men (Englishmen), and Boston men (Americans), travelling through their country brought the scourge of liquor and the inducement to prostitution. Worst of all, they brought the smallpox, leaving the Chilcotins numerically weak and broken in spirit.

The whites as individuals could be considerate—they often gave the Indians presents—or they could be cruel, refusing to feed them when hungry, or mistreating squaws. Tyhee (Chief) Waddington's men who were building a trail which now approached the boundary of Chilcotin territory were no different. They were not welcome, but they paid the Chilcotins in muskets and ammunition for packing and guiding, and these were much better for hunting than the old bows and arrows.

The Chilcotins who remained at Bute were visited toward the end of the year, in the Eagle Moon, by a band under a powerful chief from far away in eastern Chilcotin territory. He was Alexis, who controlled that part of the plateau west of Alexandria to Puntzi Lake. He was much more powerful than Tellot, controlling more territory and tribesmen, and was a more dominating figure.

The Alexis Chilcotins stayed for awhile, and the chief invited Cheddeki to come to Puntzi with them for an exchange visit. Cheddeki, however, had a bad hand and was unable to travel.

Early in the new year, Alexis and his band left. Since Cusshen wasn't around, they took with them 25 sacks of flour from the Bute Inlet Wagon Road Company's cabin.

* * *

The next two and a half months were anxious ones for Alfred Waddington. The main problem was a lack of money. The year's work had completely drained the fund provided by himself and investors. He therefore set about trying to raise more money so that work could be continued in the spring.

Writing home to his sister in Canada on Jan. 14, William Brewster remarked that the road company so far had been "very unprofitable" but that it was solidly backed. He had not yet been paid for his last period of employment, but he intended to work for Waddington again in the spring if nothing else came up.[31]

Some of the workmen had been paid by Waddington in scrip giving them a lien on the road company charter. This had not always proven popular and on one occasion during the return trip to Victoria a few of the men had threatened to "expose" the situation. Waddington had talked them out of it by reminding them any detrimental publicity would reflect on the value of the scrip in which they had been paid. When they arrived in Victoria, the men gave three cheers for the Bute Inlet project and three more for Waddington.

Another source of concern to Old Waddy was the Bentinck Arm and Fraser River Road Company Ltd. The company had been in existence for a couple of years. John G. Barnston, a lawyer newly arrived in the West from Lower Canada, had explored with a party from Alexandria to North Bentinck Arm with a similar aim to that of Waddington. From Alexandria to Puntzi Lake the route was the same as Waddington's; from there it went north and west to North Bentinck Arm instead of south to Bute.

Barnston had writen after his trip: "...we are firmly convinced that if the Upper Fraser turns out to be the rich mining country that is expected, goods and provisions can be laid down by this route for as low as figure at any point of the Fraser above Alexandria as they can now be had for at Williams Lake."[32]

But like Bute Inlet, the North Bentinck route had received a lot of unfavorable publicity. Waddington, of course, agreed with the criticisms of The Arm. It was farther from Victoria, it was longer with less favorable pasturage, and unlike the Homathko Valley, the Bella Coola had no gradual ascent— the only way out was straight up the mountainsides. Waddington was building a pack trail which was to be converted later to a wagon road. It seemed impossible that the Bentinck route could ever be more than a crude trail.

Nevertheless, the Bentinck Arm Company was now hoping

to start construction. On February 1, British Columbia's Colonial Secretary forwarded to the Attorney-General the draft of an agreement for the Bentinck Arm road, along with plans for the road. The agreement was to be put in final form. The route itself was well-defined through common usage and Palmer's survey, and a number of parties had gone through using Bella Coola and Chilcotin Indians to pack.

Should the Bentinck Arm route become established, it could draw valuable business away from Bute Inlet. Based on the volume of the Lillooet route, it was conservatively estimated that Bute Inlet would realize returns of $24,000 a month on freight tolls during the season, and $150,000 a year on live-stock and water transportation tolls.

But Waddington found that confidence in his project had been shaken by the delays. A prestigious group of directors had been elected a year before at a shareholders' meeting. They included Waddington, prominent banker A.D. Macdonald, Dr. W.F. Tolmie of the Hudson's Bay Company (well-known in local politics), D. Lenerue, R. Burnaby, and Hugh Nelson of the firm of Dodge and Nelson which packed on the Douglas-Lillooet route. Support from these men and others who might have invested withered away. Waddington was forced to sell all his personal holdings to buy them out at bargain prices and get enough money to continue the work.

*   *   *

The Indians encamped on the Homathko were nearing starvation by early spring. Most of their fish were gone, and until the big run of oolichan—sardine-like fish which saturated rivers of the B.C. Coast—there would be little to replace them. The natives either could not find sufficient game or did not choose to hunt.

They became a considerable nuisance to the white settlers, particularly to John Clark. One "amusing" incident was later related to the party brought up by Waddington to resume work on the trail:

"Mr. Clark last winter missed many small things from his log house at the townsite, and could not catch the thief, who came down the chimney during his absence. At last he got a friend to go into the cabin with a quarter of a pound of gunpowder, and locking the door outside himself, went away a short distance and then crept back to watch the fun.

"Soon an Indian came stealthily along, his extremities bare, sans culottes, sans everything. He got nearly down the chimney when the man inside threw the powder on the smouldering ashes, and off it went. The Indian went off also,

37

and with a terrific yell, but over the state of his nude proportions a veil must be drawn. He for months afforded a wholesome warning to his tribe, being unable to sit or lie down."[33]

*Nothing short of lead or hemp will bring the lawless tribes to their
senses. This was fully demonstrated by the lamented Captain
Robinson last summer when he sent several broadsides from his
gunboat Forward into a camp of Haidas near Cape Mudge and
brought them to their knees suing for peace in a few minutes after
the first gun was fired. The lesson then taught the savages lasted
them for some time. Those effects are now nearly forgotten and
another lesson is required to teach them how to behave in civilized
society.*

Victoria *Colonist*
August 30, 1862.

On March 16, 1864, the schooner *F.P. Green* sailed from
Victoria for Bute Inlet. On it were 20 workmen, Brewster, and
an artist Waddington had hired to sketch the inlet and
Homathko Valley. Most of the hired men were ex-sappers discharged in B.C. when the Royal Engineers had been recalled a
few months before.

Waddington did not sail with this first party, but he was
impatient to get the work started again and planned to go up in
a few weeks. He was confident the trail could be through by
late spring or early summer, including the detour around The
Canyon and a rough path south from Puntzi Lake.

William Brewster was also relieved that work on the trail was
starting again, but for a different reason. Victoria, despite its
bars, brothels, and gambling houses, was to him "a miserable,
dull place to live in."[1] He had spent a good part of the winter ill
in bed, and the prospect of good employment pleased him.
Waddington had paid him wages owing from the last year, and
there would be several months steady work to look forward to.

The artist, an Englishman named Frederick Whymper, was
also looking forward eagerly to visiting Bute Inlet. He had
become well known in British Columbia and Vancouver Island
over the previous two years for his sketches of the Cariboo
goldfields, done during an extensive hike through the region.
Waddington wanted drawings to send back to London to
attract investors, and Whymper would get the chance to see

some new country.

As the schooner neared the mouth of the Homathko River, some Chilcotin Indians paddled out in their canoes and came on board. "Among them one old hag attracted some notice, from her repulsive appearance and the short pipe which she seemed to enjoy."[2]

John Clark greeted the schooner as it put up at the wharf. He related the difficulties, caused by the Indians, in looking after the stores and mules during the winter, and he said he had been threatened on various occasions. His story about the chimney got a good laugh, however.

As in the previous spring, there were Homathkos, Klayoosh and Euclataws camped at the inlet, in addition to Chilcotins. The Chilcotins were in poor condition, having long ago run short of food. A few had stayed in the Homathko all winter while others were newly arrived. Whymper soon found that he agreed with the unsympathetic attitude towards them.

"The Chilcoatin Indians are a dirty, lazy set, and although a few Homathco Indians raise good potatoes at the head of the Inlet, the former prefer half starving in winter to exerting themselves."[3]

"These people appeared to be very bare of provisions, and disputed with their wretched cayota dogs anything that we threw out of our camp, in the shape of bones, bacon-rind, or tea-leaves, and similar luxuries."[4]

Waddington was not happy to discover that the flour left under Cusshen's care had disappeared. Brewster said he would find out who did it, and talked to Cheddeki. The Indian was of no help.

"I said, you know I have been three years with you and I have never stolen anything from you. The White said, "No, but I want to find out who did take it."[5]

Brewster decided to hire Cheddeki again to help with the mules. Cheddeki's wife, Tellot's daughter, stayed at the coast camp and was given flour and bacon to live on until he could return.

The foreman got his men organized and started up for the ferry. Whymper went with them. Snow was still deep and in some places the trail had to be cleared away for the heavily-laden mules. Despite the snow, the mosquitos were already out and bit through the clothing of the men.

At the ferry, the mules were unloaded and the provisions were stored. The ferry was put in good working order and Tim Smith, one of the ex-sappers, was permanently stationed there. As work progressed, Chilcotins would have to be hired to pack food and equipment from the cabins at the ferry crossing to the upper campsite located nine miles further up on the far side of The Canyon.

Cheddeki was retained to pack the big blasting drills, and he went with the work party to the site. Cheddeki's wife joined him a short time later. Tents were pitched on a grassy flat beside the Homathko near the third bluff to be tackled.

Cheddeki had been with the whites about three weeks when a half dozen Chilcotin families came up from the Waddington townsite, the men asking for work. Before hiring them, Brewster demanded to know if any of them had been involved in the theft of the flour. If they wanted to pack, he said through interpreter Baptiste Demerest, they could pack for the 25 sacks of stolen flour.

The Indians would admit to nothing in regard to the flour but one said, "You are in our country, you owe us bread."

It was true that the Bute Inlet trail was now entering Chilcotin Indian territory, but Brewster was angered at their stubbornness and insolence. He took out a notebook and pencil and told Demerest to start listing the names of the Indians present. When he was finished, he instructed Demerest to ask them if they knew what he had been doing.

The Chilcotins did not like to see their names written down. Writing was a mystery to them. Their names were very important, indistinguishable from the people who owned them. The writing of a person's name was like theft. But they did not know why Brewster would want to do such a thing.

"I have taken down your names because you would not tell me who stole the flour," stated Brewster. "All the Chilcotins are going to die. The whites will introduce sickness into the country which will kill you all."[6]

Brewster made the threat easily in a moment of anger, with the intention of frightening the Chilcotins and impressing them with the power of the whites. But he could not appreciate the dread of smallpox held by the Chilcotins. Two years before, a white man at Puntzi Lake[7] had made a similar threat to get them off the land, and it had been followed by the epidemic which had killed or scarred so many. Brewster's words were therefore taken seriously.

The foreman then relented and hired the men for packing. Their ability in this regard was their only attribute that impressed Whymper.

"Many of them were subsequently employed in packing goods on their backs, always carrying their loads fixed to a strap which came round and over their foreheads. As they

41

would pack 100 lbs, and upward this way, their heads must be regarded as tolerably strong and thick! Some of them were also employed in building the road."[8]

Two Homathko Indians were also hired. The Chilcotins established their own camp beside the Homathko near that of the whites. With squaws going about their work and children playing, it became a busy place.

Whymper hired one of the Indians as a guide and started in search of the Great (Tiedemann's) Glacier, a 15-mile long sheet of ice west of the fork of the river. Since he did not know Chilcotin, and the Chilcotins did not know much Chinook, it wasn't a very successful expedition. His first problem was explaining what he meant by a glacier. The only equivalent in Chinook was "Hyu ice, hyu snow"— plenty of ice and snow.

While Whymper was looking unsuccessfully for the glacier, a Chilcotin Indian appeared at the Waddington townsite engaged in a different kind of search. Like most of the Chilcotins now in the valley, Klatassine had not been seen by Waddington's workmen before this year. But he knew of Waddington, and he hoped the white chief could help get back his daughter from the Euclataws, who had stolen and enslaved her.

Klatassine was a respected and feared Chilcotin war chief, and a near relative of the Nancootlem chief Anahim.

"His was a striking face, the great under jaw betokened strong power of will. The eyes, which were not black like most Indians, but of a very dark blue, full of a strange, what might be a dangerous, light, were keen and searching."[9]

Probably in his late thirties, he was tall with a big nose and dark brown hair. He wore no moustache as was the custom among many Chilcotin men.

Among the Chilcotins, there were certain men who gained power not through heredity or skill in providing for the band or family, but through bravery in battle. These men were not necessarily well-liked, but they were accepted as tyhees, "big men" or chiefs. Since they preferred fighting to fishing, hunting or gathering, these men were often poor. But when it came time to do battle with an enemy, it was the war chief who took charge, and everyone including the tribal chieftain became subordinate. With only two or three, or perhaps a dozen warriors, he would seek out the enemy.

Klatassine was one of these men. He had participated in many fights with Carriers, Homathkos, and Shuswap.

"He was a great man amongst the Indians. Indeed, although not a hereditary chieftain he was looked upon as their chief by all the Chilcoatens. His physical strength, his power of will, his courage, his unscrupulousness had won him this pre-eminence. He was the terror of the foes of his tribe. By his clansmen too, rather dreaded than loved. The little children would peep in through the holes in his tent to catch a sight of the terrible chief and run away crying with fright."[10]

The taking of slaves was common among the tribes of the region. Usually they were women or children, or young men, captured on raids. Although slaves could be sold and were worked hard, the Chilcotins allowed their slaves to otherwise become full members of the tribe. Chilcotins enslaved by other tribes were often returned to their families and regained full status.

Klatassine was aware of the peace negotiated by Wadding-ton, and looked to him to get back his daughter without need of bloodshed or barter. He was disappointed to find Wadding-ton had not yet arrived, and kept asking Alfred Sampson and George Cadman, two packers stationed at the townsite, when Waddington was coming. Klatassine had brought his family with him and sent his son Piell, a boy of 17 or 18 who followed his father unquestioningly, up the pack trail to Brewster's work camp to make enquiries there. Piell had a long dark face with long hair, and was thought to look like a priest. He had travelled with some road workers and arrived at the camp April 20. Tellot also arrived at the camp.

Whymper, meanwhile, returned to the camp without having found his glacier. He made a deal with Tellot to guide him to it and this second trip was much more successful. Tellot was "an Indian of some intelligence"[11] and "a good Indian."[12] Accom-panied by four Chilcotin men and their families who had decided to return to Tatla lake, Tellot led Whymper through thick timber strewn with windfalls and prickly thickets to a flat below the glacier. There they camped.

Before the Indians who had travelled with them continued their journey, they asked Whymper for a gift. The artist gave them a little flour and tobacco, and handed one of the children a sixpence. He explained in crude Chinook that the picture was of "Victoria, Klootchman tyhee copa King George illi-he" —"Woman-chief of the King George land," or England. The youngster indicated with his hands that he would hang the coin from his nose.

Whymper was "not overgrieved"[13] to see the Chilcotins leave.

The next morning, April 24, he left Tellot in camp "to look after the traps, as he was unwilling to take any more trouble,"[14] and struggled up to the base of the glacier two and a half miles away. Between the boulders and driftwood flowed numerous large, swift streams.

"On reaching the glacier, its presence was rendered very obvious by the cracking of the ice and the careening of the stones from its surface. This was incessant; now a shower of pebbles, now a few hundred-weight of boulders, and now a thimble-ful of sand, but always something coming over. The ice—very evidently such at the cracks, where you saw its true color, and its dripping lower edges of stalactite form—yet appeared for the most part like wet, smooth rock, from the quantity of dirt on its surface. At its termination the glacier must have been three-quarters of a mile in width; it was considerably wider higher up. While sketching it, all around was so supremely tranquil that its action was very noticeable. Rocks and boulders fell from it sufficient to crush any too eager observer... The day was extremely warm, and the glacier in full activity."[15]

Whymper spent the entire day sketching the scenery, returning to his camp late in the evening. "From his (Tellot's) manner, I should suppose that he thought me a fool for my pains, although he showed some little interest in my sketches."[16]

Whymper remained at the main camp for another day or two, sketching Tellot during a few spare moments.[17] He talked with Brewster, who gave him some letters to take back to Victoria for Waddington. The bluffs remained troublesome, but the trail was inching ahead.

Tellot, meanwhile, was hired by Brewster to pack.

On his way back down to the ferry, Whymper did a few quick sketches. He visited with Tim Smith, the ferryman, and some workmen under Brewster who came down from the upper camp for supplies. A pack train from the townsite had arrived and Whymper left with it the next morning on its return trip. About 11 miles from the inlet, Whymper left the pack train and went alone towards a glacier which could be seen from the trail.

*　*　*

Piell had returned from the work camp to the townsite with some frightening information. He told his father about Brewster's threat to bring smallpox.

Klatassine was extremely upset at hearing this. He had intended to wait for Waddington to get back his daughter, and then go up to Puntzi Lake via the Memeya and Bridge Rivers. But he decided instead to go up the Homathko so he could stop and see Tellot on the way.

Klatassine first went into the camp of the Euclataws and bought back his daughter for a canoe, six blankets and two muskets, a steep price. He informed Sampson of this and then took his family up the trail.

With him were Piell, Cusshen, the scarface McNeill had caught stealing the year before, his young, pregnant wife Toowaewoot, and two daughters by another wife.

They slept the first night at a cabin called the halfway house, and continued the next day up to Boulder Creek camp, three miles below the ferry.

At about 9 a.m. on Thursday, April 28, they arrived at the ferry. It never became entirely clear exactly what took place that day and why. What is known is that Cusshen and the scarface continued on to the upper camp, but Klatassine and his family were joined by two other Indians at the ferry, one about 45 years of age (perhaps Yahooslas) and the other Chessus.

Neither of these two were liked by the whites and they in turn did not like the whites. Yahooslas stole from them and Chessus was a naturally rebellious individual. Chessus had been sick at the work camp and had received some care from the whites despite his hostility towards them.

Klatassine was clearly in a vile mood himself, resulting both from his frustration at Waddington's absence and from the smallpox threat he had heard about.

As for Smith, the ferryman, he was a rough individual who had gotten into several arguments with the Indians during the few weeks he had been at the crossing. Klatassine, apparently, asked for blankets and food for himself and his family. Holding to Brewster's policy, Smith arrogantly refused. There was a scuffle over the goods in question, but Smith retained possession.

Klatassine seethed over the rebuke. Chessus and Yahooslas urged action.

That evening, Smith went about preparing his dinner over the outdoor campfire as was his routine. The Indians stayed nearby watching him cook the food which he had refused to share.

When he was finished, the ferryman leaned against a big tree beside the fire and lit his pipe. As he puffed contentedly on the pipe, Klatassine aimed a musket at him from a short distance away. Smith died with no inkling of his doom. The musket ball pierced his head and dug into the tree behind him. The dead man's body bounced off the tree and onto the ground.

Klatassine had killed many enemies. Smith was the first white man to die at his hand, but to the warrior he was little different from the others.

The killing was some cause for celebration. The body was stripped, Klatassine taking the red-striped shirt for himself, and then dragged over to the river and dumped in.

Following that, the Indians ransacked the cabin.

* * *

Brewster ordered Junga Jem, or Squinteye, a Homathko Indian he had hired, to go down to the ferry on the morning of April 29. He was to wait there until the next pack train arrived and then help bring provisions up to the camp. Tellot obtained a promissory note to take to Smith, who would give him a blanket in payment for hauling three loads of provisions. He told his son-in-law Cheddeki that he was going down with Squinteye and would be back that night.

At about 11 a.m. Tellot and Squinteye were descending the hill a mile above the ferry when they were met by Klatassine's group, carrying some blankets and baked bread.

Tellot and Klatassine were old acquaintances, and the greetings were hearty. But the tale of what had happened the evening before quickly came out.

"Our master has killed a white man at the ferry," stated Chessus.[18]

Klatassine and Piell confirmed it.

Tellot became angry, threatening to go back and inform Brewster.

Squinteye asked why the Chilcotins had killed Smith.

To protect himself Klatassine should have killed him, but instead handed him two blankets and warned him not to tell anyone of Smith's death when he reached the townsite. It was a characteristic gesture on the part of Klatassine, who was as generous as he could be deadly.

The frightened Squinteye hurried away down the trail. When he came to the ferry landing he whistled for Smith, but there was no sign of life on the other side of the river. He continued past the trail downriver to a calm spot and swam across.

Klatassine convinced Tellot to wait until they could talk to the other Chilcotins at the camp. Tellot was reluctant, for he had been respected to a certain degree by the whites as a good Indian—even if his followers had not—and had gotten on well with them. But Klatassine, backed by the other three men, spoke of the smallpox which the whites had threatened to bring.

46

Tellot joined them and they went over the mountain trail and slipped into the Indian camp. Klatassine began talking to the Chilcotins there, and by evening had gained unanimous support.

There were 12 warriors altogether. Besides Klatassine, Piell, Chessus, Yahooslas and Tellot, there were Cusshen and Scarface, Chraychanuru (formerly a slave of the Homathkos, known as 'Bob' to the whites), Tellot's son-in-law Jack (about 22), Lowwa (a stout man of about 23 or 24), Cheddeki, and another young warrior of 23 or 24 (perhaps Hachis or any of a half dozen others later identified by Klatassine), who had killed a white man on the Sechelt Peninsula. Cheddeki, as was his practice, was staying in the white camp.

Klatassine's mind had assessed the situation carefully over the past few days and he had concluded that all the whites should be killed. They were building a trail which had now entered Chilcotin territory and before long would go right through it. The whites had no right to be on Chilcotin land; they had offered no compensation for it. The whites would travel the trail, steal land, hunt the Chilcotin's game and take their fish, bringing madness with their whiskey and death with the small pox. The whites must be stopped now before they went further into Chilcotin territory.

The practical means of accomplishing this aim were at hand. All but four of the Chilcotins had muskets (one of these being Chraychanuru, who had bought a musket from John Clark on credit and then sold it to another Indian). They all had knives (made by sharpening the whites' silverware or files) and hatchets. The whites were few and were poorly armed. It would be a simple thing to kill them and take the provisions which had so often been refused the Indians even when starving. They could rid themselves of the whites and return home to the Chilcotin plateau laden with plunder.

Klatassine's words were attractive to Tellot's men. Many of them had a deep-seated fear and hatred of the whites while others, like Tellot himself, would not go against the wishes of the majority.

The war chief was indeed correct in regard to the ability of the whites to protect themselves. There was only one revolver in the entire camp. While muskets had been used in the past as a common trade or payment item with the Chilcotins, almost nothing in the way of arms had been brought up this year. Waddington had suggested to Brewster that he take a good stand of weapons with him, but the foreman had declined.

The previous afternoon Brewster had taken three men and

an Indian cook and gone further up past the next bluff to start blazing and clearing. The white cook, Charles Buttle, who had worked for Brewster for two months the last season, was put in charge of the men who stayed in the main camp. The whites were therefore further weakened by being split into groups of four and twelve.

That evening there was the usual intermingling between the white workmen and the Chilcotin employees. A few jokes were shared in their limited ability to communicate with each other, and the Indians appeared to have quite a party going in their camp. It was noticed that they wore war paint, and some of the whites were nervous about it, but there was nothing else suspicious.

Buttle ordered the workmen to turn in early, as he wanted them up early the next day, a Saturday. Brewster liked to get as much work done as possible on Saturdays, since the men were given Sundays off.

In the Chilcotins camp, there was singing and dancing to the accompaniment of a round, single-headed drum. Each singer or dancer had his turn to recount famous battles. The music was a volatile lacing of rhythm and scale, the dancing light and graceful.

All this activity was a prelude to the planned attack. The Chilcotins always attacked an enemy at dawn, attempting to surprise and kill him quickly, then mutilating the corpses and celebrating on the plunder. Sometimes they scalped their victims and hung body parts from trees. The attack on the road company's camp was sure to be vicious.

* * *

It was late evening on April 29 before Whymper got back to the town of Waddington, and he paused only to eat and drink before turning in for the night at the lodge. There were four other men staying in the lodge that night—Sampson and Cadman, and two workmen named Curtis and Blaire who had resigned and were waiting for the next day's canoe back to Victoria.

The artist slept soundly after his tiring expedition, but at 3 a.m. he and the other lodge inhabitants were suddenly awakened by a big ruckus. Several Homathko Indians had burst into the building shouting and jabbering excitedly at the white men.

Among them was Squinteye, who related his experience with Klatassine and his hurried trip down the trail. But he admitted he knew only what Klatassine and the war chief's companions had told him, and the whites had serious doubts

48

about the story.

If something really had happened to Smith the road party would find out about it and somebody would be sent down to Waddington, especially since they knew a canoe was embarking for Victoria the next day. As far as they knew, the road party was armed.

It was decided to wait a few extra hours before leaving, in case someone came down with a message for Waddington about the supposed murder. There were no volunteers to go up river and check out the story.

Whymper was anxious to leave, partly because he had letters from Brewster to Waddington. And, with Waddington scheduled to leave Victoria for the inlet soon, it would be best to tell him of Squinteye's story so he could bring up additional arms with him if he felt it necessary.

The two workmen, Whymper, and the Homathko canoeist agreed they would wait until noon and no longer.

* * *

Cheddeki was the only Chilcotin unaware of Klatassine's plot. Because of his close relationship with the road company employees he was not trusted with the information. His wife was away and he went to bed in one of the whites' tents after waiting in vain for Tellot to come.

The darkness was just beginning to fade when Cheddeki awoke but, deciding it was too early to get up, he lay down again to sleep.

Somebody shook his leg and, looking up, he saw Tellot.

"Why sleep you so long, get up, for Klatassine wants you," Tellot told Cheddeki.

Cheddeki, suspecting something was wrong, put on only a blanket and immediately went with Tellot, taking his gun with him. When they reached the Chilcotin camp, all the Indians there were gathered around. The musket was taken away from him.

Klatassine told Cheddeki to sit down beside him. Did he like the whites, Klatassine asked.

"I like the whites, because I live by them for a long time."

"Will you help us?"

Cheddeki asked in what way.

"I am going to kill all the whites. You know they have our names in a book to do that with us," Klatassine told him.

Cheddeki remained silent for several moments.

"If you do not want to come in with us, give me your gun," Klatassine said. "If you will not go with us, remain with the whites and we will serve you the same."

Cheddeki did not wish to die with the whites. He said he would go. His gun was returned.

Some of the Chilcotins quietly recited Christian prayers. Near this same spot 20 years before, a Chilcotin war party had annihilated a band of 19 Homathkos.

* * *

Daylight was just beginning to break over the Homathko Valley as Charles Buttle dressed and went out to ready the fire for the work party's morning meal. The ex-miner and Boundary Commission sapper must have things brewing by the time the men awoke.

Except for the prattle of the river it was a quiet morning. The dancing and singing carried on by the nearby Siwash encampment had ceased a couple of hours ago or more. The only sound in the main road party's camp was the knocking together of wood sticks and the dull clang of pots and pans as Buttle stooped beside the fire. A black terrier kept by the work party wandered up and sniffed around.

Intent on his work, the cook was unaware of any movement in the surrounding bush; the explosion of animal-like gasping whoops chilled him. Uncomprehending, Buttle had only started to turn and rise when two bullets caught him in the back, killing him instantly.

Klatassine sprang in among the tents with his dozen warriors while the squaws and children came up to the edge of the camp to watch. Simultaneously the Chilcotins headed for the tents of the workmen. What happened next took only a few terrifying minutes.

John Newman, a Norwegian, and his tent-mate, James Oppenshaw, were easy victims. Newman was hit twice in the groin with shot; Oppenshaw died without waking as a slug tore through his brain.

Next door, Alexander Millan and George Smith died similarly.

In another tent, Philip Buckley was both awakened and dazed by a glancing blow to the head delivered by Tellot with a musket butt. His quick reflexes saved his life. Without knowing that his companion, John Hoffman, had been shot as the gun butt was aimed at him, or who his assailant was, he jumped to his feet by reflex action, knocking down the Indian, but at the door of the tent he was met by two more Chilcotins. Together they slashed at him with their knives and he fell.

The shooting had awakened Peter Petersen, the Dane, a few seconds before. He jumped from his blankets, in doing so avoiding a roundhouse musket swing. Petersen recognized the

Indian as Cheddeki. He saw two Indians firing into a neighboring tent.

Fortune again protected the Dane as a wide-mouthed, moustached Chilcotin, dressed in red blanket leggings and wearing a glass bead-embroidered belt with a knife in it ran up wielding an axe. Petersen leaped aside as Chessus' double-handed blow dug harmlessly into the ground.

"I then ran to the bank of the river and got behind a tree to hide myself as I saw the Indian who first struck at me coming up with a musket to shoot. The Indian...was gradually getting closer to me. At last he fired and shot me in the left arm, the ball passing through my wrist. I then jumped into the stream which was running fast, the blood poured profusely from my wound and discolored the water."[19]

Inside Petersen's tent, Robert Pollock lay bleeding from a serious gunshot wound in the abdomen.

A few scant seconds after the attack had begun, Klatassine's men employed their most deadly tactic. The supporting ropes of each tent were cut and the canvas flopped down on top of those who were still inside.

In the tent nearest Buttle's (the cook) slept Joseph Fielding, head propped on his rolled up pants, James Campbell, and Edwin Mosley who had moved in from another tent only the evening before.

Shots were aimed at the heads of Fielding and Campbell, but Mosley, sleeping between them under heavy blankets, wasn't noticed in the dull light which momentarily entered the tent when the flap was lifted. Then the tent was collapsed.

"A man was killed upon each side of me almost instantly. The pole of the tent fell lengthwise upon me and to this I attribute my escape."[20]

Helpless, he saw the big knives of the attackers hack through the tent and into his two writhing companions.

The other workmen were finished off the same way. Under the tent which Buckley had barged out of, the wounded Hoffman was hacked up with knives and hatchets. Likewise, Pollock and Newman. Wherever there was movement, the knives, hatchets and musket butts fell.

As Klatassine's insurgents concentrated on the tents, Buckley revived long enough to crawl into the bush undetected.

Mosley, after the attackers had satisfied themselves that no one was left alive in his tent and had left, crawled out from under the canvass on the river side and headed for the banks of the Homathko.

He was sighted in the grey dawn as he reached the river and a rasping whoop was followed by shots. The startled Mosley tripped over a log and tumbled over the sheer bank onto the rocks at the edge of the water. The shots had missed and, quickly recovering, he moved downriver to get out of sight.

An Indian approached the bank and peered over toward the dark rush of water. There was no sign of the white man; the obvious inference was that he had been hit by a musket ball and fallen into the river, which would have quickly claimed him.

Even after all movement had ceased under the tents, the Chilcotins continued to hack away to ensure the kill.

Petersen was pulling himself up on shore several hundred yards downstream after a rough ride over snags and sharp boulders.

Buckley had dragged himself into the bush and ran as far as possible before fainting from his wounds.

And Mosley, before continuing his flight along the river-bank, risked one more look at the scene of the massacre. Poking his head over the edge, he saw a large group of squaws and children milling around Buttle's provisions tent. The murderers were wasting no time in grabbing their plunder.

He could also see a body being dragged toward the river.

After his attack on Petersen, Cheddeki had shrunk back from the battle, cowed at the bloodshed wreaked on those who had employed him for so long and against whom he had nothing directly but the word of a war chief.

His inactivity did not go unnoticed. Klatassine approached him, breathing heavily from his exertion, but in control. He demanded to know why Cheddeki had stopped fighting.

"I am standing here to stop an escape by any of the whites."

Klatassine studied him, as if deciding the fate of the reluctant conspirator, but made no move against him.

Cusshen came over and grabbed the unfired gun. He said they must hurry to the axe men higher up.

"I am no good without my gun," Cheddeki said. "I will not go."

Cusshen gathered up five of the other men and set out on the trail to where Brewster and his "axe men" were camped. They left behind them a disorganized scene of butchery. The bodies of the dead roadworkers were being stripped and quartered. The procedure remained as it had through generations of battle between the Chilcotins and enemy coastal or neighboring interior tribes.

* * *

Two miles farther up the trail over treacherous terrain, Brewster's camp had remained completely out of earshot or suspicion of anything amiss. Brewster's cook, Qwhittie, called Tenhas George or Little George by the whites, had awakened, as had Buttle, ahead of the other workers. The young Homathko had prepared breakfast for Brewster and the three road company employees with him at the advance camp: John Clark, the inlet settler, earning extra money; Jim Gaudet, the half-breed son of a widowed pioneer who had settled down in Victoria; and Baptiste Demerest, another half-breed who spoke some Chilcotin and got along well with them.

Brewster sent them out to clear the route over which the road would run in this part of the country, while he himself would work ahead of them blazing.

As he shouldered his axe, he told Qwhittie they would be back for lunch.

Clark, Gaudet and Demerest were already beginning work a short distance from the tents. As Qwhittie began washing up the breakfast dishes in a big pan of heated water, he could see Gaudet off in the bush working.

Brewster walked two hundred yards ahead to where he had left off marking trees the day before. The crude trail at this point rose above the river to a small flat on the edge of a sharp precipice. The foreman picked out a fir tree in line with the projected route and aimed a couple of light blows, peeling off the bark and leaving a blaze of white wood several inches wide and long.

His second swing was followed by a sharp click from somewhere in the bushy area near the trail. Chessus' musket had misfired.

The startled Brewster looked around him, unsure of the sound.

"Who is it?" he asked, thinking he may have heard one of his own men, or perhaps a Chilcotin messenger from the main camp.[21]

"We have killed the others and we are going to kill you," Chessus' voice boomed out at him.

"Why do you want to kill me?" was all the surprised Brewster could say, not knowing who his enemy was or how many there were.

His question wasn't answered. A second shot barely missed him and he took off down the trail toward camp. But there suddenly came more shots from that direction.

Qwhittie was alarmed by the shooting and looked toward

the work party just as Gaudet fell. Four shots had been fired from ambush; Gaudet, wounded in the shoulder, had plunged off the trail into the bush and down the hill before a second bullet went through his left temple.

Clark, who had been working further along the trail, also attempted to escape into the bush, leaving behind the only gun the work party carried. It was unloaded. Scarface and another Indian trained their muskets on Clark. He was hit twice, in the groin and thigh. Crippled and whimpering from the fear and excruciating pain, he attempted to crawl. The bushes rustled beside him and a hatchet smashed his skull.

Demerest had stopped behind a tree, nervously wiping his brow, to look back toward the trail to see if his initial panic had been justified. Two Chilcotins burst through the bush a hundred yards from him and he plunged down the hill gripped by terror.

There was no way of eluding his pursuers. As Demerest cleared the bush and hit a mossy flat at the edge of a turbulent place in the river, one of the Chilcotins stopped and drew a bead on him. The shot rang out; Demerest didn't miss a stride as his body hurdled over the bank into the surging water. When the Indians reached the flat a few seconds later and looked into the Homathko, there was no sign of him. Even an unwounded man could not beat the river here.

Qwhittie did not have time to make any decisions about his own safety before Chraychanuru, who had been befriended by Qwhittie while a slave of the Homathkos, came running up. Grabbing his hand, Chraychanuru started pulling Qwhittie away.

"You must go, quickly, before they kill you too. They are going to kill all the whites."[22]

"Why do they want to kill the whites?" the boy asked him.

"I don't know. Go home to your own illahe!"

Qwhittie took his former friend's advice, fleeing down the trail toward the main work camp.

Brewster helplessly hid behind a big rock as the Chilcotins closed in. One axe was useless against the muskets. Surrounded, he could only wait to be killed, holding on to life for a few more precious moments.

Before a musket ball hit him in the chest, he must have had time to reflect on his own refusal to fully arm the work party. These red men whom he had trusted with his life would now claim it.

He slumped back on the ground and the firing ceased. When he looked up there were half a dozen Chilcotins standing over him.

The road foreman asked them to finish it.

Chessus put down his gun, raised Brewster's own axe into the air, and brought it down, cleaving into the white man's brain with a thump. The body kicked and was still.

The corpse was quickly stripped for the clothing. Chessus drew a big knife fashioned from a file and castrated the dead foreman. Then he plunged the knife into the chest, twisting and pulling at it until there was an accessible hole. Soon he stood and extended a blood-covered arm. In his hand Chessus held the still-warm heart.

He put it to his mouth, clenched it with his teeth and cut off a piece with his knife, grinding it up as red drool seeped over his thick lips.

Cushen took the muscle from him and did the same. The other four followed. Just as Brewster's manhood had been taken from him for punishment, his power as a white tyhee would now be assumed by his executioners. The strength from this heart would give them great advantage in the time ahead.

* * *

Klatassine and Tellot hastened along the squaws carrying what plunder they could from the main camp. They had divided up most of the clothing, food and other items of use according to need and reward, taking the rest along towards the upper camp to Chessus and the splinter war party. A few stragglers lingered behind at the first camp to scavenge and dispose of the remaining bodies.

Qwhittie blundered into them as they rounded a corner in the trail. He had no wish to be judged along with the whites or to be conscripted into the war party and was frightened. But instead of being harmed he was given a $20 bill and told not to say anything. He was allowed to continue down toward the first camp. His intention was to get back to the Waddington settlement at the mouth of the Homathko to warn the other whites, unless they had also been killed already. The ferryman was probably also dead, and those at the first road camp obviously were.

The boy's expectation was confirmed. At the camp he saw the bodies of four of the white men laid out on their tents. They were naked and mutilated, some headless or limbless.

* * *

Following his escape, Mosley had continued down along the river bank, jumping from boulder to boulder or edging along the slope. Several hundred yards downstream he detected movement. Crouching motionless against the bank, Mosley felt his heartbeat quicken. But the shadowy figure ahead did not move like an Indian, and Mosley could see no good reason why one of the Siwash killers would be grubbing around at the river, anyway.

It was with relief that he found it to be Petersen, and the Dane was likewise glad to see one of his own party. But his arm was a mess and his strength was gone. They had to get down to the ferry for Smith and his boat, and Mosley helped Petersen along as much as he could.

Finally Petersen had to stop. He urged Mosley to continue and to come back for him when he'd gotten help.

Neither of them liked the idea of leaving Petersen alone for possibly one or two days so close to the scene of the murder, but there was no other way to do it.

* * *

When Buckley revived, his first thought was to warn Brewster. "I fancied the men were engaged in packing away the things from our camp. I managed to crawl a distance of about 150 yards to some water where I drank eagerly and remained there till about 5 o'clock. I felt stronger after quenching my thirst and started off for Brewster's camp."[23]

When he got close to Brewster's camp the Irishman heard dogs barking. Brewster had no dogs...the Indians were there.

Down below, Klatassine and Tellot and their bands were celebrating their great victory—dancing, singing, and feasting on the food from the first camp. The men drank great quantities of water and forced themselves to vomit in order to purify themselves.

Buckley turned back to the spot he had left and remained there all night.

* * *

Mosley reached the ferry after what seemed an eternity. He cupped his hands to his mouth and shouted for Smith.

There was no reply. Mosley shouted again. There was no answer. Tired, the workman looked for a comfortable spot to rest.

Petersen caught up with him shortly. Regaining some of his strength after the brief interruption in his flight, and feeling more than a little nervous about being only two miles away from a band of murderers, he had soon resumed the journey down the remaining few miles to Smith's ferry.

Together they yelled at Smith across the river but again there was no answer. They thought he was either asleep or off somewhere, and they decided to try again in a while.

Qwhittie by this time was also fleeing down the right bank of the Homathko. When he reached the ferry landing he saw two white men whistling and shouting across at Smith's cabin. They suddenly saw Qwhittie and, recognizing him as a Homathko, spoke to him but Qwhittie ran away. Mosley followed him for a short distance and then went back.

Anxious to get to the Bute settlement and nervous about any human between him and his objective, Qwhittie went downstream to the ford, swam across and continued on the trail.

* * *

Buckley spent the evening hiding in the bush near the upper camp, alternating between spells of unconsciousness and periods of being able to do nothing other than listen to the barking of the dogs, unintelligible Indian conversation, and general noise coming from the camp as the Chilcotin war party and its entourage celebrated its victory. He slept the night, but early next morning he determined to make for the ferry.

Returning back down the trail and skirting the grisly remains of the camp where his fellow workmen had been cut to pieces, the Irishman made the best time he could toward the crossing.

When he reached it about noon on Sunday, Bulkley found he wasn't the lone survivor. Mosley and Peterson were there, having remained since their arrival the day before, continuing to call across to Smith from time to time, hoping he had returned. They had slept uneasily at the landing's tiny cabin with boarded door and clubs in hand and resumed their calling that morning, to no avail.

None of them knew of any swimmable places in the river nearby and Buckley and Petersen weren't in much shape anyway. Continuing down the right side of the Homathko through the thick timber with no trail was out of the question. The guy rope for the ferry still stretched across the river, but in their condition the three survivors could hardly monkey their way that far.

Buckley found the answer. The ex-sailor discovered a discarded length of rope which he looped around the guy and, in a sitting position, began hitching his way across. It was even slower and more difficult than the hike had been. Holding the guy rope with one hand, he would push his loop rope along it with the other, then pull himself forward.

When he got to within 12 feet of the opposite shore, the river appeared placid and shallow enough to risk, so Buckley slipped out of his loop and dropped in. He swam and waded to dry land.

He found the ferry skiff badly damaged, apparently by axes.

Smith was nowhere in sight. Although the ferry was gone, the travelling block was intact, and he rigged another loop onto it and sent it back to the other side. Petersen and Mosley joined him.

The reason for Smith's disappearance quickly became evident. Near the fire where Smith usually prepared his meal, the survivors found a large pool of blood. From there, a trail led to the river, as if a body had been dragged. Smith's cabin was a shambles. Whatever stores weren't missing were strewn around on the floor and outside on the ground.

Once again, there was the question of what to do. The choices were limited. They could rest and then start out down the trail again to the mouth of the river. It was 30 miles and the shorter leg just completed had almost finished Buckley and Petersen. Mosley could, however, go alone.

But an hour later their problem was solved. The usual brief moment of fear at the sound of an approaching human was allayed as the two French Canadian packers, Sampson and Cadman, rode in with five Homathko Indians, all armed to the teeth. It was the rescue party sent by Qwhittie.

They did what they could for the wounds of Buckley and Petersen, and gave them food and water. The skiff was repaired enough to float.

On Monday morning Mosley, Petersen, and Buckley got in with one of the packers and two of the Indians while the other packer and the rest of the Homathkos took the trail back to the townsite. Several miles downstream the skiff was put in at the halfway house where the party found another friendly Homathko who gave them the use of his large canoe for the rest of the way.

On Tuesday they continued to Waddington. The townsite's few dozen residents were anxiously awaiting details and rattled questions at them. But even the three survivors could not answer them all. They thought most or all of their own party other than themselves had been killed, but they hadn't had time to count heads. Qwhittie had seen Clark and Gaudet shot, but Brewster and Demerest might have gotten away, and the three knew less about that than the Indian lad.

At noon the next day the survivors, two Homathko Indians and one of the packers left via ocean canoe for Nanaimo.

* * *

On May 5 Whymper arrived in Victoria following a canoe trip that was uneventful except for his party accidently setting off a forest fire on a small island. His news of Smith's alleged death caused a stir, but if the story was true there seemed no need to worry—the other whites at Bute would surely take care of it. Indians murdering individual whites was a common tale.

In a statement to the Victoria *Daily Chronicle*, the artist first felt it necessary to praise the scenery and the Bute road at length before getting around to Squinteye's story about Smith.

"Victoria may fairly be congratulated on the fact of such being within a 16 hours' steamer-boat ride of this city, and I do not doubt that as this coast becomes peopled and settled this part of the country will be visited by numbers of tourists and travellers.

"I am sorry to be the bearer of a report which I would fain hope will prove false."[24] Then he described how he had been awakened by Squinteye and told about Smith's supposed death. The *Colonist* carried a similar article.

A week later the complacency regarding the Waddington party's safety was shattered. the morning *Chronicle* hurried out an extra on the evening of May 11 with the headline "HORRIBLE MASSACRE" and an article, based on the stories of the three survivors, sketching out the deadly work of the Chilcotin "fiends."

"The news is of a most dreadful character and its promulgation has raised a feeling of alarm among all the settlers in the outlying district."[25]

Waddington, of course, was presented with the news as soon as the survivors arrived on the *Emily Harris* from Nanaimo. He spoke with Mosley, Buckley, and Petersen at the Royal Hospital, a small wooden building on former Indian land. Their wounds were not serious enough to endanger them and they seemed relatively fit considering their ordeal. All expressed ignorance as to the reasons for the outbreak other than the few minor altercations between various members of the work force and the Indians. Buttle had had occasion to deal with them roughly when they had tried to steal provisions, and Smith had had arguments with some of them, too.

Waddington could not believe that the Chilcotins would murder white men over such petty grievances. Tellot had on occasion called Waddington his *tillikum* or best friend.

Mosley had one theory based on an idea that Klatassine had gone crazy, and had convinced the other Chilcotins to do likewise. Suppose, said Mosley, that Klatassine and Smith had had an argument and the Indian had killed Smith. Fearing retribution from the whites, he may have determined to kill all the workmen to conceal the first murder and gain anonymity and time to escape.

While news of the attack was extremely upsetting to Waddington, he had another fear. A pack train was scheduled to leave Bella Coola soon under the leadership of Alex McDonald. It was to go to Puntzi Lake, from where McDonald was to start clearing a trail toward Bute. McDonald's party would be heading right into the territory of the murdering Chilcotins.

That afternoon, Waddington visited Gov. Kennedy to inform him of what he had learned. The governor decided that rather than going to the trouble of sending a naval vessel on a special trip over the strait to New Westminster to inform Gov. Seymour, the regular sailing of the steamer *Enterprise* the next day would be soon enough.

After seeing Kennedy, Waddington made a deposition to police authorities outlining the Bute project as did Buckley, Petersen and Mosley. The three survivors put in writing their denials that the murders were provoked. There was, they stated, no tampering with the Chilcotin women or abuse of the men. The depositions would be sent over with the *Enterprise*.

Unfortunately, the *Enterprise* experienced difficulties and did not sail on the 12th as scheduled. New Westminster thus remained ignorant for yet another day of the massacre in its territory.

But by now everyone in Victoria knew about it. The *Chronicle* reprinted its story of the day before and the *British Colonist* gave the news extensive coverage, running five different stories on the subject. The *Colonist* called it: "...the most startling thing of the kind that has yet taken place in either colony. There is something almost fiendish in the manner in which this treacherous massacre was perpetrated.... The cause of this Indian outbreak was so far as present can be ascertained entirely one of plunder. The men who have returned say that the Indians have been hitherto treated in the kindest manner and that there was not the slightest indication of ill-feeling among them prior to this murderous attack."

The B.C. government was scored for allegedly not dealing with the Indians of the mainland firmly enough. "It takes little acumen to perceive that such a shiftless sort of policy has inspired the natives with suspicion of our integrity and contempt for our power." There were at least 150 able-bodied men, harangued the *Colonist*, "ready or not to act under the proper authorities."

While admitting that injustices had been done to the Indians, the *Colonist* saw no excuse for letting the situation develop.

"Let justice follow inevitably on the footsteps of Indian crime, justice uninfluenced on the one hand by a morbid sentimentality, on the other by a reckless and brutal indifference to savage life and we shall not likely have again to recount so heart-rending a story as we present this day to our readers."[26]

Impatient at having to sit around for another day, Waddington sent a message to Nanaimo to go out on the *Emily Harris* to Bute for the employees at the townsite. In it were orders to search for survivors and bury the victims.

The *Enterprise* set sail on the afternoon of the 13th, with Waddington and the depositions on board. It was 10:30 that night before Seymour received news of the massacre. The new governor was furious at Kennedy's slackness in informing him. There were half a dozen naval ships based at Esquimalt, yet the Vancouver Island governor had waited two days to send the news by regular mail steamer.

Seymour immediately wrote formal application to Esquimalt to provide the frigate *H.M.S. Tribune* and gunboat *Grappler* for whatever action would be necessary. He issued two orders: one that the *Enterprise* be unloaded immediately so that it could return to the Island with the application for naval assistance; the other went to Chief Inspector of Police Chartres Brew to start getting together a force of special constables to go to Bute.

The decision to raise a volunteer force was one of necessity and strategy. After the Royal Engineers were withdrawn Brew had envisaged a permanent police force of 150 constables for B.C., but expense had allowed only a few. Seymour wanted the situation treated as a civil dispute, not as a war. He did not ask for marines from Esquimalt naval station. Only if Brew and his volunteers ran into immediate trouble would marines be sent in. The governor also did not ask for help from Victoria. It was a matter for British Columbia. Brew's expedition must check for survivors and feel out the situation, not go on a shooting spree. Seymour would have nothing to do with "men bent on vengeance."[27]

Seymour acted quickly and decisively for someone who had been in B.C. only about three weeks. James Douglas' retirement as governor of both colonies had necessitated two new governors: Kennedy for Vancouver Island and Seymour for British Columbia. Seymour was a former Lieutenant-Governor of British Honduras. On April 20 he had arrived in New Westminster on the gunboat *H.M.S. Forward* with his Colonial Secretary Arthur Birch, a tall, polite young man who had been a junior clerk in the Colonial Office.

The new governor himself was thin, bald, and rather ineloquent, but he was given a rousing reception by the 300 residents because they were pleased at having their own governor in New Westminster. Judge Matthew Begbie administered the oath of office.

Seymour was so far not enamoured with his capital city, which he found a "melancholy...picture of disappointed hopes."[28] The streets still had not been cleared of fallen trees, many of the houses were unoccupied, and the public buildings were largely makeshift accommodation.

But he was determined to make something of this crude place, and to be a good governor. His rapid formulation of strategy in regard to the Indian rebellion owed itself in large part to a call paid by Seymour on his predecessor, Douglas. Sir James had told the new governor: "A party should be at once sent in the gun-boat to the Inlet to pick up survivors and to give information of the Indians' movements. Then a party should be organized to consist of about thirty men, well mounted, equipped and provided with ammunition under a proper leader to go round to Alexandria and that rewards for each man concerned in the murder should be offered, say one hundred dollars to two hundred dollars."[29]

At 3 a.m. on Saturday the 14th the Enterprise crossed the Strait of Juan de Fuca back to the island colony. That same morning Birch sent a letter to Gold Commissioner William George Cox at Richfield. Backgrounding the situation, Birch said Brew's expedition was "merely to assert the supremacy of the law."

"This strong body of men will follow up, in case of necessity, the Indians to their fishing grounds on the lakes, but the governor trusts that under the experienced management of Mr. Brew, the well-disposed Indians will be induced to capture and hand over the murderers.

"The Governor in Council has considered it would be very desirable to have some steps taken from Alexandria towards the same object sought to be obtained by the force proceeding from Bute Inlet. He has in Council determined to request your assistance. He feels that he must leave you a very large descretion as to the number and race, of the men you would employ and as to the course to be adopted, but he suggests for your consideration that you should not be sufficiently weak to invite attack, nor your force so numerous as to form a heavy burden on the Colonial Treasury."

Cox was told to avoid "collision" with the Indians, but "you are at liberty to offer such rewards as you may think fit to the

Indians for the apprehension of the murderers."[30]

Seymour also had Birch issue a proclamation offering a $250 reward for: "the apprehension and conviction of every Indian or other person concerned as principle or accessory before the fact, to the murder of any of the 14 Europeans, who were cut off by Indians on or about the 29th and 30th days of April now past, in the valley of the Homathco River, in Bute Inlet."[31]

Seymour felt that "in every respect my predecessor's suggestions have been exceeded by my actions..."[32]

Brew's call for volunteers brought quick results, and he accepted 28 men for the expedition. By Saturday night his small force was ready and waiting for word from Lord (Richard J.M.) Gilford, the acting senior naval officer.

Gilford got into New Westminster at 10:30 Sunday morning, but instead of the *Tribune* and *Grappler*, he brought only the *Grappler's* sister gunboat, the *Forward*. He also brought with him a request that the *Forward* be detained as short a time as possible on this mission.

Seymour was not happy with the lack of enthusiasm being shown in regard to support. The situation left the possibility of success by Brew's force considerably in doubt, as he could not now be confident that communications between the force and New Westminster would be kept open as efficiently as they should be.

The governor, however, could do little else but accept Gilford's excuses. The senior naval officer had told him that the *Tribune* did not have sufficient steam power to go to Bute. The 31-gun screw frigate would have made an impressive show in the inlet and she was fast—Lord Gilford himself had made alterations in the rigging for greater speed. As for the *Grappler*, a 104-foot vessel with two howitzers and one gun, it had been damaged on a northward cruise and simply wasn't available. Neither was the sloop *Columbine*, which was out of range on another cruise.

Waddington received a message to meet with Seymour. The Executive Council was to meet later that morning and the governor wished first to discuss the situation with the Bute road's promoter.

Waddington gathered up his plans and surveys of the road and surrounding country and went to Seymour's home. Gilford was there with Seymour and sat in on the meeting.

What, the governor asked, were Waddington's views on the best means of capturing the murderers?

"First. An expedition from Alexandria of not less than 150

men, so as to be able to form detachments capable of scouring the country and hindering the Indians from frequenting their fishing grounds, until they give up the murderers.

"Second. An observation corps at Bute Inlet to keep the Indians in awe, proceed to the scene of the massacre, ascertaining if there are any survivors and inter the dead. But as the trail is not yet open, it would be most difficult to proceed from there into the interior or to establish a line of operations on this route.

"Third. An observation corps to be sent forthwith to Bentinck Arm to save McDonald's party, if there is still time, capture the unpunished Indians who committed the murders there two years before, and protect the settlers at the head of the Inlet."

Waddington stated his conviction that the rising of the Indians was a general one and that "they will murder all the white men they can meet with."[33]

Seymour listened carefully to Waddington's proposals; he had obviously put a great deal of thought into them. But he disagreed as to the extent of the uprising. He believed it to be an isolated occurrence which would not be joined in by other tribes. However, Waddington's first two points agreed substantially with his own views. They must first see to any survivors and obtain what information they could from the Coast Indians.

As to the third point, Seymour paused, turning to Lord Gilford. "Unfortunately there is no vessel disposable."

Gilford nodded.

Waddington hesitated, wondering whether to press the point. Then he commented only, "Well, that certainly is most unfortunate."[34]

He offered to place his pack mules and stores at Bute Inlet at the disposal of Brew's party. On Seymour's request, Waddington agreed to escort the expedition, and the message on the *Emily Harris* was cancelled.

Edwin Mosley also wished to go.

Arrangements for the trip were completed and at 6 p.m. the *Forward* left the dock at New Westminster to the sound of cheers from a good crowd, including Seymour.

The 104-ft. *Forward,* armed with two howitzers and a 32-pounder, already carried 40 officers and men, so the volunteers had a cramped and tedious journey.

The schedule called for recoaling at Nanaimo early next morning and then continuing on to Bute Inlet.

It was a reluctant alliance that had been formed between

Brew and Waddington for the expedition. They represented most of the competitive jealousies that had been building and raging between New Westminster and Victoria, and if not for Seymour the two men would never have joined together in such a venture.

The stubby, gruff Brew, now 48 and a bachelor like Waddington, had spent 14 years in the police force of his native Ireland and had served in Crimea before coming to B.C. six years before. Heavily involved in maintaining law and order in the Cariboo and other parts of the mainland as police inspector, chief gold commissioner and now as chief inspector and stipendiary magistrate, he owed his allegiance to the new mainland colony.

Brew saw Waddington's Bute Inlet road scheme as simply an opportunistic plan by Victoria speculators to rob New Westminster of its Cariboo commerce at a nice profit to themselves. They were deluding people into thinking the Bute was a practical route, but, from what Brew heard, the enterprise was not all it was said to be. If it ran into trouble, it undoubtedly deserved it.

As for Waddington himself, Brew couldn't stand the man. It took somebody like Waddington to promote such a scheme as the Bute road. The Victoria merchant had a ridiculously overconfident zeal for hair-brained schemes like building a railroad all the way across the continent from Canada to the Vancouver Island capital. His mind seemed to jump from grandiose idea to grandiose idea, lighting wherever lay the greatest promise of glory and profit. In short, he found Waddington to be "one of the most sanguine imaginative men I have ever met, prompt to delude himself on any matter of which he makes a hobby."[35]

Waddington was well aware of Brew's disdain for the Bute Inlet project. In fact, many people in New Westminster would have done almost anything to see the project destroyed. Brew was undoubtedly one of those who was perfectly happy to see the Chilcotin break out in rebellion.

The future of the Bute Inlet Wagon Road Company weighed heavily on Waddington's mind as the *Forward* steamed through the dusk toward Nanaimo. But more than that, there was the fate of the road party to ponder. There were families in Victoria waiting and hoping for miracles; there were relatives elsewhere who would not hear of the tragedy for many weeks or months.

While there seemed little hope for any of Brewster's two work parties other than the three men who had escaped and returned to Victoria, McDonald's pack train was a complete mystery. It seemed so probable that it would eventually encounter the rebellious Chilcotins, that a gunboat should have been dispatched to Bella Coola immediately to try to catch the party and warn the men.

It was 4:30 a.m. by the time the *Forward* reached Nanaimo, and it wasn't ready to leave again until 11:30. It headed out north into the channel and in the early evening entered the imposing fiord of Bute Inlet. At 8 p.m., 12 miles in, the captain dropped anchor for the night.

When the *Forward* neared the mouth of the Homathko in mid-afternoon the next day, Tuesday, May 17, the volunteers crowded against the railing for a look at the river where it entered the sea, and at the tiny cluster of buildings upstream.

As the volunteers unloaded their gear and prepared to camp, a steady drizzle of rain hit the flatland townsite. Brew consulted with Waddington and the road company employees and Indians regarding the march up the river. Qwhittie would accompany them and with his guiding, in addition to that of Mosley and Squinteye, there should be no difficulty in finding the locations of the murders. But it would take another three days to get there.

While Waddington and Brew consulted in the Homathko Lodge, the volunteers were finding that their relief at getting off the crowded gunboat was premature. The drizzle became a downpour and the volunteers had no tents. Some of them teamed up and made makeshift tents with their blankets, managing to stay fairly dry. But all things considered, the expedition was not shaping up to be a comfortable experience.

When the volunteers broke camp at 7 a.m. Wednesday, Waddington's mules carried the supplies and much of the equipment, but the men packed their own wet blankets, rifles, and ammunition. They were accompanied by a small band of Homathko Indians who helped in packing.

By the time they reached the halfway-house camp seven and a half hours later and 15 miles upstream, they were so tired there was no question of going further. But Brew had them up, breakfasted, and ready to go again at 5 a.m. the next day. It was another 15 miles to the ferry.

They made similar time and reached it about noon. Mosley found the scene that greeted him and the other volunteers much as it had been two and a half weeks before.

The patch of blood still darkened the ground beside the charred campfire wood; the drag marks still traced a short path to the river bank. A musket ball was dug out of the tree against which Smith had been leaning.

Nothing in the cabin had been left untouched. Except for a few tools, everything had been taken or destroyed. Brew sent several men along paths leading into the bush off the main trail. The first plunder to be spotted consisted of five big chunks of bacon and a bag of beans hidden in the bushes. Further search resulted in the discovery of a cache half a mile off. In it were cooking utensils, 500 pounds of bacon, 200 pounds of sugar, and 120 pounds of dried apples. A 50-square-foot area was covered with sugar, coffee, tea, dried apples and beef.

It was decided to spend the night at Smith's cabin and cross the Homathko early the next morning. The ferry scow had been retrieved by Waddington's packers several days before and put back into service, but it didn't appear to be very safe and the river didn't look inviting. Brew wanted to reach the camp where the murders had occurred as quickly as possible the next day, so, to save him time, Waddington decided to stay behind with Qwhittie and several other men for the chore of ferrying the mules across the river.

* * *

As Brew's party was preparing to cross the Homathko at Smith's ferry, Gov. Seymour, back in New Westminster, was composing a letter to the Duke of Carlisle at the Colonial Office informing him of the difficulties that had arisen in the B.C. colony. The governor outlined what was known of the massacre and what steps he had taken toward controlling the rebellion.

While he was leaving the decision up to Brew whether the force should push inland or not, Seymour expressed doubts about its ability to continue over the mountains without a sufficient base of operations and supply.

"A forced retreat over the mountains would probably entail an amount of disaster which I can scarcely allow myself to contemplate. I am of the opinion, therefore, that Mr. Brew's party will not advance beyond the spot where their communications cease to be secure."

Seymour explained the tactic of sending Cox from the Interior with a second party, decrying the "immense sacrifice of the finances of the Colony for the maintenance of its honor and the support of the law."[36]

He then outlined the circumstances surrounding the tardiness with which he had been informed by Kennedy of the massacre. "Why were two days lost in communicating with me?"

The governor signed off after 10 pages, but he continued to contemplate not only Kennedy's laxity but that of the navy in supplying vessels.

During the San Juan boundary dispute between Britain and the United States in the late fifties, Esquimalt had taken on increased importance as a station for the Royal Navy, and more ships were based there. Now that the protection of the Royal Engineers was gone, the navy surely had to take some responsibility for the mainland. Governor Kennedy got on extremely well with the officers at Esquimalt, being as it was, close to Victoria. The same sort of cooperation should be given B.C., and Seymour's colony should at least get use of one or two gunboats on a permanent basis.

Seymour wrote a second letter.

"This large and important province which now costs the Imperial government absolutely nothing for its maintenance and does not absorb a fraction of Her Majesty's land forces, has claims, I conceive, at the still early stages of its existence, to receive a share of the naval protection the mother country affords to other and less exposed possessions."

Seymour did not like to complain, of course, and Gilford was "obliging and anxious to please in other respects."[37]

He added that the fear of Indians was now general along the Coast. The workmen in the Queen Charlottes copper mines were asking for protection or else a temporary stoppage of work. The governor could only reply that there was no naval protection available, and the mines charter would not be forfeited if they temporarily left the island at this time.

* * *

Shouts and curses came from out on the river as the ferry scow, loaded down with supplies and the first group of Brew's men, hit rapid water and strained against the guy rope as waves splashed over it.

The ferry's contents, including the men, were tossed around violently and for a few harrowing minutes it looked as if it might sink. But some frantic bailing and hard work got it to the other side with no injuries other than a few scrapes and bruises. It could have been serious.

Brew looked at Waddington, then went down to the river to prepare to cross with the rest of the men and their supplies.

The hike from the ferry to the main work camp was tortuous. While the first 30 miles of the trail made it appear that the bad publicity about it might be as ill-founded as the project's chief promoter claimed, this new stretch on the other side of the river was an entirely different story.

Brew described the trail at this point:

"About six miles above the ferry the mountains enclose the

river between sheer precipices. This is what is called the canyon. Here Mr. Waddington was forced to take his trail over an abrupt bluff, a shoulder of the mountain (Mr. Waddington says 1100 feet high) projecting into the river. Over this I counted 79 zig-zags ascending and 65 descending. Some of the angles were so steep that men who were with me accustomed to packing said no laden animals could turn them.

"After passing over this bluff the trail runs along a flat on the river's bank till another precipice forces it into the stream where it is carried along the base of the precipice on a timber bench, the inside of which rested on a narrow ledge blasted in the rock and the outside on the heads of posts planted in the river. The vibration of this bench caused by the torrent rushing against the posts is so great that I feared it would be carried away while we were on it."[38]

It was a muggy day and the mosquitos tortured the volunteers as they struggled up this trail which so much amazed Brew for its poorness. It took them seven long hours to reach the flat where the first massacre took place.

When they came upon it, some of the volunteers stopped short, gaping in shock at the scene of desolation before them. Others approached cautiously, scanning the area of the camp, eyes picking out sure signs of the murders.

Most of the tents had been cut up for the fabric and were gone—a few remnants, some with the encircled J.W. Keyser on them, remained scattered about. The remains of the canvas, the tent poles and other articles, however, made it clear where each tent had been pitched. The food stores and most of the utensils were gone, as was the case at the ferry; the rest had been destroyed. Baking pans had been smashed, cross-saws bent in two, drilling equipment broken or apparently thrown into the river, powder kegs broken and spilled, books and papers torn up. And everywhere there was blood, smeared on fabric, grass, tree stumps, everywhere.

Brew quietly told his men to stash their gear, and deployed them to make a search of the camp in order to inventory evidence. Although there were no bodies, it was not difficult to tell what happened to each victim. From each tent there were drag marks spotted with blood leading the few feet to the river's bank.

In the first tent, where Oppenshaw's head had lain, there was a large pool of blood. His hat was found nearby. Beside him, the shirt and pants of John Newman lay; the shirt showed two bullet holes near the right groin.

In the second tent, where Alex Millan and George Smith

had slept, was more blood.

Beside this was the tent from which Peter Petersen had escaped. Robert Pollock's blankets were saturated with blood and the straw matting was stained dark from it.

Then there was Peter Buckley's tent, where John Hoffman had been killed. There, the volunteers found a black jumper, a white towel, and a white blanket stiff from dried blood. A black necktie was also stained. An empty leather purse was covered with blood; next to it was a canvas change bag. And there was hair and brains.

Charles Buttle's tent was not stained like the others, but his dark colored jacket was found near the campfire with two bullet holes in the back.

Mosley approached the sixth tent. It was from there he had escaped after watching Joseph Fielding and James Campbell killed on either side of him. It was not a pleasant experience returning there now. Fielding's trousers, which he had folded up for a pillow as usual that night, had the tell-tale dark stain. Campbell's straw matting and blue bed cover were still there, likewise. Mosley picked up a piece of canvass, poking his finger through a hole in it. A long knife had slashed through it here, killing one of his tent-partners.

Brew again sent the men into the woods to search for caches or further evidence, but they returned empty-handed. Brew himself wandered up the crude continuation of the trail with Thomas Elwyn, his second in command.

The mild-mannered 27-year-old Elwyn was a capable and popular leader. After arriving in Victoria from England five years before he had become one of the earliest miners at Williams Creek, later being appointed gold commissioner. When charges of dishonesty forced his resignation in 1862, angry Williams Creek miners put together a petition demanding he be reinstated.

The trail rose steadily past the point where actual construction ended and, according to what they had been told, they must just about be at the camp. But suddenly, the trail seemed to terminate at the edge of a 200 foot precipice.

Brew and Elwyn searched along its edge. The only way they could see of getting across was to drop over the edge several dozen feet to a ledge. The butt end of a big windfall fir lay propped on the ledge, sloping downward over a fast stream and across a ravine to a small plain. Somewhere down there, undoubtedly, was the second camp and the rest of the dead workers.

Back at the camp three of the volunteers were sitting on

their haunches peering intently at the ground. One of them had a magnifying glass in his hand, playing it on some of the spilled gunpowder. Suddenly there was a blast and the three men were knocked over on their backs. Except for a few burned whiskers they weren't hurt, but they got a good ribbing from the other volunteers who had been watching the experiment.

Brew called up all hands to explain what was needed. He told the men about the ravine that had to be crossed and that since anyone not used to high places could easily fall, he was asking for someone to volunteer.

Several men requested a look at the crossing and they were led back up the trail. Leslie Jones, the brother of a Victoria doctor, agreed to try it. He needed a rope to make his way down the rock-face to the log. Jones got up onto the log and began inching his way down, arms outstretched for balance, wavering slightly. Ten feet out he stopped and, very slowly, half-crouching, negotiated a turn-around and headed back.

It couldn't be done, he announced when he had been hauled back up.

Brew asked if anyone else wanted to try.

There was silence for several seconds.

Seeing that no one else would offer, A.E. Atkins, an easy-going, good-humored Victoria laborer who had joined the expedition for something to do as much as for the wages, said he would like to risk it.

Brew granted him permission and Atkins went down to the log. Atkins took off his boots and hung them around his neck, preferring to feel the log under his stockinged feet. He left his rifle behind, taking only his revolver. The log didn't look nearly as big when he was on it, and it was a long hundred feet to the other side. But he made it, clambering down some rocks and disappearing into the bush.

He continued forward a considerable distance, criss-crossing several areas which looked likely, but he was unable to find any sign. "It struck me all at once what a fool I was three miles from no person and might be shot down at any moment."[39] He decided he had better report back, and there was more spring in his step than there had been going in.

It was pointless to search further, not having anyone with them who was familiar with that part of the trail or who knew where the advance camp had been, and all Brew could do was return to the other camp and wait for Waddington.

A little later in the afternoon, Waddington arrived with his seven men. He brought no mules with him. To Brew's enquiry, he explained tersely that the river was too rough at the present time to be negotiated with pack animals until the ferry was put in better condition.

As Waddington examined the murder scene, Brew explained about being unable to find the second camp.

Tenhas George would take them there, said Waddington.

Since the Homathko Indians had carried only small loads, and provisions were low, Brew sent half the men back to the ferry. With a dozen volunteers and several Indians, including Qwhittie, he and Waddington went back up toward Brewster's camp. At the precipice, Brew wondered aloud how it was intended to build a road over it.

Brewster "made a mistake," replied Waddington. "The trail should have been carried some other way."[40]

But Brew could not see any other way it could have gone.

A rope railing was rigged on the log and all the men crossed safely. Qwhittie led them quickly to where he had been washing dishes that morning, then pointed to where he had seen the first man fall.

First Gaudet's, then Clark's nude and mutilated body was discovered in the bush. Fanning out, the volunteers found no trace of Demerest, but they did find his tracks. The strides were long, the heel marks deep, indicating his panicked flight. His big red handkerchief was found near a tree behind which he had apparently taken temporary refuge. Then the tracks continued on down the hill, ending at the river's brink.

No one could have survived jumping into that, Brew mused, gazing down at the violent water smashing against rocks and the sheer bank.

Waddington had an explanation. Demerest always was a bit weak-minded.

Qwhittie explained that Brewster had been working further up the trail blazing when the shooting began.

Brewster's body was mutilated the worst of all. The air stunk even before they found him. Flies swarmed over the naked corpse. Brains protruded from the smashed skull. The chest cavity gaped open. Brewster's penis was jammed in his mouth.

It was getting late. They would have to return tomorrow to bury the bodies. At 8:30 that night the search party camped at Murderer's Bar.

The next day Elwyn and a dozen men were sent back to bury the three corpses. Because of the rocky ground over most of the area, it was more practical to cut logs and cover the bodies, then pile rocks on top of the logs. Elwyn read a burial service.

Before burial, the 12 volunteers were sworn in as a jury to officially view the bodies and then adjourn to hear evidence back at the Waddington townsite.

The party then immediately decamped and began the trip back down to the mouth of the inlet. At the ferry, the men who had returned there the previous day had discovered another cache.

After spending another night at the scene of the first murder, the entire force started down. Not a single fresh sign of hostile Indians had been found, and none was seen the rest of the way "home."

Immediately after the expedition returned to Waddington townsite on May 23, the inquest was re-opened under jury foreman Leslie Jones. Qwhittie was sworn in and testified as to what he knew of the killings. Mosley was also sworn in and examined. Brew and Elwyn witnessed the statements and Jones related the verdict:

"Having heard the above evidence we are of opinion that William Brewster, John Clark, and Jim Gaudet met their deaths by wilful murder committed by certain Chilcotin Indians names unknown."[41]

Since none of the other bodies had been found, they weren't included in the verdict.

Brew had intended to leave immediately to return to Victoria on the *Forward*. There was little else to be accomplished in Bute. The Homathko Indians for the most part knew no Chinook so the amount of information he could obtain from them was extremely limited. Brew could see no point in trying to pierce the mountains barring the interior and even Waddington agreed the circumstances made it impractical.

However, a canoe arrived with a message from Seymour dated the 19th asking Brew to report on proceedings and to await further word from him.

The expedition's leader, pestered by mosquitos and constant interruptions from subordinates, therefore sat down to pen a report. He explained what had been found and stated his opposition to extending the expedition at this point.

"Unless provided with horse transport and supplies, with means of repairing the ferry and working it, I could not keep a party fifty miles up the country. They would be starved. The lower-lower Country Indians are so scared that they would not venture one hundred yards into the interior unprotected, and they scarcely carry a load worth paying for. I had a consultation with Mr. Waddington as to the expediency of advancing into the interior if we could— the conclusion we arrived at was that with the present means at command it would be impracticable. Trails would have to be cut. Bridges made, precipices scaled and obstructions overcome which would require engineering skill and resources... If His Excellency The Governor wish me to advance in the Interior, I shall make the attempt, let the undertaking be ever so difficult."

Brew felt it necessary to state an opinion of the trail.

"No just idea of the Country or the Trail can be formed from Mr. Waddington's flattering description of it; within a distance of four miles the Trail crosses a mountain I consider 2000 feet high. Mr. Waddington says 1100. If I have to go on you will have to send me up horses, axes, saws, ropes."

He described the ravine between the two upper camps. "To get horses over this portion of the intended trail will require many days work—in fact I do not see how it is to be done.... If I have to advance, I would require a small increase of force. The Indians here are greatly afraid that the Chilcotins will come down and kill everyone, but the outrage was committed for the sake of plunder by a few men of a branch of the Chilcotin tribe and the main tribe will not become involved in war on their account."[42]

Rather than sending the letter back on the canoe, Brew put it on the gunboat to save time. He also sent five men back on the gunboat after giving the volunteers the choice of staying or leaving. Waddington, too, chose to return with the *Forward* to New Westminster.

* * *

William Manning was sawing wood with a heavy cross-cut saw outside his Puntzi Lake ranch while his klootchman Nancy, a Chilcotin, worked nearby.

The settler, whose partner Alex McDonald was in Bella Coola organizing a pack train for Alfred Waddington's Bute Inlet venture, saw two women from the nearby Chilcotin village come up to the house and talk animatedly to Nancy.

Manning continued sweating over the log for a time before walking back to the house for a drink of water.

"What were they talking about?" he asked, wiping his brow and watching the women hurry away.

"They say all the whites are being killed and they will come here after dinner. They say to go."

"I don't believe the Chilcotins would hurt me," Manning assured her. "I've known them a long time now. They like me."

"Not them. I don't know who. I afraid, want to go."[43]

Manning told her to go back into the log cabin and finish dinner. He genuinely was not worried. The local Indians had never shown any hint of violence toward him or the few other whites who had worked in the area. Manning had taken up the land here a couple of years ago, the first white settler in the central Chilcotin. To do so, he had had to force the Chilcotins off this particular parcel because it contained a spring he wanted. (He had threatened them with smallpox at one point, but there had been no further trouble.) It was a choice piece of farm land near the lake and creek which he had enlarged by clearing. As he pushed back the forest with axe and plow, the ranch became a good operation. To the local Chilcotins, this had been more than a beautiful spot with a spring—they had camped there for generations, for it was the junction of trails from all directions. Despite this, Manning had kept peace by sharing his potato, corn, vegetable, and other crops with them and had even employed some of them on the farm. One winter he had almost singly-handedly kept them from starving.

After dinner Manning went back out to resume his work. As Nancy was cleaning up, an old Chilcotin squaw came in and told her: "Maybe they kill you too. You better go away."

Nancy made her leave and then went out to Manning and repeated the warning. She was now very worried. She did not want to be killed along with Manning.

"You tell me this because you want to leave me," Manning accused her, continuing his work.

"No," she pleaded with him. "You have plenty of flour and money and other things which they will take and go to Alexis."[44]

But Manning, becoming angry at her insistence, would listen no longer.

A short distance away from the ranch house, the Indian Tahpitt hurried along, a rifle in one hand, grim determination formed on his face. Behind him strode Chief Anahim of Nancootlem. According to his own later statement Tahpitt did not relish the task he was about to perform. The unpredictable and cynical Anahim had harangued him for two days about killing Manning. Klatassine and his band had arrived with stories about a big victory over the whites and talk of wiping them all out. Anahim had started on Tahpitt, who could not withstand the pressures of the taunting which was soon joined in by others. At last he had agreed and had set off quickly.

Now, several other curious Chilcotins followed a few hundreds yards behind them. They passed three Indian women gathering sticks.

One of them, Ilsedocknell, asked where they were going in such a hurry. "They urge me to kill Manning," said Tahpitt, not stopping.[45]

A friend of Nancy's from the Indian village, Ahtit, entered Manning's cabin, telling her to "Come with me. Don't stop." Knowing that in only minutes the men would arrive, Ahtit refused to be put off. Nancy, by this time, was not about to offer any resistance. Not stopping to take any belongings, she went out with Ahtit. Manning was still working and did not see them leave.

"Mr. Manning."

Manning turned to see Tahpitt raise the rifle. There was an explosion and the settler felt only for a moment the musket ball strike him in the right side of the chest and exit through the left shoulder blade. Manning was dead when he hit the ground. Dropping the musket and pulling out a hatchet, Tahpitt rushed up and swung twice at Manning's face.

Nancy and Ahtit were 50 yards from the house when the shot rang out. Nancy rushed back to see what had happened. There was already a crowd of Chilcotins gathered at the ranch house, some hacking and pulling at the body, some inside the house gathering up food and clothing.

Ilsedocknell and other squaws came rushing to look at the body and fight over the spoils. Nancy entered the log house to retrieve her blankets and other belongings, but they had already been taken. Clothing, food and utensils were being thrown about.

Outside, the men bent or broke all the tools and agricultural instruments. The subject of special attention was Manning's plow, which they had been forced to watch turning up the land of their campground. To the Chilcotins it was the symbol of the white intrusion on their territory. Several Indians attacked it together and it was soon a piece of junk.

During the mayhem, Tahpitt sat sobbing, his face covered by a blanket. He had been talked into killing a white man, and now what was to happen to him? Instead of the whites staying away, more would surely come.

Nancy came out and looked at Manning's body again. It was nude and by now badly maimed. Her brother Liscullum came with help to drag the body away, taking it to the creek. They dumped it into the shallow water and covered it with branches and roots.

The wild scene at the ranch continued into the night at a jubilant potlatch. Klatassine and his followers joined and the Tatla and Puntzi Indians sang, danced, ate, smoked, and told stories. Klatassine repeated the tales of his own great victory, urging the men to join him for a journey into Bella Coola territory to kill more whites. The Bella Coola tribe, allies of the Chilcotins, could be persuaded to rise also and retrieve their land before the white man's curse killed them all.

A starving boy fished through the ice but could catch nothing. Two hunters who bragged of their skill refused to give the boy anything to eat. Famine saw that the boy was good, and went up to where he was fishing and struck the ice with his stick. Each time Famine struck the ice the boy caught a fish. Then Famine went and found the bad hunters who would not feed the boy, and killed them.

Chilcotin folk story.

Governor Seymour had by no means been idle while Brew was trudging up and down the banks of the Homathko River. There was feeling that the retirement of his predecessor, Sir James Douglas, had left the colony's Indians confused and suspecting the whites were now without a tyhee. Seymour required a demonstration of his succession to let the Indians know they were still under the fatherly protection of the whites and, more important, that the whites were as powerful as ever. Since there were some 60,000 Indians and only 7,000 whites in B.C., Seymour considered the matter important.

He decided to throw a party for the Indians. With Queen Victoria's birthday anniversary coming up there was no better excuse. He could not, of course, invite every Indian in the colony, but he sent word up among the Fraser River Indians, whom he considered the most important, via the Roman Catholic missionaries.

It couldn't have gone much better. On the big day, May 24, 3,500 Fraser River Indians formed a colorful and majestic procession of canoes, marshalled by the priests, and paddled into New Westminster. As they rounded a point in the Fraser and approached Seymour's house, Col. Moody's former residence in Sapperton a mile from New Westminster, they broke into the singing of Catholic hymns, passing under the governor's windows. Then, as part of a plan well-rehearsed with the missionaries, they broke into cheers. The procession

78

continued on to the capital's public park where the guests were treated to a luncheon "at great expense to the government,"[1] as Seymour typically described it.

The well-choreographed event continued smoothly through the day. Governor Seymour joined the throng after lunch, and official greetings were exchanged. Through the priests, the various Fraser River chieftains had agreed on the wording of a message to Seymour, and chosen three delegates to deliver it.

"Great Chief English, we beg to speak to you. We the native Indians, are gathered to welcome you, and to show you we are of good dispositions.

"We know of the good heart of the queen for the Indians. You bring the good heart with you so we are happy to welcome you. We wish to become good Indians and to be friends with the white people.

"Please to protect us against any bad Indians or any bad white men. Please to protect our land and that it will not be small for us. Many are pleased with their reservations and wish that their reservations be marked out for them.

"Please to give good things to make us become like the good white men as an exchange for our land occupied by the white men. Our heart will always be good and thankful to the queen, and to you, Great Chief. We finish to speak to you."[2]

Seymour, not a great speech-maker, made a simple but firm reply:

"My Indian friends, I am glad to see you and to find that so many have come down to show their loyalty to our queen. You are right, the queen has a good heart for the good Indians. I shall be good to them, but harsh and severe to the bad ones. I will punish them as they deserve.

"I am glad to find that you have given up strong drinks. They are not good for you.

"As you say, there is plenty of land here, for both white men and Indians. You shall not be disturbed on your reserves. I shall protect you both from bad white men and from bad Indians.

"I am glad you wish to be civilized and raised to an equality with the white men. Cultivate your lands. Send your children to school.

"Listen to what the clergymen tell you and believe in it.

"I am a stranger here and don't speak your language, but I am as good a friend to you in heart as my predecessor.

"I give you trifling presents now, but next year, on the Queen's Birthday, I shall give better ones to all good Indian Chiefs. Those who behave badly shall have none.

79

"I wish you all goodbye and hope you have a pleasant day."[3]

The day did, indeed, pass pleasantly, with little in the way of disturbances. The atmosphere was cordial and many of the Indians stayed several days to trade in the local stores. The day after the celebration the Indians helped put out a fire that had started in the New Westminster theatre.

The whole affair much allayed Seymour's fears of the general insurrection which had been rumored and which he had been publicly denying as exaggeration. Weeks later he proudly reported to the Colonial Office that, "I'm now as well known as my predecessor on the valley of the Fraser and Thompson. No white man better in the Bella Coola and Chilcotin country."[4]

Seymour also made good on his promise to provide better presents than the trinkets he had managed to get together for the first celebration. He decided to ask the home office to approve for next year's party 100 canes with silver gilt tops "of an inexpensive kind" and 100 "small and cheap" flags suitable for 20 or 30-foot-long canoes. He thought a Crown inscribed on the tops of the canes, which were to go as sort of staffs of office to the chiefs of friendly tribes, would be nice.[5]

While Seymour was satisfied he had pulled a strategic coup, serious thought was now being given to the question of why the Chilcotins had rebelled. It was difficult to accept the statements of the three survivors that there had been no provocation whatever, and public debate would continue for months and years.

As Brew sat in Bute Inlet gathering what information was possible, he at first became convinced it was a matter of simple plunder. And he found the lack of caution by the road parties inexcusable.

"It is difficult to understand how men could have such blind confidence in fickle savages as those murdered men had. There was in camp a store of all the things most coveted by Indians, clothes, powder balls, sugar, flour, meat, etc. etc."

Brew also suggested that the peace between the Homathkos and the Chilcotins achieved by Waddington had actually led to war, since previous to that the Chilcotins had never ventured into the lower Homathko River region. He continued:

"At first they were chiefly armed with bows and arrows but he was instrumental in supplying them with fire arms and powder and ball as a matter of trade.

"The Indians have, I believe, been most injudiciously treated. If a sound discretion had been exercised towards them

I believe this outrage would not have been perpetrated."[6]

Seymour himself discounted the theory of plunder. He felt the rough clothes and, to him, poor provisions of the road parties offered small temptation to the Indians.

But, with Brew's statements and perhaps talk by former employees of the road company, there was considerable conjecture in regard to the general treatment of the Indians by the road workers. Rumor circulated about the Chilcotins being treated like animals by the whites, and about the Indians' hatred for Smith and Brewster. Although concubinage was common where whites settled among Indians, the thought of young Indian girls prostituting themselves to white invaders in order to save themselves from starving to death made interesting conversation among those colonials tending toward defence of the ignorant Indians.

Waddington was inevitably drawn into the fray. The mainland press, not failing to seize the opportunity to deliver the coup de grace to a project it had opposed from the start, was scathing in its editorials against Waddington and his employees. The *British Columbian* accused Waddington of "gross deception" and "indiscretion," referring to him as "poor Waddy" and writing about "the diseased state of the old gentleman's mind."[7] It stated that "the treatment of the Indians employed in packing received at the hands of Brewster and his party was at once calculated to arouse their cupidity and provoke their vengeance."[8]

Waddington ignored what he called the *Columbian's* "nonsense" about himself, but defended the actions of his employees. In a letter to the *British Colonist* he did not deny there was provocation for the massacres; he simply laid the blame with others.

"Now, sir, I say at once that the real cause of the Bute Inlet massacre had nothing to do with the conduct of the victims themselves, who neither 'excited the assassins by ill-usage or provoked them by injustice or improper conduct,' and I am going to prove the contrary."

He wrote that he had gathered many details about the situation and "challenged contradiction" by anyone. His first accusation was aimed at the Royal Engineers' surveyor, Lieutenant Palmer.

"Is it therefore true or not, that the year before last Lieutenant Palmer or his Serjeant (sic) on their way through to Alexandria, broke through some well known Indian usage, and that Lieutenant Palmer knocked down the son of the second chief of the tribe, who resented it, and that Lieutenant Palmer then threatened to shoot him, on which the young man returned with fifty armed Indians, bared his breast, and dared him to do so? The Indians were too powerful, and Lieutenant Palmer desisted; but surely that affront has never been forgiven."

(Palmer had, in fact, narrowly averted the murder of himself and his two Royal Marine aides by Bella Coola Indians, but there were different opinions as to whether he had in fact been the direct cause of the incident or whether he had acted heroically in the face of danger brought about by no fault of his own.)

Waddington next referred to the smallpox epidemic, claiming to have seen 500 Indian graves. He outlined the actions of the traders McLeod and Taylor in re-selling diseased blankets.

And there were other reasons, Waddington said.

"A settler, who is still at Bella Coola, made a bargain to marry a pretty young Indian girl, according to the Indian fashion. This was willingly consented to, and the relations made their presents of blankets to the bridegroom, to the amount of several dozen, all which were to be returned in a month or so, in the proportion of two for one, Indian fashion. And there was great feasting at the expense of the Indians, and the bridegroom took his wife home. He was to receive vast quantities of blankets and rich presents from Victoria, by the first schooner, which never came! And at the end of four months, the relations had to take the poor girl back again, dishonored. Was that a provocation, or not?

"And did not a certain Mr. N— live for a whole year at the expense of the Indians telling them he was a great Tyhee sent out by the government, and that he would shortly receive any amount of blankets and provisions? And did he not persuade them to build him a large store, some 30 feet by 40, the Indians contributing the split boards from their own huts? For all of which he gave each of them an acknowledgement for twenty or more blankets, as the case might be, payable on arrival from Victoria, which arrival never took place, and the scrip is still in the hands of the Indians."

The Indians who came down to Bute Inlet had been "shamefully treated" before their arrival and while it was unknown to the road company it was not unknown to the government, Waddington continued.

"They found a party who in the innocence of their hearts and their confidence in the coast government, felt secure and were working unarmed, and those Indians were naturally tempted to take a cruel revenge and plunder where they had been plundered."

Waddington discounted stories originating with Squinteye, "a man whose want of veracity is so notorious that no magistrate, when aware of it, ought to believe one word he says."[9]

In a letter to the Victoria *Daily Chronicle*, Waddington stated that "the cause of their death has been commented upon with unfeeling and unmerited severity" and that "poor Mr. Brewster has been taxed with being unjust towards the Indians, and the men with being childishly careless and confiding."[10]

The *Chronicle* carried an article stating that "the upper Chilcoatens only hated Mr. Brewster inasmuch as they hated the whole enterprise" because of an "aversion... to the opening up of their country by whites."

The article also said that the settler Clark, "all interesting assertions to the contrary notwithstanding, had been charity itself to them (the Chilcotins) during the winter."[11]

Frederick Whymper, the artist who had been hired to sketch the Bute Inlet-Homathko River country, also backed up Waddington. He regarded the question of motives as answered very simply: he subscribed to the theory of plunder.

Whymper wrote that this strong desire for plunder must have been accompanied by "the knowledge of the improbability in that country of ever being taken and brought to justice. That any provocation had been given them I do not believe; Mr. Waddington was well known to have been specially indulgent to them."

The artist enjoyed philosophizing about the Indians. "The Indian is to this day but little understood. By some he is looked on as an animal, by others as almost a hero of romance. The ideal Red-skin, the painted and much-adorned native with lofty sentiments, is certainly, as far as my experience goes, a very rare being at the present day, if indeed his existence at any time is not to be considered mythical."

Beneath the "thin crust" of civilization varnishing the Indian, penned Whymper, "the savage nature lurks." He added. "It is very rare to find those who are the better for intercourse with the 'pale-faces'."[12]

The newspapers differed in their attitudes towards the Indians just as they differed in their opinions regarding the causes. The Vancouver Island press, in supporting Waddington, demanded swift revenge. The press of the mainland colony, since it had to offer some defence of the Indians in order to lay blame on Waddington and his men, was more moderate in its suggestions for dealing with the rebels.

The *Chronicle* said in an editorial:

"On the spread of the news in this city, the first feeling which showed itself was a strong desire for a bloody revenge upon these dangerous races who live around us, but whom we can never trust. Had the people of Victoria had the power, they would gladly have exterminated the whole tribe to which the murderers belong. With returning reason, however, the public are willing to discriminate between the innocent and guilty, but all who imbued their hands in blood, or connived at that horrible deed ought to be hunted down, and either punished on the spot, or brought to account for their crimes, before the regular tribunals of justice."[13]

The *British Colonist* criticized the B.C. government for letting other Indians get away with murdering whites. The natives, said the *Colonist*, should be kept in "entire subjugation."[14]

The suggestion that normal legal procedure should be done away with in this case was pressed in other editions of the *Colonist*: "It is hoped that the ridiculous farce of bringing them down to New Westminster and trying them by jury will not be attempted in case of their apprehension. A summary examination and a hempen noose reached from the nearest tree in the presence of all the tribe would have a 100-fold more effect on all the Indians of the coast than the solemn and, to them, unintelligible mummery of a trial by jury."[15]

Again:

"It is mere folly to await the tardy action of the authorities. Let the citizens take the matter in hand at once, today. A steamer should be chartered from Victoria for an armed hunting party. Let them not stay their hands till every member of the rascally murderers' tribe is suspended from the trees of their own forests, a salutary warning to the whole Coast for years to come."[16]

The *British Columbian* had a more orthodox approach to justice. There was no questioning the need for fast action:

"Let the guilty parties be hunted up if they should cost the country ten thousand dollars a head, and let them be made an example of to the rest of the native population, such as will not readily be forgotten. In this matter promptitude is everything. Let the fleet be ordered at once to the Inlet and let volunteer forces from here and Victoria go with it.... Well planned and prompt action now may save much trouble in the future. The country will look for it at the hands of both Governments—the blood of fourteen butchered men, all of them British subjects save one, demands it."

But the paper cautioned against "indiscriminate slaughter for that would not mend, but aggravate the matter."[17]

In another editorial the *Columbian* stated:

"We are too apt in the first flush of excited indignation to cry out for utter and indiscriminate extermination of the savages, dealing out to them lynch law instead of British justice. A knowledge of the treatment to which the ignorant and un-tutored Indians was often subjected in his intercourse with the white man ought to lead us to receive with caution the *ipse tixit* statement of the latter concerning the affray such as that has recently transpired at Bute Inlet. We do not desire to excite sympathy for the Indians concerning this bloody tragedy for, so far as is yet known, they are entitled to none at our hands, but we hope to see the same impartial justice brought into requisition in dealing with the aborigines that we would desire to have meted out to ourselves."[18]

And, in another article:

"We are quite aware that there are those amongst us who are disposed to ignore altogether the rights of the Indian and their claims upon us—who hold the American doctrine of 'manifest destiny' in its most fatal form, and say that the native tribes will die off to make way for the Anglo-Saxon race, and the quicker the better; and, under the shadow of this un-christian doctrine, the cry for 'extermination' is raised at every pretext. Very different, however, are the views and sentiments held in reference to the Indians by the British Government. The representatives of that Government may not, in every instance, faithfully delineate the Imperial mind in this respect. Depend upon it for every acre of land we obtain by improper means we will have to pay for dearly in the end, and every wrong committed upon these poor people will be visited upon our heads as sure as justice is one of the immutable attributes of Him who avengeth the wrongs of the weak and oppressed of whatever color or caste."

The *Columbian*, which had always been critical of Governor Douglas, blamed him for the "total absence of policy" in regard to the Indians.[19]

* * *

Brew's despatches convinced Seymour that an expedition inland would be impractical, as he'd suspected it would be. The governor decided to go along for the ride with the *Forward* back to the Bute townsite to pick up Brew and his force. The *Forward* left May 26 and returned May 31.

Waddington was in New Westminster and he quickly decided to petition the B.C. government not simply for compensation, but to take the charter off his hands.

Claiming to have spent $50,000 on the road and lost much more in addition, Waddington attempted to make a case for government responsibility in the matter.

The two or three months delay before the expected quelling of the Indian uprising would "...cause me the loss of the season, the loss of keeping up an establishment to take care of my property, mules, etc. at Bute Inlet, the loss of the toll I should have the right to levy immediately on the trail, the loss on the deferred sale of the townsite, and the loss of the Company about to be organized in England, besides my loss by the plunder of the late expedition (to say nothing of the upper one) and $1000 per month interest on my present outlay, making a total that could be counted by tens of thousands of dollars.

"I would rather under such circumstances and after the melancholy events which have taken place, prefer the sacrifice of all the hard-earned profits which I had looked to and surrender my agreement."

The promoter claimed: "There can be little doubt that the future toll would give a dividend (and an increasing one) of 25 percent on the capital invested, for ten years making $12,500 per annum on my present outlay.

"For all this and my past labor, I would ask the simple reimbursement of that outlay, and as much more, as a compensation for future profits and other losses, making in all $100,000."

Waddington called the need for the Bute road "indispensable" and urged the government to act quickly.[20]

Waddington was to be disappointed, however, as the issue dragged on for weeks. As might be expected, Brew was outraged when he learned of Waddington's request, and led the opposition to it. He stated:

"Mr. Waddington says that his aim in developing the Bute Inlet route was to advance the general prosperity of both colonies. I believe his chief aim was to make a profitable speculation and the aim of those who trusted in his representations and supported him with their money was to divert the trade which passed through New Westminster to the upper country into another channel and crush New Westminster which aspired to rival Victoria as a port of direct import."

He pointed out that while the Fraser River route was opened up naturally because of the discovery of gold on it, there was no gold in the Bute. Brew blasted the route and Waddington as being more dream than reality.

"I do not understand how Mr. Waddington estimates that his enterprise would have brought 100,000 pounds sterling of foreign capital into the colony. He would sell his charter to the route for $50,000 if he could.

"It seems impossible unless the money was squandered that Mr. Waddington could have expended $63,000 on the Homathco trail—there is not work done for it to be seen—besides the cost of what work was done did not all come out of Mr. Waddington's pocket."

Brew charged that when Waddington's promises weren't kept, shareholders sold their stock to him "for a trifle." He rejected Waddington's claims that the trail would soon have been opened and producing revenue.[21]

As usual, Seymour agreed substantially with what Brew had to say. As far as the governor understood, Waddington had been granted the road charter only grudgingly by Douglas in the first place and had been warned many times about the project's drawbacks.

He also rejected Waddington's claim of government responsibility in the matter of providing protection. Despite what Waddington said, the government had never really been asked for protection and certainly never promised it. But if Waddington had requested it, he wouldn't have received any, either.

"Suppose we had sent a few constables there. What could they have done?" he asked.[22]

Neither was anything done about Waddington's urgent requests that a message be taken to Bella Coola to warn Alex McDonald, who had accepted a contract from the Bute Inlet Road Company to build the trail from Puntzi Lake to the Homathko Valley. McDonald had hired a few men in Victoria and had taken a ship up to Bella Coola a short time before, planning to take the Bentinck Arm trail to his and Manning's ranch at Puntzi.

Speculation about McDonald's fate was almost unanimous that he and his party had no chance to survive the trip.

* * *

On May 29, William George Cox received Birch's letter at the gold commissioner's office in Richfield asking him to raise a force against the Chilcotins.

He replied immediately:

"I have the honor to acknowledge the receipt this morning of your communication of the 14th instant referring to the murder of Europeans by Indians near Bute Inlet.

"I shall leave this place for Quesnelmouth tomorrow

morning where I intend making the necessary arrangements for proceeding immediately to the scene of the late outrage and will use my utmost endeavors to bring the perpetrators to Justice."[23]

* * *

Nancootlem was in a beautiful spot, like a rest after a long march which, in fact, it was. It was a stopping place on the crude Bentinck Arm trail from the sea, the first Indian village of any consequence after the tough climb up out of the Bella Coola Valley.

Anahim and Nimpo Lakes are a few miles apart on the gently undulating plain. The latter is particularly pretty, with coves edged by evergreens and aspen or poplar.

Near the shores of the lake a dozen tents were pitched in a cluster. Hobbled horses grazed nearby as coffee simmered and beans boiled over open campfires.

A short distance away was the Nancootlem Indian village of Chief Anahim, picturesque with its lodges and totems carved in imitation of those of the Bella Coola. Anahim's people also had constructed stockades in the area for their own protection against enemies.

In the camp of the whites several Indians were talking and bartering with its inhabitants. The camp was that of the missing McDonald party, the fate of which was much wondered about down in New Westminster and Victoria. Here, hundreds of miles from colonial civilization, the party had come, unaware of the murders.

As scheduled, Alex McDonald's party had left New Aberdeen, or Bella Coola, on May 17, a week after the Bute massacre was known in Victoria. It numbered eight white men: McDonald; Peter McDougall, a packer; Barney Johnson, an old Bentinck Arm pioneer; Clifford Higgins, an Englishman, and John Grant, both miners heading for the Cariboo; Charles Farquharson; Fred Harrison; and Malcolm McLeod. There was also a young Alexis Chilcotin named Tom employed by McDonald as helper, and McDougall's squaw, Klymtedza.

Pack animals were not taken directly from Bella Coola. The packers kept them at Noocultz, the ranch and ferry operated about two dozen miles up the Bella Coola River from New Aberdeen by John Hamilton and his family. McDougall had a big string of pack animals he was taking through to Alexandria, and he and his two men decided to join McDonald's party. McDonald and McDougall were old friends—McDougall sometimes wintered with his pack horses at the Puntzi ranch. At Puntzi Lake, McDonald was to start southwest toward Bute

Inlet to begin construction of Waddington's pack trail.

McDougall sold a large quantity of furs to Hamilton for cash, being unable to obtain the quantities of the various goods which he had wanted to take to the Cariboo to sell. Of the 42 pack animals, only 28 were loaded with goods for the mines, worth between $4,000 and $5,000.

The pack train had left Noocultz on May 23, travelling on the opposite side of the river and then up out of the deep valley over the Great Slide, a huge fan of boulders and loose rock. Then it had been onward toward Nancootlem.

McDonald was in one way a strange choice to be building a trail for Waddington, even though he operated the ranch with William Manning at the junction of the Bute and Bentinck trails. McDonald was one of those who was unimpressed with Waddington's route and who publicly proclaimed the superiority of the Bentinck trail. McDonald knew both routes well. He had accompanied Major Downie on his exploration of Bute Inlet. And, in February and March of 1863, he had packed his gear in a toboggan and snow-shoed his way down the lakes and through the forests from Puntzi Lake to Bute Inlet. He had to agree that while Waddington was deluding himself about the Homathko, the upper plain through the Tatlayoko and Bluff Lake region was good trail-building country. The water travel wasn't as good as Waddington had thought, but the country was fertile and good for stock. McDonald, though, had spent a lot of time in the Bella Coola, trading or tending store for Peter Baron, and he liked that route better.

As the pack train travelled toward Nancootlem, it had broken again into two parties travelling a day apart. McLeod, McDonald, Johnson, Farquharson and Harrison joined them the next day.

Now, McDonald and McDougall were standing in their camp with McDougall's squaw. Klymtedza was a young, excitable woman the packer had bought from a Chilcotin family headed by her aging father, Chilhowhoaz. The plump squaw had adapted well to the ways of the whites, usually wearing white women's clothes, and working hard for McDougall. Unlike most or at least many Indian concubines or slaves of the whites, she was loyal to her master rather than remaining true to her family or tribe.

Klymtedza was jabbering excitedly to the two white men. They must go in a big hurry, leave everything, take the horses and go. She kept repeating herself, now in her native tongue, now in Chinook and broken English.

Nancootlem or Sitleece was her home village. She had visited her family and friends across the lake and had learned of a plot against the whites. A nomadic war chief named Klatassine had come to Anahim's village three or four days ago with several families, talking of great victories over the whites who had threatened to bring smallpox back on the Indians. This Klatassine spoke of killing many in the Homathko, and of the supposed death of Manning at Puntzi. He was urging Anahim's men to join his own and go down to Bentinck Arm to attack the whites there. When the pack train had arrived, Klymtedza was told, Klatassine had been exulted at the good fortune. He now had a visible enemy and plunder with which to tempt the Nancootlem warriors.

At first, McDougall had dismissed his squaw's story as extreme exaggeration. But she had insisted, adding to it from time to time new pieces of information about the alleged plot. Now he and McDonald were becoming worried.

McDonald suggested they would be better off going forward. The trail back to the Arm was just too tough to travel in a hurry with all those loaded animals.

No! They must leave everything and run! said Klymtedza.

She may be right, McDougall told McDonald. If McDonald's partner was dead like she said, they would be heading into a trap anyway. Ahan, a Nancootlem subchief in his late twenties, had said he was willing to go on to Puntzi and see if there was any truth to it.

Two young Indians were standing a short distance away. One was Ahan and the other was Lutas, a young and rather mild-mannered Chilcotin in his teens. They had visited the camp two or three times since the train arrived, and they professed total ignorance of any talk of plots in the Indian village or even news of trouble elsewhere. Ahan, in particular, was a sensible and straight-forward sort of Siwash, and seemed trustworthy.

McDonald did not feel they should worry too much about what had taken place before. The important thing was what was going on in Anahim's camp now.

The white men were reminded that the brother of one of their party had been killed two years before by Chilcotin Indians near Puntzi Lake. Bob McLeod, besides being Malcolm McLeod's brother, had been Alex McDonald's cousin. He had been leading a pack train to Alexandria when he had been jumped.

Anahim was away from his village right now, but there was much activity there. Klatassine was using his by-now polished oratory about the white man's threats. While Ahan appeared helpful to the packers, he was, in fact, well aware of Klatassine's plans and was substantially in agreement with his feelings about the whites.

Klatassine had brought many gifts, and had talked for days with small and large groups of Nancootlem men about the smallpox threat. If the whites were allowed to continue their invasion of Indian land, there would soon be no more Indians left to fight. The whites wanted to kill the Indians and take their land, and this time the dreaded smallpox would be fatal. The white tyhee at Bute had said the disease would come in the next warm (year). For all those who joined Klatassine to help him wipe out the whites there would be many presents.

To Ahan, Klatassine's words were true, for he had seen many of his friends die of smallpox. It was good that the white men should be killed.

Lutas felt the same way, and Chacatinea, an important Nancootlem Indian like Ahan, also found wisdom in what Klatassine was saying. Chacatinea had personal reasons for backing Klatassine—he hated McDonald. He therefore joined in trying to persuade Ahan, Lutas, and the other men to join Klatassine, even threatening them. "Atl'a'risen!... He speaks the truth!"

Achpicermous, a half Bella Coola and half Nancootlem Indian who listened with the others, did not trust Klatassine, but did not attempt to challenge him.

While Klatassine was whipping up support, McDonald and McDougall moved their camp to a knoll near the lake. The small hill, lightly wooded with poplars, commanded a view in all directions. At the bottom of one side was a large pool edged with rushes and lillies and teaming with minnows. Past the hill it drained in a trickle toward Nimpo Lake. The eight white men dug out a protective earthwork 20 feet square at the top of the knoll.[24] By digging down and piling the dirt and a few rocks around themselves in banks, they soon had a secure post from which to stave off any attacks. They hobbled the pack mules and horses nearby.

This situation relieved Klymtedza's fears considerably. With plentiful provisions and a good water supply only a few dozen yards away, they could stay there many weeks.

But it was uncomfortable and tedious in the earthworks, and these weren't men who could sit around in cramped quarters doing nothing for long.

Klatassine's plan was to hide in the woods near a broken bridge a few miles further on towards Puntzi Lake. The bridge could be rigged to entangle the horses, and in the confusion the Indians could attack and kill the white men quickly.

When two of the pack animals were discovered to be missing, Tom, McDonald's helper, was sent out alone to look for them. He never returned. Klatassine captured him for a slave even though he was Chilcotin.

After two days in their makeshift dirt fort, the packers and miners had had enough. They wanted to move out, in one direction or the other. McDonald, known to the Indians as "Aleck," wanted to push on toward Puntzi Lake. But McDougall, "Mac" to the Indians, sided with his klootchman. Klymtedza knew there was no chance of getting through the Chilcotin to Alexandria. If the men insisted on moving, they must withdraw towards Bella Coola, and they must leave their supplies and pack animals and ride quickly.

McDougall, though, wasn't about to leave four or five thousand dollars worth of goods, in addition to valuable pack animals, to the Indians. So, the animals were loaded up and on May 31 the long pack train started its noisy and obvious journey back to Bella Coola. McDougall and Higgins rode in front leading the way. With McDougall was Klymtedza, who declined the choice of leaving her master to return to her family where she would have been welcomed back, and would have been safe. Riding behind them was McDonald. Grant was next. The other men were strung out along the train.

They had not gone more than two miles towards Anahim Lake before the wary Klymtedza became frightened. There were Indians running through the woods, she told McDougall. But McDougall, Higgins, and McDonald could see nothing through the dense growth of stunted spruce which covered the area like giant strands of grass.

They must leave everything and go to the woods, Klymtedza urged. They must now leave even the horses, she said, for here they would be useless.

But once again her warnings were ignored, and the pack train continued on for another three miles.

The departure of the pack train, especially in the direction of Bella Coola, had caught Klatassine by surprise. He got together as many men as he could in a few minutes, numbering only about a dozen. As those who had horses gathered them up, Achpicermous saw Ahan going to help them.

"What are you going to do?" Achpicermous asked him.

"I am going with the rest."[25]

At that Ahan hurried off. Achpicermous followed behind. Besides Ahan, there were only three other Nancootlem

Indians who joined Klatassine's Tatla and Puntzi warriors. They were Lutas, Chacatinea, and Chilhowhoaz.

The Indians on foot ran through the woods past the pack train while the horsemen took a wider route to come out ahead. Five miles from the earthworks, Klatassine deployed his party in ambush on both sides of the trail. They were to aim at both the men and their horses. They were armed with muskets, guns and hatchets, each having several weapons.

The attackers waited until the train was between them, then opened fire. Achpicermous, not yet arrived, said later that he heard very rapid firing, with many shots in the first volley.

"My God, I'm shot!"[26] screamed McDougall in pain, clutching his chest as he fell. Higgins also fell, shot through the chest. As Klymtedza ran to McDougall, she too was cut down.

The main marksmen were Ahan, Klatassine and Yahooslas, the Lower Chilcotin Indian.[27]

McDonald's horse collapsed under him though he himself was unwounded. Grabbing the reins of a loose animal, he mounted again.

Grant, on foot behind McDonald, shouted at him to run.

"I'll give them all I have, first," McDonald replied, blasting into the midst of several Indians with his double-barreled shotgun.[28]

The panicked pack horses bucked and stamped around, getting between the attackers and their quarry. This proved lucky for several of the party.

Grant saw an opening in the stubby trees and made for it. A ball ripped through his arm, but he wounded his pursuer and got into the woods.

Grant's example was being followed by the rest of the pack train members. Instead of grouping and helping each other fight off Klatassine and his followers, the whites made it every man for himself and scattered. They had been expecting an open attack, not an ambush. Though McDonald was in a difficult position, none of the packers made any attempt to save him. They were too much thrown in confusion and panic by their own predicaments.

As Malcolm McLeod raised his rifle to shoot at the Indians, a ball grazed his face and stripped the flesh from three of his fingers to the bone. A moment later, his horse crumpled, dead from shot.

Harrison was stunned by a ball skimming by his forehead, opening the flesh over his eyes. Another ball hit him in the hand and a volley of buckshot got him square in the back.

Farquharson's horse was shot, but he made it into the

woods unhurt and ran for his life.

Johnson, the old pioneer, remained relatively calm, and his presence of mind was to save his life. As buckshot hit him in the face and chest, a musket ball struck his horse in the head. Regaining his feet, Johnson made for the woods pursued by two attackers, who fired as they ran. Seeing a small lake ahead, Johnson headed toward it, gaining as the Indians stopped to reload. Exhausted, the old man jumped into the water, tossed his hat out a few feet, then ran through the water along the shore and exited back into the woods. Diving into some bushes, he panted quietly as the two Indians reached the spot where he'd gone into the water. They seemed confused by the ploy. Had he drowned? He was nowhere in sight, and after a brief probing of the immediate area, they rejoined their companions.

McDonald's second horse had been shot down by Piell, Klatassine's son, and he was once again spilled to the ground. This time he, too, ran for the woods.

Grant, hit again by shot in the thigh, side and chest, saw McDonald in the distance hiding behind a big tree.

Yahooslas fired and McDonald fell on his back, wounded in both legs. Chacatinea saw his chance. Running up to McDonald, he levelled his musket at his old adversary, but it was a foolish move. McDonald raised his six-shooter and shot the Indian through the heart. Chacatinea, who had been one of those most wanting to attack McDonald's train, died without firing a single shot.

As Grant limped off into the woods, getting as far away from the scene as possible, McDonald was still behind the big tree. It was the last any of the party saw of him alive.

With the rest of the pack train dead or scattered, the war party now turned its full fury on the courageous McDonald. He held them off until the other five balls from his handgun were gone, then grabbed for his unloaded rifle. But he didn't have time and he knew it. The Indians moved in. A shot from Klatassine broke both his arms as he tried to load his gun.

He lay on the ground gasping for air as Klatassine came up, aimed his rifle at McDonald, and finished him with a shot to the head.

Higgins, who had been shot first by Yahooslas, was already dead, killed by a second shot from Ahan, but McDougall lay unconscious near his dead klootchman, Klymtedza. Ahan, who had first shot McDougall, urged Lutas forward. The youngster aimed at McDougall's head and fired, then walked quickly away without looking at the result.

It was the last shot of the attack. Between 50 and 60 shots had been fired within the few minutes it lasted.

Achpicermous and others (including Tom) who had been following behind the war party arrived at the scene, looking for their share of the spoils. There was plenty for all. Klatassine gave Achpicermous a sack of flour, two pairs of pants, two shirts, a knife, some powder and some shot.

"Entltcu't!" the chief urged him. "Take it!"

Had he joined them he would have had a larger share, Klatassine told him.

The war chief was generous with the booty, making sure none was left out. Not all the Nancootlem Indians were as honest with him, however. While scarcely more than a dozen of Klatassine's men did all the fighting, dozens more had followed up to watch from a safe distance. As the pack mules and horses panicked and ran into the bush, these members of Anahim's tribe gathered them up and made off with them. By the time Klatassine's braves were able to search for them, there were few left.

Whether or not Anahim was part of the conspiracy, he did not take a direct part in the action. But he benefitted by it just the same. Klatassine kept several horses for him, a large quantity of provisions and money.

For the moment, there would be more celebrating for the victory and for the spoils. But not for Chilhowhoaz. He wept over the body of his daughter, Klymtedza. For betraying her people and staying with the whites, she had had to be killed. Therefore it was better that her life would be taken by her own father—it was Chilhowhoaz' bullet that had finished her.

Chacatinea looked as savage in death as he had in life. The tall, brawny warrior had been fearless and scornful in the face of danger all his life. His face was blackened like those of several of the other attackers. A large brass ring hung from his nose. Two weeping brothers wrapped his body in blankets and interred it beneath logs on the field of battle, decorating the grave with stakes, feathers and flags as befitted a great chief.

Klymtedza was also buried nearby.

The bodies of the three whites were left to rot in the sun.

In the forest, the five surviving members of McDonald's pack train began making their separate ways back toward Bella Coola on foot. All but Farquharson were badly wounded. It was some 75 miles to Hamilton's ferry, another 22 to Bella Coola.

* * *

As if by a miracle of communication, a story circulated in

Victoria the very next day, June 1, about the McDonald party being attacked. Under the headline "Another Massacre,"[29] the *Colonist* gave the alleged details:

"...McDonald and all his party, nine in number, have been murdered on the Bentinck Arm trail by the Chilcoaten Indians. The news was received at Bute Inlet by Judge Brew, from two friendly natives who had come down from Bentinck, via Benshee (Puntzi) Lake and the Junction. These Indians stated that they had met McDonald and his party somewhere near Benshee Lake, and told them of the murder of the Bute party, warning them not to go on any further or they would assuredly meet with the same fate. Their story was not believed, however, and the party pushed on and met the returning murderers a short distance this side of Benshee Lake, where, according to the statement of the two Indians, they were all brutally murdered. The informants came straight down to Bute..."[30]

Though the story had certain elements of truth, it was quite by accident, or perhaps resulted from anticipation of Klatassine's success. The two Indians, of course, had not run to the Waddington townsite in one day to tell the story of the massacre, and the *Forward* had not steamed to Victoria and passed on the information to the newspaper to print within 24 hours of the incident. Neither had the massacre taken place at Puntzi Lake. The entire story was nothing more than a rumor resulting from public anxiety and conjecture plus the readiness of the press to publish anything at all to do with the Indian rebellion. When Brew and Seymour had come back on the *Forward* from Bute it had made its usual stop at Nanaimo for refueling. Brew had been told about rumors in the Victoria press that McDonald and his party had already been killed. Brew said it was possible. A report was sent back to the Victoria papers that Brew said McDonald's party had, indeed, been massacred. With a few embellishments, the "news" of the massacre was published. In fact, the Victoria papers were reprinting their own rumors now attributed to Brew.

At the same time, stories of Manning's murder were reaching Victoria and New Westminster.

All this "news" of new murders by the Siwashes was enough to set Victoria buzzing once again.

That afternoon Capt. D.M. Lang got a public meeting going in the Victoria Rifle Corps drill hall. Rather than waiting for word on whether or not Victoria volunteers would be used, he wanted to get some basic training done now so that the colonists would at least know how to use a rifle.

Just about everyone seemed indifferent to Lang's idea, wondering why anyone would have to be trained to chase after Siwashes.

Reported the *Colonist*: "The audience generally seemed totally ignorant of the purpose of the meeting, nor were they much enlightened by the various speakers who in turn occupied the floor. One of the two civilians who took up a considerable portion of the time of the meeting created roars of laughter by declaring his readiness to go up and "murder every Indian he could lay his hand on."[31]

Capt. Lang told the meeting the drill room would be open the following night to all comers who wished to drill. Most interested Victorians, however, were busy elsewhere.

Angry at the news of further killing and anxious to do something about it, a group of citizens petitioned Victoria mayor Thomas Harris to call an emergency meeting "to consider the best means of strengthening the hand of the Sister Government to secure and punish the perpetrators of the recent massacres and to protect the lives of her Majesty's subjects in the settlements of the Northwest coast of British Columbia."[32]

At 8 p.m. on June 2 the Victoria Theatre was crowded with colonists wanting to know and wanting to express views about what could be done.[33] The theatre was filled to capacity long before the scheduled meeting time. Among the audience was Como, a Lillooet Indian chief.

On the stage with Mayor Harris were Waddington, MLA Amor de Cosmos, Rev. A.C. Garrett, George Cruikshank, C.J. Hughes, Dr. Dickson, C.B. Young, P.M. Backus, Robert Bishop, A.C. Elliott, R. George, E. Mallandaine, and a few others. Young had nominated Waddington for mayor at the public election in 1862 when Waddington had received only a few votes and withdrawn in favor of Harris.

The mayor rapped his gavel on the podium and the meeting came to order. "This meeting was called by the people of Victoria," he stated. "I hope it will be the last time I will have to appear before you in such a cause. I hope the people will concur in aiding the government of British Columbia in bringing the perpetrators of the late tragedies to justice, and that the meeting will be able to lend manly protection to the lives of their fellow creatures."

A few "hear hears" responded.

"I invite all persons who so wish to come on the platform and express their views, but I first ask Mr. de Cosmos to move the first resolution."

The oddly handsome de Cosmos took the podium. Born Bill Smith, he had changed his name during a residence in California. He'd come to Victoria six years before and started the *British Colonist*, but gave it up to pursue politics, his main interests being the achievement of responsible government and union of the Vancouver Island and British Columbia colonies.

A charismatic personality, he was a fine speaker, eloquent and emotional.

"I regard the occasion which called this meeting together as one from which none should flinch," he began. "I believe I was one of the first to have mooted the subject of the Bute Inlet route, and I did not then think I should be now compelled to express the feelings of the community at such outrages."

He read the first resolution:

"Resolved—that the whole community have received with heartfelt sorrow and the greatest indignation the intelligence of the murder of a number of our fellow countrymen, by Indians in British Columbia, and view with extreme anxiety the dangerous condition of the outlying settlements and mining localities in this and the neighboring Colony."

De Cosmos said that this resolution summed up his views well. "We are all sorry that men engaged in this undertaking have lost their lives; we are all highly indignant, and justly so.

"It is a matter of self-protection and we are bound to take action against the Indian offenders in a practical manner. Our treatment with the Indians should be this: whenever life is taken, life should be sacrificed in return. The Indian knows no law but blood for blood," he proclaimed, to cheers from the audience.

"Any leniency only adds audacity to their crimes. I inherited an antipathy and hatred to Indians and I do not entertain with others a morbid sympathy for them," he continued.

"I have lived among Indians and I know their treachery. I have known what it is to crawl on all fours after them with my Bowie knife in my mouth, and my antipathy to the savages results from outrages committed on my own family."

Nicely getting wound up, de Cosmos got to the point. "On the broad principals of humanity we should render our settlements safe, and I know of no means except by distributing our ships of war and armed volunteers on the coast, to put down crime immediately it occurs with a strong arm, and show the natives they cannot commit atrocities with impunity.

"It is reported that Mr. McDonald, a pioneer with Major Downie, has now also fallen victim to them. This meeting should express its sympathy to Mr. Waddington, for I believe that worthy gentleman is not only entitled to sympathy, but also to compensation for the losses which have overtaken him through the acts of the savages."

De Cosmos took his seat to the applause of the audience, and Rev. Garrett arose to second the resolution. Rev. Garrett had worked hard to help the Indians during the 1862 smallpox epidemic, but he now endorsed de Cosmos' sentiments.

"There was a time when I differed with Mr. de Cosmos in my views of Indian character," he said. "My views have now changed.

"I have learned that we must deal with the Indians with truth, justice and severity,..."

There was at this point an interruption as someone attempted to gain a seat in the press box, much to the annoyance of the reporters.

"White men can not look on calmly when their brethren have their hearts torn from their bodies, but by the most determined resolution must show the Indians that such crimes must meet with the most condign punishment."

He said he was satisfied that "but a very short time will elapse before this night's proceedings will be translated into every native tongue" and "carried by their swift canoes" to the most distant tribes.

Garrett was acquainted with the Indians well enough to know there was hostility between the various tribes as well as to the whites. But he could not accept their culture or their mentality as deserving consideration alongside the European, and he was determined to convince this meeting of his own views.

"The savages are happy enough together gathering up the spoils and drinking the blood of the whites," he stated. "I don't believe they can keep up any combined effort for long, but nonetheless the most vigorous steps of repression are necessary."

Such steps should have been taken sooner, he felt.

"While the Indians felt the strong hand of the whites they were as meek and as cowardly as kittens, but when they saw our gunboats traverse the narrow inlets without firing a shot—" the audience interrupted him with prolonged applause.

"Without firing a shot, what could we expect but that the spirit of demons which possess their blood should be roused to fiendish atrocity? While we are here we can but express our sympathy for the pioneer of civilization and progress (applause again) and also for the wives and children of our murdered fellow men, and we must take such means as may preserve those offshoots of our city whom we are bound to nourish and whom we should regard as the mainstay of our future prosperity."

He sat down to even more applause than de Cosmos had been given. Now it was Waddington's turn, and he was greeted with a further round of loud hand clapping and cheering.

"I'm not here to tell my own story, but although I'm an old man I still have a little blood in my veins and I cannot refrain from expressing my feelings," he told them.

He stated again what had happened on the Homathko, and added mention of the attack on McDonald's train. "I pressed Governor Seymour to send a war vessel to Bella Coola to prevent further murders there, but for some reason or other it was decided that no vessel should be sent. Why, I cannot say, though it's said the *Columbia* was being repaired and the gunboats also could not be sent."

The audience interjected some loud hissing and cries of "Shame! Shame!" in agreement with his complaint.

"It is my firm belief that ere this time the Indians, glutted with blood, have murdered every living soul in Bella Coola, and they number twelve on my fingers."

This caused a considerable stir as he named the Hamiltons, Wallace, and White, and referred to others whose names he didn't remember.

"If a gunboat had been sent up to Bentinck Arm when the news of the first murder was received here, all these lives might have been saved," Waddington claimed. "I will only add that when I saw the mangled body of my poor foreman Brewster, I simply looked up to Heaven for forbearance, but I look to my countrymen for justice."

Again, thunderous applause.

The first resolution was carried unanimously and the second was then read out:

"Resolved—that in view of the fact that many of the victims of the recent Indian massacre belonged to this Colony, and that their families reside here, the colonists of Vancouver Island deem it their bounden duty to request His Excellency the Governor to tender to His Excellency the Governor of British Columbia the services of not less than 100 men fully armed and equipped, to aid the British Columbian authorities in the detection and capture of the murderers.

"I hope whenever they catch one they will hang him there and then," appended P.M. Backus, the resolution's mover, to loud cheers.

The motion's seconder, C.J. Hughes, spoke in substantially the same fashion. "I hope that the force will not be limited to 100, but that such a force will be raised as will show the savage he cannot trample upon the blood of white men. We can't recall the dead, but I trust we should avenge their death. I speak from experience of the difficulties of Indian warfare and I would hope that we could muster 300 to 500 men."

His words also went over well, receiving cheers throughout.

The next speaker, however, took a more moderate approach. C.B. Young, prominent in local political and business circles, agreed that "a cold-blooded and atrocious crime had been committed," but "there is still a small voice within me which I value more than the voice of those who have spoken before me, and I ask you to bear with me. I have heard of justice to the Indians, but I consider that justice has not been meted out to them.

"What of the failure to appoint any Indian agent? Hudson's Bay Indian policy won't do now..."

At a meeting designed to whip up enthusiasm for an Indian hunt, it wasn't a popular way to talk, and a rising crescendo of booing, hissing and heckling forced Young to sit down. When it subsided the mayor called him back to finish and he briefly related how the Indians had been turned off their potato patches at Bentinck Arm.

"How did the Saxon feel towards the Norman during the invasion? Indians have feelings as well as ourselves and should be treated with justice."

The meeting got back on the track with Rev. Dr. Evans who stated support of the resolutions, believing that vigorous efforts were necessary to "strike a heavy blow upon the cruel and dastardly perpetrators of the late crimes, though I, at the same time, believe the Indians have not been fairly dealt with in the matter of compensation.

"But this matter calls for prompt and decisive measures, a drum-head court martial if necessary."

"Hear, hear," came from the crowd.

"And hanging!" came another voice.

"Yes, and hanging on the spot, too," said the speaker, followed by cheers of approval.

Several other speakers gave their views, one being forced to sit down when the crowd grew tired of him and assailed him with hisses, groans and cries of "Sit down!" and "Chair, chair!" Another aimed some shots at Young, and there were also statements of earnest cooperation with New Westminster advocating, in effect, letting bygones be bygones.

A third resolution was made:

"Resolved—that an enrolment list of persons anxious to volunteer in the force be opened tomorrow for signature at the office of Selim Franklin & Co., the names to be submitted to the governor; and that a committee be appointed to wait on His Excellency with a copy of the foregoing resolutions, and with authority to confer with him on behalf of the meeting as to the means necessary to carry the said resolutions into effect, such committee to be named by his Worship."

There was further discussion, this time in regard to arrangements for the volunteer force, and the mayor added that Governor Kennedy said he had received no indication that the people of British Columbia would not cooperate "heartily" with those on the Island.

The mayor appointed the special committee, naming de Cosmos, Rev. Evans, Waddington, Young and Garrett.

After a formal vote of thanks to the mayor, what had been a lively and at times rowdy meeting quietly dispersed, the citizens of Victoria content that appropriate measures would now be taken.

The next day, the Victoria committee met with Governor Kennedy. A retired army officer and former governor of Western Australia, Gambia and Sierra Leone, Kennedy had arrived in Victoria to take over from Douglas in March. He was an amiable individual who was also an able and honest administrator, but to many his shy manner seemed cold, and he was not naturally popular. The new Vancouver Island governor was disgusted with the low state to which the Indians of the colony had sunk, with the way the men prostituted their wives for food and money, with the degrading effects of the whiskey trade. Kennedy wanted justice and honesty returned to dealings with the natives. Yet he could not sanction violence against the whites, either. He told the citizens' committee that he agreed totally with the spirit of the resolutions passed at the public meeting.

"I assure you that no one feels more strongly than I do about these events. Unfortunately, there's nothing I can personally do about it other than what's been done—sending the depositions of the survivors to New Westminster as soon as possible."[34]

He continued: "I've stated to Governor Seymour that if he would accept aid from this colony we would furnish any requisite number of volunteers.

"I must say, the Indian policy in recent years in these colonies has been a mistaken one. This 'bread and treacle'

102

system may have been efficacious at one time, but not now. We need strict justice, good faith and great firmness."

"Your Excellency, we must first obtain a good leader for such an expedition," said Rev. Garrett.

"Yes, and adequate arms. I found out the other day there are a thousand stand laying rusted up in some shed. This may be something for the House to look into, Mr. de Cosmos."

Young suggested that Donald McLean, the retired HBC Chief Trader, be obtained to lead the Victoria volunteers. He also mentioned the possibility of Lillooet Indians joining an expedition against the Chilcotins.

"We are extremely concerned about the safety of our own Vancouver Island inhabitants," remarked Garrett.

"Your committee must fully understand the situation," Kennedy told them. "I've had something to do with savages in my time and I know something of the mode of dealing with them. There are only two paid magistrates on the island; what is to prevent massacres in Comox or Cowichan, as Rev. Garrett says? And there has been the licensing of whiskey settlers. Every man in the colony should know how to handle a rifle as we do, because we don't know how soon we might be called on to fight for our hearths and our homes."

"We must be guaranteed funds for the expedition," said Garrett.

"His Excellency must first sanction the expedition," de Cosmos interjected.

"No," said Kennedy, "Governor Seymour must first accept our help."

Waddington estimated the cost of such an expedition to be $5 per day per man, and that was a lot of money, for the force could be in the field weeks or months.

"And I have felt from the start three different parties should be sent out," added Kennedy.

"I asked for a gunboat to be sent to Bella Coola after the Bute murders, but I understand there were none disposable. One should be sent now."

"Yes, yes," mused Kennedy. "It's been most unsatisfactory. I'm amazed those men of yours had no arms, it must have been a terrible temptation."

"Your Excellency, there's an urgent necessity for a law preventing the sale of arms and ammunition to the Indians," de Cosmos said.

"The existing system lost its effect when Governor Douglas left," stated Waddington sullenly.

Kennedy looked at him. "I fear the system failed before my

The Chilcotin War
MAPS & PHOTOGRAPHS

The Colonies: British Columbia and Vancouver Island, highlighting Victoria, New Westminster, Bute Inlet, North Bentinck Arm, the Chilcotin, Alexandria, Quesnellemouth, and the goldfields.

Bella Coola Route: Based on "Bella Coola-Alexandria Trail," no date or author, PABC; and current B.C. government maps.

Chilcotin Plateau: Showing Waddington's proposed route, Palmer Trail, and main search area including place of McLean's death, Manning's murder, Klatassine's fishing and hunting grounds, and surrender point. Based on Waddington's map of 1863, Sketch B, PABC; map of "Waddington Murders" n.d., no author, PABC, and current B.C. government maps.

Waddington Trail: In lower Homathko Valley from bute Inlet, based on Waddington's map of 1863, Sketch A, PABC; and current gov't maps.

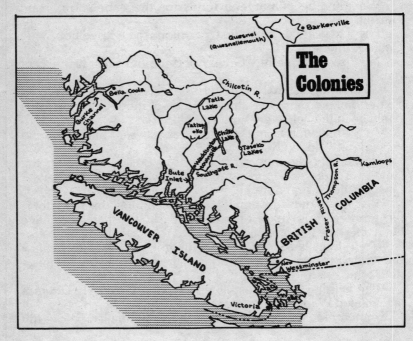

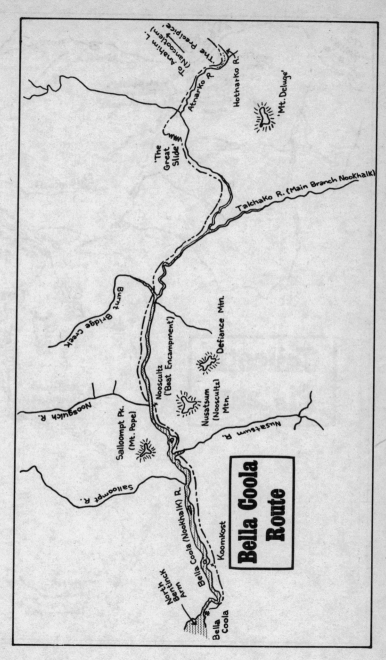

Bella Coola Route

To Anahim L.
(Nancooten)
"The Precipice"
Atnarko R.
Hotnarko R.
'Mt. Deluge'
"The Great Slide"
Talchako R. (Main Branch Nookhalk)
Burnt Bridge Creek
Nooscultz ("Boat Encampment")
Defiance Mtn.
Nooscultal Mtn.
Nusatsum (Nooscultal) Mtn.
Salloompt Pk. (Mt. Pope)
Noosgulch R.
Nusatsum R.
Salloompt R.
Bella Coola (Nookhalk) R.
Koomkost
North Bentinck Arm
Bella Coola

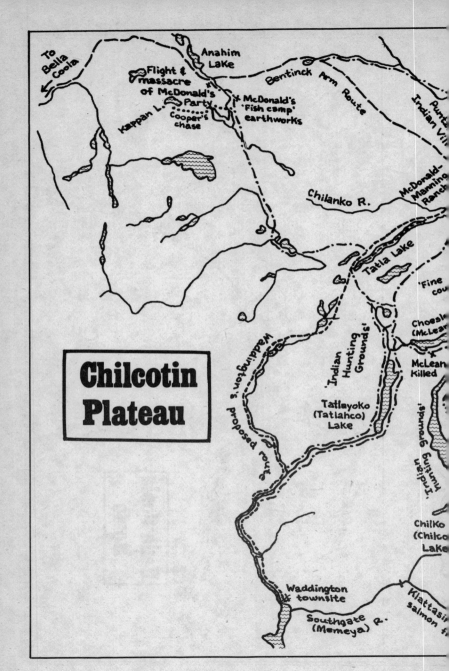

Chilcotin Plateau

To Bella Coola

Anahim Lake

Flight & massacre of McDonald's Party

Kappan L.

Cooper's chase

Bentinck Arm Route

McDonald's 'Fish camp' earthworks

Punti Indian Vill

Chilanko R.

McDonald-Manning Ranch

Tatla Lake

'Fine cou

Choesl (McLear

Indian Hunting Grounds'

McLean Killed

Waddington's proposed route

Tatlayoko (Tatlahco) Lake

Indian Hunting Grounds

Chilko (Chilco Lake

Waddington townsite

Southgate (Memeya) R.

Klattasi salmon fi

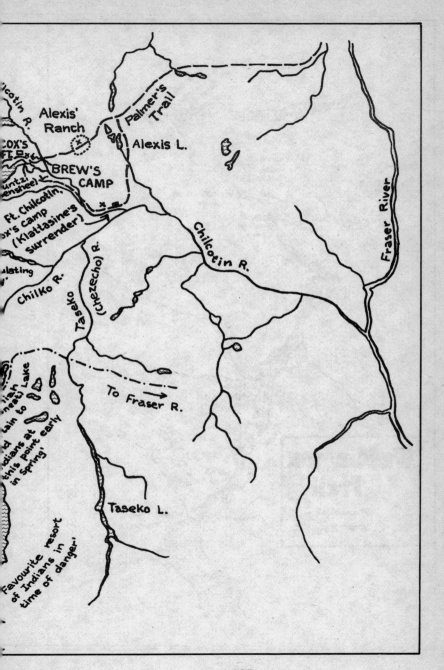

Alexis' Ranch

Palmer's Trail

Alexis L.

COX'S F[...]

BREW'S CAMP

[...]untzi [...]ensheel[...]

Ft. Chilcotin.
[...]x's camp
(Klattasine's
surrender)

[...]ulating

Chilko R.

Chezecho) R.

(CHEZECHO) R.

Chilcotin R.

Taseko

To Fraser R.

Fraser River

[...]iah
[...]neath Lake

[...]d
[...]ain to
[...]ndians at
this point early
in Spring'

Taseko L.

Favourite resort
of Indians in
time of danger'

107

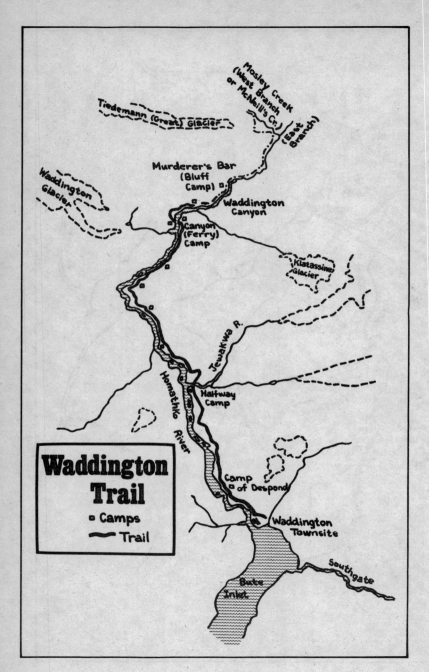

Mosley Creek (West Branch or McNeill's Cr.) (East Branch)

Tiedemann (Great) Glacier

Waddington Glacier

Murderer's Bar (Bluff Camp)

Waddington Canyon

Canyon (Ferry) Camp

Klatassine Glacier

Jewakwa R.

Homathko River

Halfway Camp

Camp of Despond

Waddington Trail
□ Camps
── Trail

Waddington Townsite

Southgate

Bute Inlet

The Author

Puntzi Lake looking from the north toward the south side.

The Author

Puntzi Creek, in which William Manning's body was hidden by Chilcotin Indians.
Pastoral scene near Tatla Lake, looking toward the Cascades.

The Author

Depression in earth at top of hill still remains from the McDonald party's earthworks dug out over 110 years ago.

'Fish Trap Earthworks' plaque on rock near spot where Alex McDonald's party dug in to protect itself against the Nancootlem Chilcotins.

THE CHILCOTIN WAR

In 1864 Alfred Waddington's crew constructing a road from Bute Inlet to "Cariboo" was almost wiped out by resentful natives about 65 miles to the south. The war party then killed members of a pack train here and spread terror across the whole interior. Governor Seymour's armed patrols captured the suspects who were convicted and hanged at Quesnel.

PROVINCE OF
BRITISH COLUMBIA
19 66

Sketch of activity in Bute Inlet, 1862 (by Edward Parker Bedwell).

'Mouth of the Homathco River, Bute Inlet' (by Frederick Whymper, 1865).

Remains of old Waddington bridge near foot of Waddington Canyon, 31 miles from Bute Inlet, Oct. 13, 1928.

"Upper entrance to the defile at the head of Bute Inlet, Mr. Waddington's road on right." Sketch by Frederick Whymper, 1865, Reproduced in *Illustrate London News*, Sept. 5, 1868, p. 232.

Remains of Tim Smith's cabin near foot of Waddington Canyon. Smith, Waddington's ferryman, was murdered here by Klatassine. Photo taken Oct. 13, 1928.

Waddington Canyon looking upstream.

The Waddington Trail about half a mile above the head of Waddington Canyon. Trail wound over canyon about 1300 feet above river level and wound down again to river. Photo 1928.

Bluff above Murderer's Bar, Homathko River (from watercolor by Herman Otto Tiedemann).

B.C. Government Survey Camp, October 1928, on Tragedy Bar, Homathko River, four miles above Waddington Canyon.

Alfred Waddington.

Chartres Brew.

Donald McLean

Thomas Elwyn

Governor Frederick Seymour

John D.B. Ogilvy

Frederick Whymper

Governor Arthur Edward Kennedy

Sir Matthew Baillie Begbie

Rear-Admiral John Kingcome

119

predecessor left," he snapped. "There were murders before I arrived and nothing was done."

The meeting ended with Kennedy assuring them he would "lose no time" in laying the offers of assistance before Governor Seymour. "I will inspect the volunteers myself," Kennedy said.

That morning, a couple of dozen men were waiting at the doors of Franklin's when they opened at 7 o'clock. Throughout the day there was a steady traffic of them signing the volunteer roll. It read:

"We the undersigned are desirous of enrolling ourselves as volunteers to assist the authorities of British Columbia in the detection and apprehension of the murderers, on the condition of being armed and equipped at the public expense."[35]

There were 129 signatures when Franklin's closed for the day.

The offer was sent over by steamer that night. Seymour resisted the temptation of being too busy to reply for a few days, instead sending a letter back to Kennedy the very next day. He declined the offer, but thanked Kennedy anyway.

"These volunteers will, I have no doubt, attribute to none but proper motives the hesitation I feel in accepting their offer of assistance; the time may perhaps come when I may have to call for their services, but it has not yet arrived.

"There is nothing unfriendly or disrespectful to the people of Victoria in my declining to avail myself immediately of their offer of assistance."

Noting the "much-delayed receipt" of word on the Bute massacre from Kennedy, Seymour said he now expected to complete arrangements for capture of the Chilcotins "without any more wearying delay."

Seymour expected to obtain a ship for a Bentinck expedition and should he need the Victoria volunteers "I would inform them at the outset that their duties would not probably be of that exciting kind which tempt young men from their homes. We are not at war with the Indians and the energy of the volunteers restrained by their oaths as special constables will probably have only to be directed to making passable for themselves and packers the many swamps and rocks which impede their progress."[36]

In other words, Seymour did not want a rabid bunch of Victorians intent on a Siwash shoot.

* * *

The village of Bella Coola consisted of 16 white people living in log houses along the river and among the Totems and thunderbird-painted lodges of a large Indian community called Great Village by the whites. The Indian name for it was Koomkootz and it was a fairly impressive settlement, established on both sides of the river.

Alexander Mackenzie had reached it in 1793 during his overland search for the Northwest Passage, and Captain George Vancouver visited it that same year by sea. Eventually a few whites had become established to trade with the Bella Coolas and to farm.

Bella Coola had much in common with the Waddington townsite in regard to geography. It was situated at the head of a deep fiord, the North Bentinck Arm of Burke Channel on the B.C. coast. A lush green valley reached inland under the Atnarko or Nookhalk, or Bella Coola River, shadowed by rough peaks frothing this time of year with waterfalls. Numerous rockslides fanned out from the crevices.

Mackenzie had given the Indian community at the head of the inlet the name Great Village. He had also called it Rascal's Village. Later, with the white intrusion, it became New Aberdeen, and then Bella Coola. But none of the names entirely disappeared, and they were interchanged with equal stature.

The explorer Mackenzie found the Bella Coola Indians to be a proud, artistic, and industrious people, excellent rivermen and fishermen.

Lieutenant Palmer, when he visited the Bella Coola Valley during his 1862 road survey, found them quite different:

"Hudson's Bay blankets and shirts are the usual articles of native attire, and they adorn themselves with nose-rings, earrings and fantastic head-dresses of wampum. They have not yet come within the influence of Protestant or Roman Catholic Missions and adhere pertinaciously to the old Indian superstitions and customs, maintaining, as regards their religious and other ceremonies, a jealous secrecy which defies the scrutiny of the white man. The language is the most guttural and difficult on the Coast.

"In moral character the Bella Coolas are degraded specimens of the red Indian. Prostitution, polygamy, and other worse vices at which civilized men shudder are of frequent occurence amongst them. Thieving is an art that all attain to perfection, and, in intercourse with them, I had unpleasant opportunities to becoming acquainted with the incredulity, falsehood and avarice which form prominent traits of their character. Sir Alexander Mackenzie christened Koomkootz 'Rascal's Village,' and I willingly contribute my testimony to

121

the justice of the title.

"To their immoral habits of life, and partly also to wars with the Hydahs, the bloodhounds of the northwest coast, may be attributed the gradually progressing extinction of the race, clear evidence of which is afforded by the sight, at different points further up the river, of the ruins of deserted lodges, once the habitations of large families of Indians that have gradually dwindled away by death until the few survivors have incorporated themselves with the larger bands."[37]

But it was the smallpox encountered by Palmer and other explorers which was undeniably the main factor in the degeneration of the Bella Coola Indians.

Twenty-two miles upriver from Bella Coola, John Hamilton had taken over the trading post of merchant Peter Barron, who had explored an Alexandria route before Palmer and was now living mostly in Quesnel. It was at Hamilton's post that it was necessary to cross the Bella Coola River in order to continue the journey west up the valley and up into the interior.

Hamilton had come to the site with his wife and daughter and had the beginnings of a good farm going. Among the three enterprises—ferry, store, and farm—he was doing pretty well.

The whites called it Boat Encampment or Canoe Crossing, but it was actually the site of an Indian village called Nooscultz, sometimes Anglicized into Newsculles by the whites. The village was all but gone, but there were often quite a few Indians camping there on their way back and forth along the Bella Coola, and many also came for the sole purpose of trading with Hamilton.

On this particular day, Hamilton had a special visitor from among the ranks of the Indians. Chilcotins often descended into the valley to visit and trade furs for blankets, pants, gunpowder and other articles. Of the Chilcotins, the Nancootlem tribe were the most frequent visitors.

Today, Chief Anahim himself entered John Hamilton's store with several of his tribe, asking for gunpowder. Anahim was not liked or trusted by the whites of the country, but his power was respected. Hamilton got the chief a quantity of powder.

Anahim produced a $5 piece, much more than enough for payment, and Hamilton pocketed it. Then Anahim asked for another pound of powder and showed a second $5 gold coin.

Curious by now, Hamilton asked where he had gotten all the money.

There was no reply. Anahim turned and smiled at the other Indians.

Hamilton shrugged and got him the rest of the powder. His partner, Adam Ross, had left for the Cariboo with four others in April with supplies to sell. A letter had come back from Ross via a traveller that they had had to buy snowshoes from Anahim's tribe and had paid $5 a pair. That was probably how Anahim had gotten the money.

The Indians left, and Hamilton had no way of knowing until three hours later that Anahim's money had come via Klatassine from Alfred Waddington's Bute Inlet work party, most of which were now dead.

That clue came in a letter from A.H. Wallace, the customs house officer at Bella Coola. Wallace had heard of the Bute massacre and suggested Hamilton take appropriate measures to secure the safety of his family, namely forsaking Nooscultz for Bella Coola.

A Chilcotin Indian boy who worked for Hamilton was also nervous. He had talked with Anahim's men and received broad hints about the Indians taking their land back from the whites, and that the war had already begun.

It gave Hamilton plenty to think about. If the Chilcotins had come into the valley to kill the whites, Anahim could have done so. But he did buy a lot of gunpowder.

When John Grant slowly rode into sight, bloody from the gunshot wounds he had received at the hands of the Chilcotins, Hamilton finally believed. Grant hurriedly explained what had happened. He did not know if there were other survivors. He did know for sure that McDougall, Higgins and McDonald were dead. The Chilcotins, Grant said, could be right behind him.

Hamilton's wife tended to Grant's wounds as best she could. A few belongings were gathered together quickly and put into a canoe. There might be no need to hurry, but it was better to be safe than dead.

With food, clothing, and arms packed into the big river canoe, the party prepared to shove off into the Bella Coola. The Chilcotin helper suddenly ran off into the woods.

Hamilton pushed the craft off from the bank and as it began to turn downriver, the hearts of the occupants froze. On a slope above them were several mounted Chilcotins. They were not recognizable by name, but it was certain they were there with but one purpose in mind. Hamilton and Grant readied their weapons, though Grant's arm made him almost useless for fighting and there wouldn't be much doubt of the outcome of an attack.

But they didn't attack. They didn't fire a shot. Seeing they could not reach the drifting canoe, they rode down upon the family's house. The Chilcotins settled for plunder.

The canoe began the journey to Bella Coola at the head of North Bentinck Arm.

The man who had sent up a letter to warn Hamilton of possible Indian attack had his own trouble with the Chilcotins. After the rout of McDonald's pack train, Klatassine had continued his efforts to recruit more followers. While the Bute Inlet massacre had attracted several to his cause, the McDonald victory served to eliminate any doubts about the possible success of the rebellion. Now there were men from several bands joining Klatassine or striking out on their own in smaller groups. The immediate object was to convince the Indians of the Bella Coola valley to join with their Chilcotin cousins. The whites there were all that stood between Klatassine and almost total victory over his foe. To wipe them out would mean the elimination of every white man between the Coast and Alexandria—the entire Chilcotin territory, except for Alexandria itself, would be back in Indian control.

While an attack on Alexandria was in his mind, the advantages of another victory, at Bella Coola, were obvious to Klatassine. If the Bella Coola Indians allied with the Chilcotins, war parties could grow to hundreds of warriors, and those Chilcotin chiefs who now refused to bring their men into the fray would have little choice.

Klatassine did not go down to Bella Coola himself, but one of the small groups of Chilcotins confidently went down into the coastal valley and into the town of Bella Coola.

The Chilcotins barged into Wallace's store and demanded powder and ball. Wallace refused, claiming he had none left, but one of the Indians drew a knife and slashed at him. The frightened and angry customs officer ran into a back room and returned with a long sword. He charged at the invaders, "who incontinently left."[38]

The incident was enough to convince Wallace that even the Bella Coola settlers were no longer safe and that without help they might all be killed by the Bute murderers and their followers. A small schooner had recently arrived at the settlement and provided the local Indians with powder, much to the anger and alarm of the settlers, but there wasn't anything they could do about it.

Wallace spread word and soon the entire white population was in council in his store. Among them were four women.

The consensus was that the Indians, in light of past successes and the small numbers of the whites, would attack them. It was decided to suspend business, barricade the houses and send a canoe upriver to fetch the Hamiltons.

But the Hamilton family, accompanied by the wounded Grant, soon arrived on their own after a six-hour journey down the river. When Grant told his story again, the men felt they should go back up to see if any other survivors from McDonald's pack train had made it back down.

They manned two canoes each with four trusted Bella Coola Indians and started up. They were armed with revolvers and rifles, White with a new repeater. Hamilton left his daughter and wife and went with them, anxious to see what had happened to his home, but Wallace remained in his store.

Hamilton was surprised to find that the war party had not burned his house.

White, experienced with the Indians, now took charge, reconnoitering alone. He returned, reporting there were no Chilcotins, or their horses, in the immediate area. The party searched the house, finding the stores and belongings plundered, but little actual damage done.

There was a shout from the bush. White and Hamilton went out to investigate. A voice came demanding that they identify themselves. That done, two wounded men walked into the clearing—Fred Harrison and Malcolm McLeod.

The pair had teamed up after Klatassine's attack at Nancootlem and made it down to Hamilton's ferry. They were happy to learn that Grant was alive, but they didn't know if any others from the party were. They had seen no one, neither white nor Indian, since fleeing from the scene.

The night was spent at Boat Encampment, with the three white men alternating at guard duty, watchful against marauding Chilcotins and their own Bella Coolas. When dawn came, there had been no disturbances, and a check of the area by White again turned up no Indian sign. The canoes were loaded and, with their two extra passengers, the rescue party pushed ten more miles upriver.

The Bella Coola canoe captain of one of the vessels pointed to the river bank. A white man led a horse and on the horse slumped another man. Farquharson, though he had escaped unhurt, had become completely lost in the strange country and had wandered around without any food ever since. The bush-experienced Johnson had found him and, though he was the wounded one, was in better shape than the greenhorn. So, it was Johnson who was walking, and Farquharson who rode Johnson's horse.

The canoes were taken further upstream, but nothing else

was found. Boat Encampment was checked again on the way back down. Nobody had been there.

At Bella Coola, the settlers were becoming more and more uneasy. More Chilcotins had arrived at the Indian village the night before and were doing their best to persuade the Bella Coolas to revolt. The Chilcotins were saying that the whites must be forced out of Indian territory, that anyone attempting to pass through or settle the Bute or Bentinck Arm routes must be killed.

The Bella Coola whites, now numbering 21, sealed themselves inside Wallace's store and determined not to repeat McDonald's mistake. They would wait there until they starved to death, the Indians left, or help arrived.

* * *

Bella Coola was not being ignored even though New Westminster had no knowledge of its immediate difficulties. Governor Frederick Seymour was pressing ahead with plans to take a force to North Bentinck Arm. Had the river steamers been seaworthy he would have commandeered them, but instead he had to wait for the Royal Navy for transportation. The crotchety old Admiral John Kingcome now came through with approval to use one of the big warships for the expedition to Bentinck.

Until Brew got his new force picked and supplied, the main thrust would be from the Cariboo expedition.

An elightened Indian is good for nothing.

George Simpson,
Hudson's Bay Company.

If my will was only concerned, the black, ungrateful, blood-thirsty, treacherous, and cowardly scoundrels should have prompt justice for it; hang first, and then call a jury to find them guilty or not guilty.

Donald McLean,
Hudson's Bay Company.[1]

Donald McLean was a 59-year-old Scotsman who had served with the Hudson's Bay Company for 28 years before retiring to his ranch and roadhouse at Hat Creek in the Bonaparte country.

During his long tenure with the Company he had grown to know the B.C. Indians as few other white men had, though it did nothing to increase his respect for them.

He had joined in London as an apprentice clerk and immediately been shipped to the Snake River country in Idaho, serving nine years there before being transferred to New Caledonia in what was now the colony of British Columbia. He worked his way up as postmaster and clerk, finally being appointed Chief Trader in 1853, after considerably longer employment than usually preceded such promotion.

McLean was in charge of a number of posts during his years with the company, ending with the Thompson's River Post (or Ft. Kamloops) for six years before his retirement.

He had had a lot of dealings with the Indians, and most of them were in an unfriendly capacity. When an Indian stole a horse or killed a white man under his jurisdiction, McLean made certain that justice was done.

The Hudson's Bay Company based most of its dealings with the natives on the theory that they were best kept ignorant and that they were children who must be controlled with a strong and firm hand.

127

Donald McLean had no argument with this philosophy. To him the Indians were "rascals" who had little use other than providing the Company with furs.

Those who found fault with HBC policy in administering the new lands angered him. "I wish the glib-tongued speakers and ready-penned writers against the Company were placed for a few years in the un-Christianed Indian country. They would, I suspect, change their sentiments. I know my own, and shall not be easily induced to change them."[2]

One of his most famous dealings was with the Quesnel Indians. One of them had killed an HBC employee of low rank and lower reputation.

McLean at this time was in charge of Ft. Alexandria. His superior, Donald Manson, ordered McLean to capture the murderer, Tlhelh. So, in January 1849 he trekked the 25 miles north to Quesnel village with a posse of 16.

The Indian village was deserted, but on the opposite side of the river three huts appeared to show signs of life. McLean took the posse across and entered one of the huts, finding Tlhelh's uncle Nadetnoerh with his step-daughter and baby.

"Where be Tlhelh?" demanded McLean through his interpreter. ""Tlhelh tatqa?"

"Tlhelh huloerh," answered Nadetnoerh. "Tlhelh is not here."

"Where is he? Ye better tell me quick," warned McLean.

"How can I know his whereabouts? All I know is that he is not here."

"Then fer today ye shall be Tlhelh," McLean decided, drawing out two pistols. Both shots missed, but the determined Scot took out his musket and finally killed the docile Indian.

A son-in-law, in an adjacent hut cutting up venison, ran out upon hearing the shots, but was dropped with several bullets from the posse members. His half-breed wife attempted to hide in their hut, but one of the party went in and fired almost point-blank with his musket. The ball crushed the baby's head and wounded the mother in the shoulder.

An old man blocked the entrance to the third hut and when McLean cut a hole in the roof and looked in, almost blew his head off with a rifle shot. McLean left him with the remains of his family.

Months later, McLean got his man by threatening another uncle with the alternative of death for refusing help, or 100 skins reward for Tlhelh's scalp. The uncle reluctantly chose life and the reward, and found his nephew and killed him, later whipping Mclean's face with the scalp.[3]

Despite his disrespect for the Indians, McLean was a devoted family man and an efficient administrator. He resigned under something of a cloud after he became embroiled in a dispute with the Company over two new Fraser Canyon posts. Rather than be transferred east of the Rocky Mountains, McLean took his family with his accumulated stock and wealth and retired to his ranch near what was later to become Cache Creek. In addition to his own operations, he served for a time as magistrate, gaining a reputation for his fairness and wide knowledge of English law.

It was not simply a general knowledge of Indians and how to deal with them that made McLean the logical choice to guide the Alexandria expedition against the Chilcotins (he was a better leader than Cox, but Seymour wanted someone currently in the direct employ of the government). McLean had specific knowledge of the Chilcotins.

Fort Chilcotin, that unsuccessful attempt by the Hudson's Bay Company to enlist the Chilcotin Indians in the fur trade, had been McLean's first assignment in New Caledonia. He had alternately been in charge of Fort Chilcotin and Fort Alexandria in the 1840's, and at both places had come to know the Chilcotin Indians well, and was as familiar to them as any white man. McLean knew most of the chiefs and subchiefs, their habits and personalities, and their territories. He was, in fact, married to a Chilcotin, a seeming contradiction to his general feelings about Indians.

McLean was tall, muscular, and handsome with long curly hair, mustache and bushy sideburns. His intelligence and aggressiveness may not have endeared him to the Indians who got on the wrong side of the HBC, but to the white population he was a fine citizen and a gentleman. Seymour had been told about him and the governor wanted McLean to guide Cox's party. He sent a message to Cox ordering him to obtain McLean as his second in command.

Cox thus sent down word to Hat Creek asking McLean to raise as many men as he could and meet him at Soda Creek, south of Alexandria.

McLean recruited 24 volunteers, including his own son Duncan. With 50 rifles and 50 revolvers they left for Soda Creek, arriving the first week of June.

Cox had still not arrived. He had gathered together some volunteers but when he got to Quesnel from Richfield he found the river steamer *Enterprise* (not the one on the Coast) out of service as she was being fixed up with a new shaft.

McLean, therefore, had to wait impatiently at Soda Creek

while Cox found a way to make it the 40 miles downriver. The former HBC chief trader sent scouts to Chief Alexis' territory some fifty miles west of Soda Creek to obtain information on the murder of William Manning. Alexis did considerable commerce with Alexandria and members of his tribe had brought the news of the rancher's death. Alexis had let it be known that his Chilcotins were not part of the rebellion and he did not intend to interfere in what he considered a matter strictly between the whites and Klatassine's group.

McLean's Indian forerunners returned with confirmation that Manning had been killed and that Klatassine was continuing his campaign against white settlements. A letter was sent down to New Westminster and the information, published there and in Victoria, was the first reliable confirmation of Manning's death since the newspapers had spread the unfounded rumors. McLean assured Seymour that "no danger or difficulty" would deter him from using his "utmost efforts to secure the object of the expedition."[4]

In Cox's absence, McLean was fully capable of taking charge, but his men quickly became impatient at having to wait. McLean himself considered returning home.

Cox, however, managed to get a raft built and transport himself and his volunteers down to Alexandria. McLean and his party went up from Soda Creek and the two forces merged.

On June 8, 50 men left Alexandria over the Palmer trail for Puntzi Lake. It was a rough, tough crew. Most of them were traders or miners, inexperienced in Indian fighting, but hardy and ready for combat. They were also not inclined to accept discipline very easily.

It was Cox's job to mold them into at least a semblance of order and discipline, but he himself had never readily accepted any orders which contradicted his own inclinations.

He was a stubborn Irishman of an easy-going nature on the surface, but of a will that could become stiff as sap in cold weather. He had been on good terms with Governor Douglas, but had often done things without getting the proper authority, and Judge Begbie had often found it necessary to annul his decisions.

He once settled a mining dispute by having the two rivals race from his office to the claim they both wanted. The winner got the claim.

Cox simply did not like being told what to do, as if an order represented an insult or a question of his competence. Thus he did his job well when it was of his own doing and poorly when he chose not to cooperate. He was a fine horseman, at home in the rugged Cariboo.

In this particular situation he had been given wide discretion by Douglas' successor and he was pretty much on his own. In the Chilcotin wilderness there could be little interference. Realizing his own limitations in a strange place, however, he relied heavily on the advice of McLean.

Cox issued a standing order that there was to be no fighting or unnecessary rowdiness. Any man who disregarded the order would face immediate dismissal from the expedition. The thought of being left alone in unfamiliar Indian territory should have been enough to keep the men in line.

But a couple of days out of Alexandria a Cariboo miner got into an argument and drew a knife and revolver. The fracas was broken up before it really got started, but Cox gave him ten minutes to leave camp. After that, Cox said, the men the miner had threatened could do what they wanted with him. The man left without his weapons, blankets or provisions on a long and frightening trek back to Alexandria, if he could find it.

It was the first and last such incident.

In the first days of travel the expedition followed a relatively well-marked trail which had been used by Indians and white packers, but it was frequently interrupted by large quantities of windfall, and paths sometimes had to be cleared with axes and muscle.

After the short climb out of the valley of the Fraser River at Alexandria, the country suddenly and dramatically flattened into a gently rippling plain cratered with innumerable lakes and freckled with marshes and meadows. Poplars, berry bushes, and tall grass formed oases among the evergreens. As the group moved west, the vegetation became more luxuriant and the Cascades gradually rose above the horizon like a frozen sunrise.

It was an impressive land, but at the same time tedious in its similarity. Even the appearance of a black swath of burned-out forest offered temporary though eery relief. As the long train passed between the tall, sharp stumps, the occasional rasping of a charred branch was the only sound from this dead land.

When the expedition reached the valley of the Chilko River some 70 miles west of Alexandria, Cox took the opportunity for a short bivouac. Here he hoped to find Alexis and employ him as a guide, for the area from the convergence of the Chilko and Chilcotin Rivers to Puntzi Lake was his most frequent habitat.

The recruitment of Alexis had been Cox's primary strategy

from the start. As Seymour explained it:

He was to "at once proceed to the headquarters of Alexis, the great chief of the Chilcotin tribe, show his warrant, and explain that the Queen's law must have its course. He will support his application for redress by showing my proclamation, offering a reward of 50 pounds...for the apprehension of each of the murderers....[5]

Cox found out it wasn't going to be that easy.

"Alexis...was not to be found, he having with his family fled to the mountains, reports having been freely circulated that we were coming to this region for the purpose of exterminating the Indians, friendly or otherwise."[6]

The "rumors" had been picked up in Alexandria by members of Alexis' band as the expedition had been preparing to move out. The miners and drifters Cox had managed to recruit from the goldfields had talked loosely of their mission, the intent being, according to many of them, to go out and shoot as many Indians as possible. Alexis was not about to take any chances, even if he did consider himself a neutral. He had decided to leave his village a few miles north of the Chilcotin-Chilko forks and go on an extended hunting trip in less accessible territory.

There was nothing for Cox and McLean to do but to push on and hope to be able to contact Alexis somewhere along the way. The expedition continued another 40 miles to Puntzi Lake, the junction of the Bentinck Arm and Bute Inlet trails, and the scene of William Manning's murder. They arrived at Puntzi on June 12, four days after leaving Alexandria.

Many of the men arrived near exhaustion, not having been in shape for the march.

Puntzi is a tadpole-shaped lake about five miles long at the head and three more at the tail. The northwest shore alternates between groves of giant cottonwoods and stands of dwarf poplars and aspens, with large spreads of juniper on the rocky slopes. Occasional sandbars or peninsulas break a shoreline otherwise thickly forested.

A mile from Manning's ranch, as the train made its way along the north shore, Cox sighted a group of Chilcotin lodges. It was the village used by the Indians after they had been expelled from the choicest spot by Manning, the village from which Tahpitt had walked to kill the rancher.

The village came into view quite suddenly as the trail crested on a hill. The whites were sighted by the Chilcotins, but the Indians did not immediately flee. In fact, thinking it was another pack train, they were preparing to let it walk into a trap.

Cox, however, was either not desirous of or not wily enough to take advantage of the situation. Had he the presence of mind, he could have broken off a party of men and sent them behind the hills ringing the lake and closed off any escape by the Indians.

Instead, he ordered the expedition into full armed view on the hill. Within minutes the Indians had deserted the village for the bush. Cox, instead of capturing at least some informants and perhaps some of the murderers, had nothing but a collection of empty huts.

McLean, through this, could surely only mutter to himself about the ineffectiveness with which this first contact with the Chilcotins had been executed. While Cox had orders to avoid a direct "clash" with them, even Seymour would have been able to see the advantages of a more tactical action.

After an examination of the deserted village, Cox called up William H. Fitzgerald, one of his Cariboo volunteers. Two Chilcotins had described to Fitzgerald in Alexandria the location of Manning's body. With Fitzgerald, McLean and several other men, Cox continued on to Manning's ranch and searched out the stream. It took less than a half hour of thrashing through the cold-running water to find the body under the roots and branches.

Considering the fact it had lain in that spot for probably three weeks, the cold water had preserved it remarkably well. The covering of roots had kept the sun off and also probably retarded decomposition. The bullet wounds were easily identified—holes in the right breast and left shoulder blade where the ball had entered and exited. The head was completely crushed.

The body was removed and an inquest was held. As it was interred on the land Manning had paid for with his life, Donald McLean read a burial service commemorating the courage of white settlers in opening up new land against formidable odds.

Cox called a conference with McLean and J.D.B. Ogilvie, a tall, thick-set and tough civil servant who was third in command. It was clear that the nature of the surrounding territory—it was thickly timbered and covered with bush— made it more important than ever to gain the services of Alexis as guide and interpreter. Without someone of his stature to act as intermediary with the rebels it would be almost impossible to make contact with them. The expedition was supposed to talk, not attack. The speed with which they were able to flee their village today demonstrated the Indians' key advantage—they were in their own environment. The trails were innumerable and impossible to sort out.

McLean would take his son Duncan, the Indian Scout Jack, and another volunteer and go to Chilcotin Forks to attempt to find Alexis or at least members of his family or immediate band. It was a dangerous mission, for they might easily be slaughtered by Talpitt's Puntzi Lake band which was probably in an angry state at having been chased out of its lodges. But McLean felt it was better that a small party should go rather than split up the expedition, and he had no fear of the Chilcotins.

Early next morning, before the sun was up, McLean's scouting party slipped out of camp, making it safely out of the area unharassed.

*　*　*

Klatassine kneeled on the needle-covered forest floor beside a big rock. From his vantage point he could see the white men milling about their campfires.

It had been with surprise and anger that he had witnessed the big white expedition bungle into Tahpitt's village the previous day. He was surprised at the show of force and angry at being caught unaware and having to retreat. These whites looked very different from those he had been used to. There were many more of them, they were well-armed, and they were better organized. He knew why they were here, and for the first time Klatassine acknowledged the strength of the whites. It was only by coincidence that Klatassine had been back in Tahpitt's village, but what if he had been taken? These whites would have to be tested. He had not previously had any conception of their numbers or power, thinking them to be few.

Now there was sudden movement in the camp below. Two whites had been searching the woods all morning and had easily been avoided, but now they were back in the camp, pointing towards the hills. Unknown to Klatassine, the pair had spotted an Indian dog which was hanging about the spot where several Chilcotins were keeping an eye on the white camp.

Eight white men and an Indian boy walked towards the bush.

Klatassine quietly spoke a command to a brave who had been squatting beside him, and the warrior moved off.

The heavily armed whites entering the woods had been picked by Cox for their experience and ordered to follow the dog "and to bring to camp any Indian they might fall in with so that I could make my mission known amongst them."[7] The Indian lad, one of several picked up by the expedition along the way, was to act as interpreter.

The party had gone a half mile into the woods when their Indian guide gestured silently that there were Chilcotins nearby. Immediately, shots rent the air and bullets brushed over the heads of the whites. Klatassine had sent several of his own men to await their arrival and fire on them from cover.

The Chilcotins advanced and fired again, retreating as the surprised whites made their first return volley. Then, reloading and running from tree to tree, they renewed their attack.

One of the whites was wounded and they were driven back toward their camp.

Cox sent out eight more men to rescue the first eight and took a third party of eight, including himself and Ogilvie, to try and get in behind the Chilcotins and cut off their escape.

Suddenly, the Indians were gone. The whites dispersed and beat about the bushes over an area of four miles, but found nothing. Cox finally gave up and they all returned to camp. The commissioner, nervous over the battle, ordered the construction of a small fort.

In his first encounter with well-armed and prepared whites, Klatassine had not won a big victory. But outnumbered two to one his braves had outfought and outfoxed the whites, wounding one of them. Despite Cox's efforts to surround them, not a single Chilcotin had been captured—several times during the day whites had passed within a few feet of hiding Indians.

The incident gave Klatassine greater confidence in the ability of his men to cope with these whites, and he set out to still the fears of Tahpitt and those others who wailed that the Chilcotins would be wiped out and should offer the whites presents to atone for the deaths.

Klatassine realized the folly of such thinking. The whites wanted war now, and either the Chilcotins must win or die.

The fighting had not been without its casualties among Klatassine's followers, either. While Chacatinea had been the only one to die directly from the war, there had been two other deaths indirectly resulting from that. Chacatinea's younger brother Niko had been almost as strong in his words against the white's as Chacatinea himself, and urged Chacatinea to fight them. But Chinanihim, an older brother, had been against it, and after Chacatinea was killed by McDonald Chinanihim berated Niko for causing the death.

A quarrel ended with Chinanihim shooting down Niko. As frequently happened in such cases, the agony of guilt was too much for Chinanihim, and if he had maintained his sanity long

135

enough he probably would have committed suicide. As it happened, he went crazy and hung about the camp sobbing and screaming that everyone was doomed.

Chinanihim's own sister finally talked her husband into going out and shooting him to put him out of his misery and stop the noise.

But Klatassine could not allow such incidents to divert him from his objective. His own life and many others depended on his strength.

About 11 a.m. the next day, the whites heard firing from the direction of the same area in which they had skirmished with the Chilcotins the previous day. Then, five Indians appeared at the edge of the bush, fired guns into the air, and waited for the whites to react.

Had they given chase as Cox had ordered the day before, they might all have been killed, for Klatassine had set a sure trap for them. Cox, however, was not willing to risk any more casualties, and found that by ignoring the five Indians they soon went away.

As he put it, "I concluded not to risk the lives of my men in any way until the arrival of Alexis, as the Indians hold complete advantage over us in the bush."[8]

Cox had the Indian lodges burned and a truce flag raised over the fort.

Two days later, Donald McLean and his three companions returned safely to the Puntzi Lake camp. He had not been able to find Alexis, and had run into problems with members of the east Chilcotin's tribe whose first reaction was to prepare to kill them and worry about their intentions later.

But McLean managed to convey to them his good intentions before any harm was done, and the Indians promised to send for Alexis in the mountains. They estimated that this might take four or five days.

They also told McLean that the Chilcotins directly involved in the killing so far numbered only about ten, but were solidly banded together.

Cox decided to stay within the relative safety of his new fort for the time being. On June 19 he wrote up a dispatch outlining events to that date and sent it back with a small party toward Bella Coola for Governor Seymour. He wrote:

"I am now sending for fresh supplies, as it is possible we may be here or elsewhere in this vicinity for some weeks, as the murderers and their tribes have retired into the woods and their position must be discovered before we can think of taking them with certainty; and for this duty we require Alexis, who is well acquainted with their haunts and hiding places.

"I believe our force is sufficiently strong to perform our task. The Indians, friendly and unfriendly, do not number more than 70 at the furthest. I expect Alexis to arrive here tomorrow; should he disappoint me, which is unlikely, I shall proceed towards Bentinck Arm, about 65 miles, and obtain Anahim, an influential and good Indian as guide."[9]

Cox and his men remained penned up in their fort, but there was not a hostile Indian within dozens of miles. Klatassine had left the area to visit his close relative and friend, that "good Indian" Anahim whose village had been the rallying point for the attack on McDonald's pack train, and to turn his attention to Bentinck Arm.

While Cox was making his way toward Puntzi and subsequently hiding in his fort, Seymour and Brew were busy planning their own expedition via Bentinck Arm.

The governor decided to go along with Brew on his trip from Bella Coola into the Interior to join up with Cox. It would make a grand show, the governor tramping about the wilderness personally seeing to it that justice prevailed, and he could then continue on to the goldfields for a personal inspection. Despite the control Douglas had exercised over the influx of miners into B.C., he had never had direct contact with them. Seymour thought a visit would be a good thing both for his own edification and for the entertainment of the miners.

Brew made all the arrangements for the expedition after Seymour finally wrung assurances from Admiral Kingcome that naval support would be available. The plan was for the *Tribune* to pick up the volunteers and their supplies and pack animals at New Westminster. Unfortunately, that ran afoul when the *Tribune* ran aground in the Fraser River on its way to the B.C. capital, and there was concern about its ability to get back down to the sea fully loaded. Another problem was that a train of pack mules hired from upriver failed to arrive.

Brew therefore went to Victoria and bought 17 pack horses and got them loaded on board the H.M.S. *Sutlej* on June 14. The *Forward* went over to New Westminster and brought back the 40 volunteers the same night.

At 11:30 a.m. June 15, the *Sutlej* sailed out of Esquimalt Harbor for Bentinck Arm, sent off by a large cheering crowd and the band of the Russian flagship playing "God Save The Queen" and other British national airs. Kingcome himself was in command. Seymour travelled on the *Sutlej*, but his own personal steam yacht, the *Leviathan*, had left at 4 a.m. for Nanaimo to pick up the two Homathko Indians, Squinteye and

Qwhittie. A small party had gone back to Bute Inlet to assure the cooperation of the Homathkos should the Chilcotin rebels return to their area, and had brought Squinteye and Qwhittie over to Nanaimo. From there the *Leviathan* would take them to Bentinck Arm to join the expedition and identify the murderers when they were found.

The *Labouchere* and the old HBC steamer *Bearer* were also to sail into North Bentinck Arm to impress the Indians there with a show of strength.

Brew's new volunteers, some of whom had been with the first Bute Inlet expedition, were as well suited to the job as any available. He had pared them from the dozens who had asked to join and he was pleased with their calibre. Most were former Royal Engineers who had come from England with Col. Moody. When the Engineers were disbanded late in 1863, most had remained in B.C., taking up occupations ranging from small business to farming to blacksmithing. Thomas Elwyn would again be second in command. Among the volunteers was William Buckley, one of the Bute Inlet survivors.

Offers of assistance from New Westminster's Hyack Fire Brigade and the New Westminster Rifles were rejected in favor of this small force of special constables. The tactic was in keeping with Seymour's intention not to put the expedition on a war footing.

Victorians had at first been indignant at Seymour's rejection of their proposals to send an expedition of their own, but grudging approval was allowed Seymour's actions and the ability of the men who had been picked. As the *Colonist* editorialized:

"It is needless to say that it would be difficult to obtain a better set of men than these.

"The Royal Engineers have had abundant roughing experience while on the other hand they possess habits of discipline and obedience which are the very greatest importance in an expedition of this kind and which we fear might be sadly wanting among some of our Victorian volunteers. It is not desirable that every Indian north of Victoria should be killed, but it appears to be the idea of some of our heroes that are 'spilling for a fight' amongst us that all they had to do was to elect their own officers and start out on a general hunting expedition in which the Indian race generally were to be the game. If we wanted to bring about an Indian war, we couldn't do better than indulge this highly irresponsible and anti-discipline element, while, however, there were at the same time a goodly number of valuable men ready to start from Victoria. We believe all things considered, that it is fortunate Governor Seymour, by having so effectual a force ready to leave, is able to dispense with extraneous assistance."[10]

* * *

The *Sutlej* was an impressive warship. The big frigate had been launched nine years before at Portsmouth as a sailing ship, but had been converted to screw propulsion and lengthened four years later. Designed for 50 broadside guns, the number had been reduced to 35 plus a chase gun in conversion.

With 515 officers and men, she had arrived at Esquimalt for service in the Pacific Northwest almost a year before to the day.

E.A. Atkins lay on a topsail, which had been spread on the gundeck, muttering to himself. Here he was, fool enough to have signed up for another expedition, and things were looking even less comfortable than the Bute Inlet trip. He'd thought that with a ship the size of the *Sutlej* things would be done up better, since there was a lot more room than on that little gunboat *Forward* they'd been squeezed into, and this was a full-fledged expedition, not just a search for dead bodies.

But no, here he was laying on a damn sail mashed in between two cannons with nine other volunteers. They had been told to have a "quiet sleep." Sleep, on this hard deck, with the ship rolling around, and a big lantern hung right in front of his face, was a joke.

"Damn thing's just like the rising sun," he complained, but Atkins had quickly found out complaining did little good on this boat. He'd warned a marine that if the bloody thing wasn't moved there was going to be trouble. The marine refused and left.

Atkins got up and picked up the lantern, preparing to throw it overboard when the lieutenant of the watch showed up and took it from his hand. He left with the lantern and it looked like sleep was finally going to be a possibility.

Atkins laid back down and was drifting off when another volunteer started yelling.

"Whatinhell's going on here, there's water all over the place."

Sure enough, somebody had decided to wash the deck and forgotten to stop the scuppers, flooding the volunteers. The volunteers got up cursing and went outside on deck, but were soon ordered back down between decks again.

This time they were split up, five to a mess. Atkins stumbled around for half an hour before he found the right mess, but he finally got fed. The meal consisted of "some hard beef that had been round the Horn two or three times and some coco." He was hungry enough to swallow it all, and then went back on deck for a smoke.

He took out his pipe and tamped in some tobacco, lighting a match and sucking in the flame.

"No pipes!"

Atkins ignored the sailor and continued puffing, but a few minutes later he came back again.

"Put out your pipe," the sailor ordered.

Atkins complied, but he made like he was going for a casual stroll, in fact looking for a good place to hide. He came across a lifeboat. He climbed inside, lay down and lighted up. Sure enough, the same sailor happened along and spotted him.

The volunteer gave up. He eventually "got into" the rule of smoking only during the half hour after official meal times. "Just think of it, to men that can smoke for two or three hours."

The next night, Atkins had the same problem of finding Number 1 mess, but he finally got his dinner of hard tack, salt beef, and coco, and struck for the deck to have his smoke before the half hour was up.

As he stood puffing contentedly another sailor came along. Atkins was about to start swearing profusely and to put out his pipe when the man asked, "Interested in a drink?"

"Can a duck swim?" replied Atkins, and followed the sailor below.

Even Atkins wasn't up to the strength of sailor's grog, however.

"For Godsake, drink it yourself!" he wheezed, retreating back up to the deck.[11]

* * *

On Saturday, June 18, Admiral Kingcome took the *Sutlej* up the North Bentinck Arm of Burke Channel to Bella Coola. Even the volunteers who had served on the first expedition to Bute Inlet were impressed anew at the dramatic dimensions of the fiord.

Seymour and Brew planned to land the following day, consult with the Bella Coola whites, and proceed immediately inland. The expedition, however, didn't get off to the auspicious start that might have been wished.

Kingcome dropped anchor both bow and stern, but a sudden wind swept the stern onto a shoal.

"Well, it would make you laugh if you saw 500 of us that is crew and all, running from aft right out to the Bosprik end to

140

jump her off," recalled Atkins. "But we did and here got her anchored all right so next morning we landed with the horses and the provisions all right and then commenced the Chilicooten Expedition proper."[12]

As the unloading was underway, three of the five survivors of McDonald's pack train came on board to relate the details of the attack and the probable deaths of McDonald, Higgins and McDougall.

As they spoke, the full proportions of the mistake that had been made in sending Brew to Bute Inlet first became apparent. Had Seymour been given another ship by Gilford, he would have sent it to Bella Coola to try to stop McDonald. But the one ship he did have could have done the same thing, and three more men and thousands of dollars worth of merchandise would have been saved.

The tiny white population of Bella Coola, though, wasn't about to start laying blame on Seymour. When the *Sutlej* had sailed into North Bentinck Arm, the Chilcotins who had been there quickly disappeared, and the Bella Coolas very suddenly started acting friendly to the whites again. The "siege" that had kept the 16 whites barricaded inside Wallace's store for most of three weeks—during which they ventured out only periodically to trade—was ended.

The Bella Coolas, in fact, now offered to help Seymour and Brew hunt the Chilcotins. Seymour thought this was a fine idea, and provided uniforms and Lancaster rifles to the 30 Bella Coolas Brew conscripted.

The Indians had a fine time parading about the settlement in their new uniforms, imitating white soldiers.

The Bella Coola settlers were highly skeptical of Seymour's tactic in employing the Bella Coolas. Besides being extremely unpredictable, it was well known that many of them were closely connected both by blood and marriage with the very Chilcotins the expedition was going in search of. Some of them were undoubtedly prepared to join with the Chilcotins, and could easily lead the expedition into an ambush or turn on their white employers without warning just as the Chilcotins did at Bute Inlet. Seymour and Brew might well be placing the entire force of New Westminster volunteers, as well as the Bella Coola settlers, in serious danger.

As a gesture of trust, the Indians offered to give up the man who had killed a marine a few months earlier, but Brew did not want to be bothered with that now. He organized his volunteers and pack animals and moved out of the village that same day.

McLeod of McDonald's pack train, though still suffering from his wounds, decided to join the expedition.

Seymour stayed behind, saying he would join Brew the next day. Monday was the anniversary of the accession of Queen Victoria and something of a celebration was planned.

As Brew's train made its way up the trail near the Bella Coola River, a *British Colonist* reporter marvelled at the scenery.

He later wrote in his news story: "Bentinck Arm is a wild, desolate country. The scenery is striking, bold and grand; the mountains are covered with snow, which is now melting, forming torrents and streams, the noise of which is heard on all sides."[13]

When Lieutenant Palmer of the Royal Engineers had explored the area two years before, he had noted "countless tributaries, of every size from tiny cascades to impetuous mountain torrents," feeding the Bella Coola River on its passage through the mountains.

"The Nookhalk (or Bella Coola) valley, which averages from one-half to one-and-a-half miles in width, opening out considerably at the confluences of the principal tributaries, is walled in by giant mountains of from two thousand to six thousand feet in height, presenting the usual varieties of scenery met with in mountain travels in this country. Some of the slopes...are perfectly devoid of soil, timber or covering of any kind, and rise very abruptly from the valley, massive, unbroken walls of granite and trap standing in stupendous contrast to the forest scenery on the river banks and islands."[14]

Though the floor of the valley was flat, the river weaved drunkenly back and forth between the mountain ridges, and the swampy delta landscape turned into thicker underbrush and forests of cedar, cottonwood, and fir occasionally replaced by alder and willow groves or open patches of low berry bushes and small timber.

The narrow Indian trail in the lower part of the valley followed the river closely. It was soft and covered with fallen timber, and there were no bridges over the streams which tumbled into the Bella Coola River. Palmer had found it impractical to pack horses over the trail and instead transported his baggage by canoe the first 35 miles. Other whites who used the trail did the same thing, transferring their goods to horses upriver.

The first day out, therefore, was not an easy one for the New Westminster volunteers. In fact, it turned out to be one of the most difficult.

The expedition was the first to take its own pack horses from the sea. The volunteers walked with the loaded horses while most of the Indians—four to a canoe—were engaged in taking freight upriver.

The trail had to be cleared and in some places corduroy roads or bridges had to be built to get horses across quagmire or rushing streams.

But the big problem was with the half-broken, unmanageable pack horses Brew had picked up in Victoria to replace the mules which hadn't made it to New Westminster in time for the departure of the *Sutlej*. Much of the men's time was spent in getting them into reasonable order. It was a tough job, especially since they should have been loaded with about 150 pounds and were forced to carry between 200 and 350 pounds per animal. Every once in a while one of the frustrated horses would lay down and start kicking until the load went flying, so frequent halts had to be called.

Seymour, meanwhile, slept in the comfortable quarters of the *Sutlej*. The next morning, the frigate weighed anchor and sailed out into the Arm. In salute to Queen Victoria, she fired off 21 guns, and added 17 more for the governor.

The natives were suitably impressed by the roar of the cannon and the echoes bouncing off the mountain walls.

At mid-afternoon, the *Labouchere* sailed in and dropped anchor near the *Sutlej* and *Beaver*. The *Labouchere*, a side-wheel steamer, was not as big or impressive as the *Sutlej*, and had been to The Arm before, but together the three ships presented the desired picture of colonial power.

The activity of the volunteer force the previous day, the sight of the naval vessels and the demonstration of fire power seemed to have reduced the local Indians to a state of total submission. When the *Leviathan*, bringing Squinteye and Qwhittie, tardily joined the other three ships, it only added to their awe.

Hamilton chose not to chance another outbreak of violence at The Arm, however, and put his family on the *Sutlej* for Victoria until the insurrection was put down. He sent with them a quantity of good furs which had escaped the Indians.

The *Sutlej*, which was to be replaced at Bentinck by the gunboat *Grappler*, would have another important passenger. Achpicermous, the Indian who had been one of the spectators at the attack on McDonald's pack train, had come down to Bella Coola to join the other Chilcotins there. He had been captured by Morris Moss, a trader, and had been identified by the survivor Farquharson as a participant. It was more likely that Farquharson remembered him from before the attack and simply took him to be one of Klatassine's men, but as far as the whites were concerned they had captured their first murderer.

Seymour, with Lieutenants Henry Cooper and Hugh Stewart of the *Sutlej* as aides-de-camp, and a personal guard, then moved out to catch up with Brew.

When he did, the governor had second thoughts about the desirability of traversing the wilds in search of Indians. But after a night in the woods, Seymour decided to carry out his announced intention.

When the expedition reached Hamilton's ferry, they found it in possession of a small group of Ansanies, a band of Chilcotins, the same ones who had threatened Wallace in his store, and whose members were responsible for Robert McLeod's death the previous winter. For a few tense moments it appeared they would refuse to give up their new-found lodging place and might even fight, but when presents were given and the Bella Coolas in Brew's employ did not take the side of the Ansanies, they left.

They might have yielded some information had they been caught or properly cajoled, but Brew let them go because they were not known to have been involved in the rebellion. This was to be common strategy, or lack of it, on Brew's part. Anxious to avoid any impression that he was on an Indian-killing campaign, he would insist that the most conclusive evidence be available against any individual Chilcotin before he would be taken into custody, and pains were to be taken not to unduly disturb any who did not appear to be guilty of anything. The policy was not unanimously popular even among the well-disciplined ex-Engineers.

Brew was a tough taskmaster despite his caution. When he made a decision or a promise, he stuck to it, and anyone who crossed him was subjected to his fiery Irish temper. Brew's years in the Irish police force, before coming to British Columbia, made him accustomed to being obeyed without question.

The horses were ferried across the river with some difficulty after a night camping at the Hamilton ranch, and the journey continued. From here it was about 20 more miles to the Great Slide, up which the men must climb to reach the Chilcotin plateau.

Inland, the Bella Coola Valley contracted considerably from its mile width at the inlet, squeezing between the mountain ridges. The vegetation became thicker, like rain forest, with huge Douglas firs towering over dense groundcover. The mountains became lower but more rugged, frequently jutting out in broken masses into the river. Dozens of slides fanned out from high on the peaks to the edge of the forest below.

Thirty miles from its mouth, the Bella Coola was formed by the joining of the Talchako and the Atnarko rivers, the trail following the latter into a deepening gorge. The river gradually became reduced to a narrow torrent.

The horses rapidly became more used to their work, but there were still frequent moments of utter confusion and mayhem. One volunteer wrote in his diary of "a Bull Run on a small scale; packsaddles here, ropes there, flour, blankets, bacon, beans, buckets, and a heterogeneous mass of 'iktas' scattered along the trail in the most admired confusion," all caused "by starting before we were ready and stopping before we wanted to."[15]

Shortly after this mishap, another one of a different nature occurred. As the train crawled along a narrow, winding section of the trail, some Indians were seen on the opposite side of the river. They appeared to be Chilcotins, and there was considerable excitement among the volunteers, being strung out as they were and momentarily defenseless.

One fellow, whose experience did not match his gallantry, rushed from the rear of the train with his government Lancaster rifle cocked and ready. A twig caught the trigger, the rifle fired and the ball shot through the wrist of the man immediately in front of him and whizzed close past the next 20 in line.

The Indians proved to be the Ansanies again, but for the second time Brew declined to make any demand on them to help in capturing the rebels.

The expedition arrived at the foot of the Great Slide on June 28.

Directly south rose Mt. Deluge[16], crowned with a cluster of peaks, the summit of which the Bella Coola Indians believed to have been the residence of an ancient chief of their tribe and his squaw who climbed there at the time of the Deluge and thus saved their race from extinction.

Palmer, when he had surveyed for the possible new trail, felt the slide could be avoided and, indeed, would have to be if a road was ever to be practicable. But the existing trail turned straight up the face of the big rockfall, which covered virtually the entire side of a mountain. The trail did not wind, but took short zig-zags up the fragmented, loose trap rock on the face of the slide, rising toward cliffs and hollows and continuing past to an altitude of 1780 feet. It was a slow and painful trip over slippery and dangerous footing, and the men were soon wishing Brew had been able to get Ladner's mules instead of these damn horses.

This sweating, cursing, snorting, stumbling train of 19 horses and some 75 men halted their toil as if by a command from the Almighty when a face-blackened and feathered Siwash suddenly leaped from behind a clump of bushes above them and fiercely shouted, "*Kar mika chako?*" As the volunteers gaped, the Indian glared for a few moments, then sunk down out of sight.

To everyone's relief, he was gone when they reached the spot, and they continued on.

Lieutenant Stewart, however, had been following a short distance behind the train, and when he reached that part of the trail he was greeted with the same surprise. Stewart, though, had the presence of mind to draw his revolver and order the savage to surrender. He then marched his prisoner on, catching up with the expedition as it was setting up camp at the top.

He was one of those same Ansanies nobody had bothered to try to question before, or at least he had been with them. The Indian was not only related to the main Chilcotin tribes, but claimed to be brother of Anahim. It was established beyond doubt that he had been among the group in Wallace's store. He yielded a description of the attack on McDonald's pack train and named some of those involved in it, but denied that he was a part of any murders. The prisoner also warned that there were Chilcotins following the party and had intended attacking as it came up the slide, but decided there were too many despite the vulnerable position. (A report reached New Westminster and Victoria a few days later that the Chilcotins had, in fact, attacked the whites on the slide and hurled them over the cliffs. However, the rumor was soon admitted to be false, after being printed in the newspapers.) Unknown to Brew and Seymour, Anahim was among the hostile party.

The captured Indian claimed total innocence on his own part, and Brew figured that was good enough. He hired him as a guide.

After a day's halt to rest the horses and the men, the expedition prepared to push on. Ogilvie and 12 men arrived with Cox's letter of the 19th. Seymour ignored Cox's suggestion that the Alexandria force be left to handle everything, and told Brew they would continue as planned to Puntzi Lake to tie up the two forces. He wrote a letter to Cox asking him to meet them half way so they could discuss strategy.

Ogilvie started back to Cox, leaving Brew and Seymour to follow behind with their men.

The Bentinck Arm trail now emerged onto an elevated rolling area almost level with the summits of the mountains. The big pines, cedars and firs of the valleys were gone, there now being stunted firs, sparser brush and grass grasping sandy soil. The trail descended gradually 500 feet to the Hotharko, a small tributary of the Atnarko, and went along its valley for several miles east and north.

At the forks of the Hotharko was a steep 100-foot-high bluff of basalt columns known as "The Precipice." The trail here was extremely steep. The top of The Precipice was 3840 feet above sea level.

From there the country became much like that which Cox's party had passed over to get to Puntzi Lake from Alexandria—a vast plain of forest broken only by marshes and lakes, with the peaks of the Cascades in sight to the west. Poor grass, wild roses and strawberries and *knnik-knnik* or *uva ursi,* the native tobacco, formed the main ground-cover. The evergreens remained stunted, but small cottonwoods formed groves along the banks of streams.

Mishaps continued to plague the expedition in fording torrents, crossing rotten bridges or negotiating the steep, sometimes almost non-existent trail. It was a pretty bedraggled party of volunteers which neared Nancootlem, and one volunteer complained that "the whole business is botched from the first from want of a proper leader."[17]

By now, 20 of the 30 Bella Coola Indians had deserted and three horses had been lost, a total which Seymour called "a comparatively trifling loss."[18]

The trek for the remaining few miles to Nancootlem was much easier, but monotonous. Being this close to the territory of the Nancootlem Indians, Brew and Elwyn enforced strict silence. No hunting was allowed, even of grouse for food.

It was known that Anahim had a palisaded fort at his village. Though Brew did not believe Anahim was himself involved in the rebellion, he was tired of the march and hoped the whole Chilcotin would make a stand there.

He was disappointed to find the fort empty, and Anahim's village deserted. He did not order the fort or lodges burned. If his opinion of Anahim proved wrong, leaving the fort could well prove dangerous later.

The first sign of McDonald's party was an aparejo, some straps, a half keg of nails, and some augers. A little further the expedition came across some broken boxes, with matches and

147

candles strewn around.

Then, beside the road near a tree bigger than the thin dwarf spruce usual to the area, was a body or, at least, part of one. It was difficult to determine whether the Chilcotins or the wolves had mutilated it more. Both legs were off near the knees. Only the thigh-bones, ribs, back and head were left—the rest apparently having been eaten by wolves. Both hands were gone, but the fingers of one were found near the torso. A knife was deeply imbedded in the skull. An examination of the clothes beside the corpse showed that one shot which passed through the left arm near the shoulder and probably exited through the right wrist had been fired from close enough range to singe the shirt. Other holes were found in the shirt and pant legs.

These were the remains of Alexander McDonald. But only 15 yards away was an even more grisly sight.

Near an Indian tomb of logs and stakes, an expedition member was startled to see a Chilcotin sitting on the ground.

A moment later he saw that the Indian was quite dead, the body also having been eaten at by wolves. A wreath of feathers sat on the head, a ring hung from the nose, and in the mouth was a pipe.

After Chacatinea and Klymtedza had been buried and the Chilcotins had left the scene, the wolves had moved in for a free meal. They not only tore apart the bodies of the white men, but managed to drag out Chacatinea's body from its grave. They had dragged the body a few yards, but had apparently been interrupted and had left it, quite by accident, in a sitting position.

A Bella Coola Indian happening by spotted the body and, rather than burying it, insulted the corpse by leaving it in its sitting position and putting the pipe in its mouth.

A dead horse was next to come in sight. About 200 yards further the body of Higgins was discovered. He had been shot in the chest and arm with balls, and in the stomach with buckshot. Higgins had been dragged off the trail by the feet. His head lay in a hollow surrounded by hair. The back of the head was smashed, obviously having been struck repeatedly with axes, knives or musket butts.

Next, there were several more dead horses and more candles and other goods scattered around. Near a small pond beside the trail lay the body of McDougall, riddled with bullets and horribly mangled like the others.

In the woods and along the trail for half a mile were boxes of carpenter's tools, yeast tins, ropes, candles, gutted pack saddles, broken agricultural instruments, kegs of nails, and personal papers and money.

The bodies were interred by the volunteers.

The next day the earthworks dug out by McDonald and his party were passed. Two miles further on another fort was found on a hill. Trees surrounding the palisaded blockhouse had been cleared away, and the walls had been loop-holed. It was probably here that the murder of McDonald and his party had been planned and Brew ordered that the fort be burned down.

The volunteers energetically went about the task, and dense masses of smoke soon rose above the trees.

Suddenly from the opposite side of Nimpo Lake came a single shot. A few hours later a dozen huts were found. The smoke had warned the Chilcotins of the presence of the expedition and the shot had been a warning to all those around to clear out. Their direction was traced for a few miles southwest.

Brew dispatched a "flying party" of 25 men under Lieutenant Cooper after the Indians. He was to chase them until he found them or until he lost them, and then go to Puntzi Lake. Brew, Seymour and Elwyn would hurry there with the remaining men.

Cooper's party left on an hour's notice, in heavy rain. The country into which they travelled had never been seen by white men. The trail took them ten miles to Lake Capana (now Kappan Lake), a small body of water on the west edge of the plateau.

Henry Cooper was an efficient young marine and the ex-Engineers under his command had confidence in him. But he didn't have the right kind of help...Brew had sent with him as guide the Chilcotin captured at the Great Slide. The police magistrate had been advised strongly against the move, but Cooper was stuck with him.

For four days Cooper kept on the trail of the fleeing Indians. But then, the trail got faint on smooth rock and snow as it neared the Cascades, and the Chilcotin guide had to be given his chance. He promptly led them into a swamp, where the volunteers thrashed around up to their thighs in mud and water, and horses became mired. The guide claimed he no longer knew where the trail was, so the party had to give up for the day and camp.

The next day Cooper formed the party into scouting groups to try and pick up some sign. The guide was left in camp to take care of the pack horses. When the volunteers returned that evening, the Indian was gone. So was the best pack horse.

Two volunteers went after him and as they were catching up the Chilcotin abandoned the horse and took off on foot, soon disappearing without trace.

Cooper suspected that the Siwash had chosen to be captured, and had accomplished his mission well.

"So much," wrote the volunteer keeping the diary, "for Mr. Brew's maudlin sympathy for the Indians, and his orders that the Chilcotin rascal should not be treated as a prisoner."[19]

Atkins, one of Cooper's party, was positive the Indian had "wanted to be caught" and that his pretensions at guiding were "only a fake." He'd intended on leading them on a wild goose chase all along.[20]

The volunteers were unable to find the Chilcotin's trail again, and turned back to rejoin the rest of the expedition. Seymour and Brew had taken the remaining volunteers and loyal Bella Coolas and gone on toward Puntzi Lake, but they had left a cache of food for Cooper's forces.

There was little change in this part of the journey from the rest of the plateau. There were the same lakes and marshes. The trail was sometimes easy, sometimes narrow and rocky, sometimes passing through burned out forest caused by lightning or a careless campfire. There was an abundance of fish and waterfowl, but few land animals. The mosquitos, hatched from the swamps, preyed incessantly on the horses and men.

"The coldness of the nights in no way appeared to hinder their existence, and, in the worst places, they can only be described as forming a dense living cloud which covers the country to a height of twenty feet from the ground."[21]

Less abundant but just as worrisome were small black blood-sucking flies which swarmed around the moving train.

The scenery toward Puntzi Lake became somewhat more pleasant, or, at least, greener. Gentle streams watered the foliage of the low-lying country which now boasted thin quantities of bunch grass.

The convergence of the two expeditions at Puntzi Lake on July 6 was cause for celebration. Cox's men—"virtually besieged by an invisible enemy"[22] as Seymour described their situation—gave the governor a hearty and prolonged cheer.

Brew's men set up camp near the fort, and the leaders gathered to discuss events to date and to plot strategy. Though Brew and Cox were ostensibly the two leaders of rank, with Elwyn and McLean the respective seconds, Seymour dominated the decision-making. He was surprised and a little disgusted to find that although Cox had been at Puntzi for two days before Brew and Seymour even left for Bentinck Arm he had accomplished virtually nothing. Cox insisted that he had had to wait for Alexis, who had not shown up as promised, but Seymour wanted some action. He ordered Cox to take his unit and scour the area beyond Tatla Lake towards Bute Inlet instead of waiting for friendly Indians who might or might not show up to help. And there would be no waiting; Cox would leave the next morning.

Though the members of the two expeditions had hailed each other and welcomed the chance to swap tales, they were two very distinct camps that night. Cox's band of miners, mostly Americans, took the opportunity to celebrate. Brew's New Westminster volunteers were more sombre. The differences between the two would be difficult to reconcile if they were to be together over a lengthy period of time.

Governor Seymour recognized the possible problem quickly, and tended to side with Brew's men.

"The few hours that the two parties had passed together sufficed to show the difference in their character. The men raised in the gold district, mostly Americans, passed the greater part of the night in dancing and playing cards to an accompaniment of war whoops and the beating of tin pots. The New Westminster Expedition, almost exclusively English, and comprising many discharged sappers, spent the evening in their usual quiet soldier-like manner. No spiritous liquor was in either camp, yet the amusements were kept up in the one long after total silence prevailed in the other, and a slight estrangement commenced between the occupiers of the fort and those encamped on the plain below, which was never entirely healed."[23]

Cox's expedition presented an impressive spectacle as it moved out of camp early the next morning. His men looked fresh and tough considering their activities of the night before. With them was William Buckley of Brew's force to identify any suspects that might be captured.

When they had gone, Brew moved his camp inside the fort. Since his provisions were already low Brew immediately sent another party back some 150 miles to Bella Coola for supplies. That left only ten men at Puntzi Lake and the protection of the fort was needed. But Cox's men had left it in such a repulsive condition that Brew preferred to live outside the walls anyway.

The presence of the Chilcotins in the neighborhood was obvious even if they were never seen. Dogs were heard barking at night, and the moccasin tracks of prowling Indian scouts were often found near the fort in the morning. Brew maintained watches through the nights.

Since Manning's murder, his squaw Nancy had stayed near the ruins of the farm. Brew was able to talk to her and assure her that the white men would not harm any innocent Chilcotins. He urged her to go to Alexis and explain this to him, and that his help was badly needed. There was no war against the Chilcotins; only the guilty individuals would be punished and then the other Chilcotins would be left alone. Alexis would be guaranteed full protection if he came into the camp of the whites.

Nancy obtained no promises from Alexis, but there was an indication he would come when he had the time. He wasn't feeling very well right now, he said.

Despite Alexis' continued hesitation in placing his trust in the whites, Nancy brought some squaws into camp. They soon came in daily to barter trout for sugar, which was the only article the whites had in plentiful supply.

Cooper reached Puntzi on the 10th and intercourse with the natives was safer. Scouting parties could now be sent out for 20 or 30 miles, and they could hunt and fish.

One day the Chilcotin squaws brought word that Alexis would come in if Governor Seymour remained there. It appeared that Brew's diplomacy was starting to pay off.

Some of the volunteers, as well-disciplined as Seymour may have boasted, were still disenchanted with Brew, and the presence of the Indians made them nervous. The women began bringing their children into camp with them and, in the opinion of some of the volunteers, were learning too much about the expedition. Somewhere out in the bush were their husbands, undoubtedly waiting with intense interest for the women and children to return with information.

One morning a big Chilcotin warrior ventured into camp with his klootchman and stayed around all day, then walked out again. During the whole day, not a word was said to him… no questions asked, much to the frustration of the volunteers who felt Brew should have been trying to wring as much out of him as he could.

An additional frustration for the New Westminster volunteers was the lack of action. While Chilcotins were all around them, the expedition did not seem to be accomplishing its objective. The inactivity was boring, even if the work was light. The daily scouting parties kept them busy, but the rigor mortis of routine was setting in.

Meanwhile, Cox was also being closely watched by the Chilcotins. Wherever he went they were close by, though he had not seen any for the first several days of the search. He pushed 25 miles south of Tatla Lake into Klatassine's favorite hunting and fishing territory, the mountainous range covering 30 miles east-west between Mosley Creek, a branch of the Homathko, and Chilko Lake, stretching like an inland sea almost 40 miles itself to the foot of the Coast Mountains. Dozens of Indian trails criss-crossed the area, and the expedition's scouting parties covered 20 or 30 miles a day in their search.

One day before any Indians had been sighted, one of Cox's scouting parties came upon a new trail in hilly country which was followed for several hours. They discovered a village of deserted Indian lodges, and in a thickly wooded area found a cache of flour, bacon, saddles and other goods from McDonald's pack train.

Cox consulted with McLean and they concentrated their efforts in the area surrounding the deserted village for a few days, but came across no further sign. By July 16 the miners were growing impatient with an expedition that was turning into a ridiculous failure. Cox decided to take them back to Puntzi Lake.

They had broken camp and started their first day's journey back toward Puntzi when one of the volunteers discovered that he'd forgotten something in the camp. He rode back to the site. As the volunteer broke through the brush into the clearing he stopped short.

Squatting by the dying embers of a campfire were several Chilcotins, puffing on a calumet of peace.

Klatassine and his companions saw the white man as he wheeled his mount and charged back down the trail. They were almost as surprised as he was, for they had thought it was safe to come and examine the remains of the camp. For days Klatassine's band had watched the King George men. It was with relief that they had seen them pack up and leave this morning, but now the warning would be sounded.

The Chilcotins hurriedly but calmly stood and walked out of the clearing. In the bush, they split up and went in different directions.

Cox's volunteers were back a few minutes later beating the bush for the half dozen Indians, but it appeared they once again had vanished.

One party of a dozen miners was getting discouraged when they picked up the footprints of a lone Indian. Hurrying up on them, they sighted their quarry, a tall, muscular Chilcotin loping along across a pasture-like opening in the forest. Three shots were fired, but they missed.

Klatassine quickened his pace, for the horsemen would be on him within minutes. He could not hope to outdistance them now that he had been sighted. He would need some luck.

His long strides carried him through the forest and over bushes and windfall, his feet deftly touching down on logs or rocks or roots and springing him onward. The great chief saw another opening in the foliage, but rather than avoid it he headed for it, though it would expose him to the whites again.

Klatassine ran onto the grassy plain; two hundred yards away rippled a lagoon. As he neared the *pengo'ntsodl,* the hunting party burst from among the trees. A musket boomed and a ball went over Klatassine's head. He plunged into the water.

The whites galloped up and peered carefully across the big lagoon, formed from a stream by one of the hundreds of industrious beavers in the area. The water still moved where the Indian had jumped in, but he had either not surfaced or he had gotten to a far bank and into the woods again.

They spread out and searched the entire perimeter of the pond, then poked amongst the nearby woods. They had lost their prey.

When he felt sure they had left, Klatassine heaved himself up onto the bank and lay resting for several minutes. He had managed to find a low over-hanging, washed-out bank, dense with drooping grass and had squeezed himself under it. Whenever whites came near he had submerged, breathing through a short reed.

The ordeal had exhausted him, but he soon regained his strength.

His pursuers, not realizing they had almost captured or killed the most wanted of all the Chilcotins, returned to the main party and told their story. They were the only ones who had sighted an Indian.

A new camp was set up on an open space near a stream running into Choelquoit Lake. Tents were unpacked and pitched again, and cooking utensils were soon once more banging over campfires. Beyond the stream rose a steep hill with a ravine breaking into a bare spot near its summit. Otherwise the hills were low and the campsite was pleasant and easy to protect.

Donald McLean had stayed largely in the background during the whole expedition while Cox issued the orders, but it was McLean's experience which resulted in most of the decisions other than Cox's snap judgements. Had it not been for the retired HBC trader, the expedition would not have done even as well as it had, for almost all of them were completely green at the job.

McLean knew the Chilcotins were near, that their camp was probably within a few miles of their own. Next morning he was up before daybreak. He strode over to where Jack, the Alexandria Indian scout, was sleeping, and awakened him.

Nobody was supposed to leave camp without permission or, in McLean's case, without notifying Cox. McLean felt strongly the presence of the Chilcotins and he wanted to reconnoitre. Jack was nervous about the two of them going out alone, but McLean insisted.

Sun was beginning to spill over the outlines of the mountains in bright ribbons as they crossed the stream and started up the hill. It was going to be a clear, warm day.

Jack was cautious from the time they left the camp. A trail led up the rocky hill by the ravine, and they followed it. At the bare summit they could get the lay of the country.

A Chilcotin named Anukatlk watched as McLean and Jack approached the top of the hill. His rifle was trained on the big, handsome white man. McLean had become a familiar figure to the Chilcotins as they watched the activities of Cox's party. He was still remembered from the time he had spent among the tribes of the area two decades ago. McLean was said to have magic, for at least twice before in years past he had been shot in the heart only to ride off unharmed.

Anukatlk, who had joined Klatassine after the massacres, was one of several scouts who were out that morning. He had settled down near the trail to keep watch, for it had been expected that the whites would send out a party in this direction. But Anukatlk had not expected to see two men out by themselves on foot, and certainly not the great chief McLean.

McLean was alert but confident, as ever, as he advanced up the trail followed by Jack. The Indian tugged at McLean's coat sleeve.

"Indians near." He wanted to go back for help.

McLean rested his rifle butt on the ground for a moment, wiping his brow and straining his senses to pick up any sign of the rebels.

"Don't be foolish, Jack," he said quietly. "We'll be alright."[24]

He continued up the trail, and the nervous and reluctant guide caught up to him. They were at a distinct disadvantage. The trail was steep and there was good cover all around. There is a tendency for a greenhorn to lower his eyes and concentrate on pumping his tired legs up the grade, so that the proper caution is not taken.

McLean, though, was ever wary. When they rounded a slight curve in the trail, it was him, not Jack, who immediately sighted the screen of fir bows piled against a tree trunk off to one side in the bush. At the same time as his eyes fell upon the hiding place, McLean's arms were raising his rifle and cocking it to fire.

But there was no one behind the screen, for Anukatlk was hiding in a clump of willows on the opposite side of the trail. As McLean wheeled toward the screen of boughs, expecting to see a gun poke through it, he exposed his back to Anukatlk.

Jack's first reaction was not to the blind, but to the click of a gunlock somewhere in the brush. He threw himself to the ground as Anukatlk's rifle boomed.

McLean fell. A second bullet passed over the guide, who tumbled a few feet down the hill, regained his feet and looked back in time to see some Chilcotins sink below the crest of the hill.

Jack plunged full speed down the trail to the camp. He almost collided with a horse ridden by Harry Wilmot, who had been on watch and had heard the shots.

McLean's son, Duncan, who had just arisen to find that his father was not in camp, was running across the meadow on foot.

Wilmot urged his mount up the trail, knowing he too might come under attack. He came upon Donald McLean lying face down, and when Wilmot turned him over it looked as though he might still be alive. But there was no pulse.

The volunteer remounted and rode back for help. As he reached the flat a few hundred yards later, Duncan McLean rushed up puffing in an obvious state of great anxiety.

He anxiously asked if Wilmot had found his father.

Wilmot's first reaction was to avoid the truth, but the young McLean insisted.

Wilmot told Duncan that his father was dead.

Duncan's face contorted, he moaned in anguish and fumbled for his revolver. Wilmot's fast action in leaping from his mount and grabbing the weapon saved the young man from suicide, for he had the pistol cocked and was about to point it towards his head. Duncan fainted.

Cox was already rushing out of the camp with 20 men on foot, for he had heard the shots too, and then Jack had come tearing in. He ordered two of them to help Duncan back to camp while the rest, including Buckley, went forward with

Wilmot and Jack.

As they filed up the slope, one of the volunteers tripped. His rifle fired and the ball went through his leg. He screamed and fell down thrashing.

The men in front of him flattened themselves.

"They're behind us!" one of them cried.

"Where?" asked the fellow who had shot himself. [25]

Two more men hauled the unfortunate victim back to camp while the rest continued on.

Passing McLean's body, Cox peeled off more men to carry it back. The remaining volunteers reached the summit of the hill and scanned the topography of the surrounding country. Cox sent a message to Ogilvy to bring up more volunteers and to form a ring around the hill.

Fitzgerald sighted in his telescope a group of Indians huddled near a big rock several hundred yards away. Shots were fired at them. One ball struck a tree five feet above Klatassine's head and the chase was on.

Cox thought he had them this time, but Indian cunning once again foiled the whites. While the area had all but been encircled by volunteers, a long lagoon at the bottom of an almost perpendicular rocky bluff left a gap in the snare.

Klatassine and his half dozen men scrambled down to the water and plunged in. Before the whites realized what was happening, the Indians swam the 60 yards to the other side and were through the line. A few parting shots followed them, but further search was useless.

The camp was both restless and morose that evening. McLean had been highly respected by the ranch hands who had come up with him from around Cache Creek and by the rough miners recruited by Cox, and his death was the crowning disaster of what had become to many of them a pointless and fruitless exercise.

An examination of his body revealed the reason for his previous escapes from attempts on his life. He wore a special breastplate. But it had done him no good against the back shot.

McLean, who had read the burial service for Manning, was now the subject of words of praise as he was laid in the ground in a field near the camp. A shallow layer of dirt was shovelled over the blankets which covered the fallen hero, then rocks and logs were placed in the grave. Finally, more dirt was smoothed carefully, level with the ground. That night flames licked over the field for several acres and a pall of smoke hung in the air. Neither wolves nor Indians would be able to find and

157

disturb the remains of Donald McLean.

Duncan remained almost catatonic for days, and when word was later received by the family in Kamloops, there was great mourning, for, despite his toughness, McLean had been a good father and husband.

Cox renamed the lake after McLean, but it was later changed again.

Though provisions were still plentiful, Cox decided to head back. It was useless to try to defeat the Chilcotins under such circumstances. They had shown time and again that in their own environment they could elude the whites forever. They had either to be deprived of their food or their leaders.

Ogilvy was named second in command to replace McLean, and the expedition pointed itself "home" to Puntzi Lake. On July 19 an advance party rode into the Puntzi camp and announced that Cox and the expedition would arrive the next day.

If the expedition southwest had been a failure, those holding the main camp at Puntzi had almost become the victims of creeping annihilation. Had it not been for the untiring efforts of the few Bella Coolas in fishing, the whole group could have starved to death. But by the time Cox returned with six days' provisions remaining, even fish were scarce. The Bella Coolas had diverted the streams so many times they were almost fished out. The diet, mainly of fish, unripe gooseberries and a little flour, was barely sustaining the men, and dysentary was spreading, attended by its bloody and painful evacuations and its intense fever.

Seymour didn't know it, but he owed his life to the whim of two Chilcotin scouts who could have claimed it without cost. The governor had strayed into the wood alone one day and had been followed by the scouts. They had gotten close enough to see him roll a cigarette and light it, but had not fired, perhaps not realizing the rank of this white man. Seymour returned to camp unaware of his danger.

The pack train from Bella Coola was overdue and if starvation neared—which would not be long—Brew contemplated a forced march to Alexandria.

Though the extra provisions from Cox's expedition could be distributed among Brew's force, Seymour was unhappy that the Irishman had not continued his hunt while he still had several days' food remaining.

With the death of McLean and the dismal failure of all attempts so far to capture any of the rebels, word was spreading quickly among the Indian bands that the whites were defeated.

That was very close to the truth. With food short and the men disgruntled, there seemed no advantage in continuing. Cox wanted the expeditions to withdraw, for he maintained that nothing useful could be done until winter. This was the best season for a war...for the Indians. Their food was plentiful now, but in winter they tended to border on starvation even at the best of times, for they were largely indolent and did not or could not stock enough to see themselves comfortably through. With a fresh expedition harassing them after the snow fell, the rebels would soon have to give up to save themselves from starving to death.

Alfred Waddington had suggested to Seymour that 15 or 20 armed men be posted on the Homathko and Memeya rivers to stop the Chilcotins from fishing there as well as to protect the Homathko Indians and whites left in Bute Inlet. The salmon from the two rivers were the lower Chilcotins' greatest resource for winter food and Waddington warned that the rebels would probably send their slaves and squaws to fish them. Putting a stop to this fishing was the surest way to catch them, according to Waddington.

Brew, however, agreed with Cox and both asked Seymour for orders to withdraw. Seymour refused. He suggested that not all had been done that should have been. Cox had wasted precious time waiting for Alexis instead of actively looking for him, and had done nothing to assure the Indians of the just intentions of his expedition. While his trip southwest had been greeted with a total lack of cooperation from any of the Indians along the way, the New Westminster party had accomplished more sitting at Puntzi Lake by the use of diplomacy. Cox had lost his best man and had returned with another wounded. McLean's murderers had not been apprehended; if Cox had endeavored to capture their women and children they might have given themselves up. There was still much to be gained by staying in the field, and much to lose by withdrawing, for the situation now was much worse than when they had started.

Seymour decided he had spent enough time in the Chilcotin country and that he should be moving on to the Cariboo. He ordered Brew to take over "the work abandoned by Mr. Cox's party," [26] while Cox would hold down the fort at Puntzi.

This was, to say the least, a slap in the face for Cox, for he was well aware that Seymour, Brew and less than a dozen men had kept possession of the Puntzi Lake camp for several days. Now Cox was being told that all his men would be needed to do the work of 10.

Thus Seymour had two extremely unhappy leaders. Cox was angered by Seymour's accusations and lack of confidence; Brew was disappointed at having to remain in a wilderness area attempting what he thought to be an impossible task at this time.

Seymour might have taken a different position on the matter had not his feelings for the Indians undergone a gradual change since the start of the expedition one long month ago.

He had joined the expedition "to secure moderation"[27] in treatment of the Indians, even though he had made a point of employing sworn special constables rather than soldiers.

But the ghastly spectacle of McDonald's pack train, the deprivations experienced in the wilderness, and the stubbornness of the Indians had tempered Seymour's emotions. He was determined that the colonial forces should not lose face either to the Indians or to the colonists of B.C. or Vancouver Island. He confided later to Edward Cardwell:

"I was determined to show, what had not previously been seen in this part of the world, a government calm and just under circumstances calculated to create exasperation. But there was no longer any use shutting my eyes to the fact that this was a war, merciless on one side, in which we were engaged in with the great part of the Chilcotin nation and must be carried on as a war with us. Happily for the occasion, our Constables knew the use of the rifle and revolver, at least as well, as the more peaceful instruments generally used in support of the law."[28]

Cardwell had advised Seymour before his departure for Bentinck Arm of: "...the great importance of moderating by every means in your power the spirit of retaliation to which such events too naturally give rise, and of confining within the limits of justice and of sound policy the measures of chastisement to which you may find it necessary to have recourse. These measures must be guided solely by a sense of justice and a desire to re-establish peace and order upon a permanent basis...."[29]

Seymour was still determined to re-establish peace and order, but the methods obviously needed reconsideration.

"...Should a real war take place between the Indian population and the whites...I may find myself compelled to follow in the footsteps of the Governor of Colorado...and invite every white man to shoot each Indian he may meet. Such a proclamation would not be badly received here in case of emergency."[30]

That remark was to bring a warning from Cardwell later on:

"I do not understand the meaning of the paragraph in which you speak of inviting every white man to shoot every Indian he might meet. I shall rely on your continued adherence to the line of conduct hitherto pursued by you, which appears to have been perfectly consistent with humanity and good policy."[31]

As if to support Seymour's determination, Chief Alexis suddenly appeared only a few hours after Cox had returned.

It was a dramatic entrance. On the same hill from which Cox's expedition had first sighted the Chilcotin camp a month and a half ago, eight horsemen now appeared. They sat looking down at the milling camp. Many of the volunteers became intensely nervous and wanted to go out after the intruders, but Alexis sent down an envoy under a white man's flag of truce to officially give notice of the visit and to make sure Seymour was still there.

Seymour sent back an invitation for Alexis to come in and talk, and watched with Cox, Brew, Ogilvy and Elwyn as the brave rode back up to the waiting chief. There was inaudible conversation, then the Chilcotins charged down toward the camp, muskets held over their heads to indicate peaceful intentions, their mounts kicking up clouds of dust.

The entire camp watched with awed fascination as the Indians galloped in amongst them, pulling up abruptly in front of what was obviously the group of white chiefs.

Alexis demanded the identity of the "great chief" and when he was informed which was Seymour he leaped off his pinto and strode toward him. He wore part of a French army officer's uniform such as that worn by Montcalm's troops a century earlier. The long blue coat, devoid of buttons in the front but still sporting shiny brass on the huge faded yellow cuffs of the sleeves, hung almost to the Indian's knees. Alexis wore the deerskin leggings of his own people, and his chest was visible under the coat, but a white sash stretched over a shoulder and under the opposite arm. He carried his musket with the butt tucked under an armpit and the barrel resting on the forearm.

Seymour extended a hand in greeting and without hesitation Alexis grabbed the governor's wrist and pumped it a couple of times.

"Nous parlons."

Seymour sent for a Canadian French-speaking volunteer to interpret, and they all sat down to talk. Alexis and his tribe, dwelling closer to white settlement for a longer time than the western Chilcotins, was much more familiar with the white man's ways. His people had been visited in their own homes occasionally by Roman Catholic priests. Alexis spoke some English, but he spoke better French Canadian.

His decision to finally come in and talk with Seymour was cause for considerable hope, though it didn't mean he would help. But that first day's talks didn't go very well. Seymour insisted on immediately going on the offensive rather than attempting pacification. His object was to impress Alexis with the strength and determination of the whites, but Alexis was too knowledgeable and too stubborn to fall for it. The chief appeared nervous and wary during the talks.

Seymour referred to the murder of Manning near the very spot where they now talked. It had happened in Alexis' territory, though it wasn't his home village.

"How could you, the chief of this country, think it right to go Cariboo hunting while your men were killing every white person they saw?" demanded the governor.

"Many white men claim to be chiefs. We do not know who to trust any longer," Alexis retorted. He said that Klatassine and Tellot's men had renounced all connections with him, that none of his own men were involved in the least way in the killing. Klatassine and Tellot had the right to make war on the whites without it being any affair of his.

But what had the whites done to cause such barbarous hostilities?

Alexis paused, then replied that Klatassine's men were "des mauvais savages, qui connaissent pas le bon Dieu"—some bad savages who do not know the good God.

Seymour carefully explained the policy of seeking justice, not war on the whole of the Chilcotins (though he had been having his doubts about that strategy). Only those involved in the deaths of Europeans were being sought. "Those we will shoot down and catch."

A slight sneer curled the Chilcotin chief's face. How long, he inquired, did Seymour intend to remain on Alexis' hunting grounds?

"Three years," Seymour lied.

Unless the whites had more surprises—and they had always been full of them—Alexis knew better. These whites could not live here that long.

The discussion ended abruptly when Alexis arose and stated he was retiring for the night.[32]

Seymour spent an anxious night, worrying about what Alexis would do next. It had not gone as he had hoped. On top of that, Alexis should have been treated to a big feast to show him the wisdom of joining with them, but there was going to be enough trouble feeding them at all. A dozen more of Alexis' people rode in, so that there were now 20 "guests" to host.

Brew, as acting treasurer of the expedition, pointed out to Seymour the low state of the provisions as well as the "frightful expense"[33] of the two months' supplies the governor was ordering from Alexandria at inflated Cariboo prices.

There was also trouble brewing with Cox's miners. Already upset at Seymour's order that Cox remain in Puntzi, they had begun talking about it among themselves in growing groups, and a demand finally went directly to Seymour that they either be allowed to march against the Indians again or they would return to Alexandria.

Their anger was inflamed by the claim by one of the Bella Coola Indians that Alexis' right-hand man, the one-eyed Ulnas, had been involved with Klatassine and Tellot in the rebellion.

Ulnas confessed that he received a coat, a bag of flour and $10 from the plunder, but claimed he had had nothing to do with the fighting and that he had thrown the gifts away. The miners considered this to be a highly unlikely act for a "greedy savage"[34] and were determined to hang him or burn him alive as an example.

Alexis understandably was not pleased by the reception he was getting. His men were prepared to fight, and waited with loaded muskets. Brew placed Ulnas under arrest for his own safety, assuring Alexis that all those Chilcotins who had entered the camp—including Ulnas—would be allowed to leave freely with safe conduct whenever they chose.

Next morning Seymour was shaving when Brew informed him that Alexis and his men were saddling up. The whites were obviously incapable of showing him proper hospitality and Alexis considered the visit to be over. Further talk was not needed, since he maintained he had nothing to do with the problem.

Seymour was anxious for Alexis to at least not leave in his current angry frame of mind, but it looked like things were going sour again.

The governor invited Alexis for another talk before he left and tried a shot in the dark. Explaining that he must soon leave to visit Alexandria, Seymour requested that Alexis escort him through his territory.

The chief was surprised at this demonstration of trust, and could not refuse. He agreed to remain for a few days until Seymour was ready to leave.

A few days later, the long-awaited pack train from Bella Coola arrived. It had been delayed in getting the provisions and in getting men to escort it to Puntzi. Now that food was plentiful again the volunteers stopped their grumbling, and good humor returned like rain after a prolonged drought. Brew's men, though unhappy, had not caused any discipline problems as Cox's volunteers had threatened to do. The Cariboo party was still determined to play an active part against the rebels, and offered to place themselves "unconditionally" directly under Seymour's command if he would stay on.

Seymour didn't want to remain there any longer, but he relented and agreed to let them try another march into Klatassine's territory. Brew and Cox would approach it from different directions.

The force was a little larger now with a few more men from Bella Coola and Alexandria.

Now that the whites were at full strength with lots of food, Alexis agreed to accompany the expedition rather than accompany Seymour, but he would send word ahead to be sure the governor's party was not harassed in any way.

There followed a fortnight of comparative idleness while preparations were made for the three parties. Cooper and Stuart and several other men would continue on with Seymour, Alexis would accompany Cox, Brew would take his men into Anahim's territory.

Since the policy of avoiding a "clash" with the Indians had now gone largely by the wayside, the question of what to do with them should they be caught was discussed. Seymour invested Brew, "a man of admirable temper and discretion,"[35] with full powers for holding a court of justice in the Chilcotin country and hanging the rebels on the spot.

Seymour rode out of the Puntzi Lake camp on July 25, going east on the trail along the lake and into the country Cox had passed through coming from Alexandria. He left with the feeling that the Chilcotin expeditions had a high possibility of success, and that it would not have been so without his own presence and perserverance.

Cox was next to move out, taking his big party, swelled by Alexis' people, to the east end of Puntzi Lake and cutting south toward the old Hudson's Bay Company's Fort Chilcotin on the Chilko River. From there he would continue south and west along the Chilko toward the headwaters of the Memeya River.

Cox had been gone a few days when an Indian came into his camp at the junction of the Chezko and Chilko rivers and asked to see him. He was known to the whites as Joe, the son of Tahpitt. He brought a message from his father and from Klatassine and Tellot and their men.

They wished to have peace with the white men. If the whites stayed out of the mountains the Indians would not attack them and were willing to talk. If, however, Cox persisted in continuing south, the Chilcotins would wipe out his expedition.

It was the first communication between Klatassine and any of the expedition leaders, and Cox sensed that it would not have come unless the rebels were becoming worried. He told the messenger to return to Klatassine's men and tell them Cox had no intention of turning back. If they wished to come in, he would welcome them, but if not, "I will follow them up and kill every man, woman and child."[36] He added that he could guarantee safety for them if they surrendered to him, but he could not speak for Brew, who would also soon be hunting them down. If Klatassine wished to talk, Cox would be encamped for several days at old Fort Chilcotin.

Brew left Puntzi on August 8, following the footsteps of Cox's previous southwest expedition, coming up Tatla Lake and turning south toward the area in which Donald McLean had been killed. He took with him the Bella Coola chief and his few warriors, and Qwhittie, but with the departure of Seymour's entourage Brew now had only two dozen men.

As Cox had suspected, Klatassine was indeed growing concerned. His band of rebels was now ranging between Tatlayoko and Chilko lakes, as free as ever from the whites. But the women and children had to be protected, and every time the whites came close they were endangered. They had not been able to accomplish much fishing, and soon winter—the ice and eagle moons—would be upon them.

Klatassine had a new child to be concerned about. As was common among the Chilcotins, Klatassine had taken more than one wife over the years. His young wife Toowaewoot had reached her time during the skirmishing with the whites. She had gone away from the camp and kneeled down holding onto two horizontal poles. With the help of a midwife she had delivered a daughter, then walked back to camp.

The tightly-wrapped infant was kept in a narrow cradle with a padded space barely big enough for its head. In this way the head could be squeezed and deformed so that the forehead would be high and flat in order to make it easier to carry packs when she grew up.

Toowaewoot herself was not a Chilcotin, but a Carrier with rather pretty features and dark eyes and long, black hair. She had come to Chilcotin country with the family of her father, a chief named Shopeadz. To stop Shopeadz from poaching, Klatassine had attacked and killed several members of the invading band. The Carrier chief escaped, but Klatassine was left with all his possessions, including his daughter.

With Klatassine's band now was also a young son, and there were many other squaws and children, so that Klatassine was worried for their safety.

His scouts had reported on Seymour's departure and on Cox's movement south. His warning to Cox had brought a threat, and the message that Brew was coming with the intention of killing not only the men but the women and children as well.

Indeed, Brew's force was now approaching the northeast of Tatlayko Lake. With Cox proceeding from the East, the Chilcotins would be forced out of their fishing grounds.

Klatassine's guardian spirit seemed to be losing its strength. All his life he had had but one spirit, and it had unfailingly served him. A Chilcotin's guardian spirit or spirits came to him only after much questing as he entered manhood. When he had reached puberty, the Chilcotin would leave his village and go through a rite of bathing, fasting, and exercising. He would swim in the icy lakes and rub leaves on his body. This preparation for becoming eligible to take a woman and be accepted as a man by the tribe could take weeks or months.

Hopefully, the guardian spirit would appear in a dream. A Chilcotin might have no guardian spirit, or he might have more than one. Each spirit acted in one specific capacity. It could make him a good hunter, a good fisherman, a good canoe-maker, a good fighter.

Always, Klatassine had been the best fighter. The other men with him now would stand by Klatassine to the death if need be, but there were the women and children....Tellot and Tahpitt were tired of fighting the whites, and counselled Klatassine to talk to them. If the man Cox could be trusted, then surrender would not mean death and the war would end.

When he had started his war, Klatassine had not realized there were so many whites or that they had so many guns. Klatassine was confident that he could elude the white expeditions indefinitely despite the increasing hardships, but he also now felt that the King George's men would not go home, and that he could not kill them all. Killing them had only resulted in more taking their place.

It was a difficult admission for the war chief to make, for it meant his dreams of running the white men out of the country were now shattered. Yet there were promises of no harm coming to the Chilcotins, and therefore the threat of the smallpox was withdrawn. Was that, then, the victory he sought?

It was becoming clear that Klatassine might have no choice in the matter, for Anahim had betrayed him and not risen to his cause, and Alexis had joined the whites, so that the whites now outnumbered his own warriors five to one. While many Chilcotins supported Klatassine, few men risked fighting by his side.

Had Klatassine been aware of how close to defeat he had brought the colonial forces, and of the desperation which accompanied this new march, he might have retained more determination. But the circumstances led him to consider Cox's invitation.

Cox was camped at Fort Chilcotin awaiting fresh supplies when Klatassine's slave Tom arrived with another message.

Klatassine wished him to know that his Indians were scattered about the mountains, but that he was sending runners to fetch them. Klatassine wanted to know what would happen to them if they came in to talk. For his own part, he sent a $20 piece and some smaller change to Cox as a gift and as a token of good faith.

Cox replied through Tom, that he would not harm the Chilcotins if they came to him. He had no authority to kill them; that had been vested by Great Chief English in Brew. Cox would "hand them over to the big chief"[37]—referring not to Seymour, but to Chief Justice Begbie. He sent along as a return gift a quantity of tobacco.

On August 12, Klatassine received Cox's message. It was interpreted as an offer of amnesty if they went to him. They would be allowed to remain free and to explain to Seymour why they had rebelled, and to convince him to leave them alone. The tobacco meant that Cox was guaranteeing the smoking of the peace calumet, that the war would end. One of the white men had shown Tom a picture of Seymour, the Great Chief English...it was further proof that they would meet.

On the day Klatassine was receiving this misinterpreted intelligence from Cox's camp, Brew was camped on a mountain two thousand feet above Lake Tatlayoko. Eight miles to the west was Chilko Lake, of similiar shape, but more than twice the size of Tatlayoko, and five miles north of both of these was McLean's Lake, lying like a crossbeam on two studs.

Inside the horseshoe formed by these three lakes and their

rivers was a mountain range broken by several passes.

Brew left a few men to watch the camp and split the rest into two scouting parties, one under himself and the other under Elwyn. Elwyn went up into the mountains while Brew reconnoitered the shore of the lake.

Brew found fresh Indian tracks and he sent two Bella Coolas back to camp for more provisions. He intended not to give up pursuit as Cox had—he would follow the trail until he found the Indians who had made it. His trackers did not let him down and they were still on the trail when dusk closed in. They arrived at a promontory projecting into the lake and went out onto it to get a look at the country.

Below them they could see almost the entire length of the lake. And in the distance, there was movement on the water. Through his telescope Brew could see several Indians on two large rafts, crossing the lake to the western shore.

Brew sent another Bella Coola and one of his volunteers back to the camp to order more men up. Then he searched in the remaining hours of daylight for sign of where the Chilcotins had been before launching their rafts, in the hope others would still be nearby.

At dark he took his men up a 5,000 foot mountain to get a better look at the character of the surrounding country. They camped there that night, but early the next morning Brew sent out William Byers, a former corporal in the Royal Engineers, and John McIver to reconnoiter. The two scouts probed along the edge of the lake and came across some abandoned Indian lodges.

When Byers and McIver returned to their camp they found Brew and the rest of their party gone, but Elwyn was there with six reinforcements and another day's supply of food.

Elwyn sent Byers and McIver out with the new men to find Brew, while he stayed in camp. During the afternoon, the men all straggled back in ones and twos, having been able to find nothing substantial despite spreading themselves out for several miles over the vicinity. Elwyn returned to the main camp to take charge of the remaining volunteers.

Brew then abandoned the immediate area and took the men out in one force at noon the next day, leaving the beaten trails and taking to the forests. He worked them down the lake towards the end, intending to come back on the other side.

An hour before dusk they came to a noisy stream crashing down a mountainside. It took them some time to get across it, as falling in could have meant death.

Half a mile past this they came upon an Indian encampment. It had obviously been abandoned no more than a half hour before, and had the creek not delayed them the expedition might have caught the Chilcotins right there. Brew pressed south, following the tracks of the Indians. It was not a big party, probably numbering only a half dozen braves or so and their squaws and children.

Darkness closed in once more, forcing them to make camp. At dawn they were out again, spreading themselves along the trail, but at 10 a.m., when they had not yet come upon the Chilcotins, Brew called them all together.

He told them that since they were out of food he could not ask them to continue if they didn't wish to, and any who wanted could return to their main camp.

"As for myself, I intend to push on if it means living on berries and roots for a week."[38]

Five volunteers and the Bella Coolas chose to go back. Brew was left with nine volunteers, a Fraser River Indian and Qwhittie of Bute Inlet. Among the whites who stayed with Brew were Byers, McIver, Ed Atkins, and Atkins' acquaintance from the Bute expedition, Leslie Jones.

Brew took them forward for another five hours at a stiff pace. Ahead of them smoke rose up and they hurried toward it, bursting upon an Indian village which had just been fired and abandoned by the fleeing Chilcotins.

Brew could feel victory within his grasp, but his hopes were soon shattered. A few hours later, hard on the heels of the Chilcotins, the determined whites struck a river too wide and too deep for them to cross.

The Chilcotins had slipped through Brew's fingers. Reflecting on their route, the police magistrate now saw what they had been up to. They had crossed the Tatlayoko on the rafts in hopes of eluding him, gone down to the south end of the lake and then gone south and west on the edge of the mountain range in order to get around the tip of Chilko Lake. Brew had been a bit lucky to pick up their trail again, but it was a dead end. The Indians crossed the river on rafts. At least a day would be lost in building his own rafts and Brew knew that was too much time lost. The Chilcotins had escaped the horseshoe and were back in wide open country.

Brew camped for the night by the river, and next day headed back for his main camp.

"*We did not want the white man's machines, nor did we want to till the soil.... Our way of life is very good for us. It was good for our fathers, and we have no wish to live differently. We want to be left alone to enjoy our country and our fishing streams and hunting grounds.*"

Klatassine, 1864.[1]

On August 14, Tahpitt's son Joe entered the camp at Fort Chilcotin and was taken to Cox's tent. Klatassine, Tellot, and six others would come in tomorrow. They had recently left the area between Tatlayoko and Chilko Lakes, but had been unable to find the other Indians who were in that area.

At 8:30 the following morning, the eight Chilcotins and their families, accompanied by Alexis and some of his people, walked down from the hills and between the rows of tents to where Cox stood. They sat down in a row in front of him and said nothing.

Cox stared back at them for what seemed like several minutes. Then Alexis said something to them in Chilcotin. Klatassine replied. His words were interpreted to Cox:

"I have brought seven murderers, and I am one myself. I return you one horse, one mule, and twenty dollars for the governor, to show our good faith.

"The names of the men present are: myself, Tellot, Cheloot, Tahpitt, Piell, Chesuss, Cheddeki, Sanstanki.

"We have been unable to shoot or to light a fire, for the smoke. We wish to give ourselves to you to save our wives and our children."

Cox asked where the rest of the murderers were.

Again, through an interpreter: "There are ten more: Quotanuski, Yeltenly, Ahan, Hachis, Cusshen, Seitah, Katelth, Lutas, Yahooslas, Anukatlk.

"These men I know cannot be caught before the early spring (snow go away moon), when they must come to the lakes for food," Klatassine continued.

"Three others are dead. One was killed by McDonald; the other two killed themselves. There are altogether 21."

Klatassine told Cox that Anahim's band had possession of most of the plunder "and are now starving and eating the stolen horses, and also took all the stolen money from me."

"We have not seen or heard of Mr. Brew's party where we come from. We don't know where he is."[2]

Wochess, one of the Indians not implicated in the rebellion who had accompanied Klatassine, handed Cox a purse containing an ounce and a half of gold dust. Chessus handed over an additional $550 in silver.

Cox glanced at the volunteers behind the Chilcotins. A large group had gathered in around where the Indians sat; several of them had muskets or revolvers at the ready.

The Irishman looked back at Klatassine, sitting proudly in his loose-fitting buckskins. Except for Tahpitt, who had a small knife hung around his neck with a hide thong, they were all unarmed, as Cox had told them to be.

"I wish to inform you that in the name of the Queen I am placing you under arrest," Cox said slowly. "You are my prisoners."[3] The translation was given.

The armed volunteers moved forward, their weapons raised. The Chilcotins looked startled and suddenly nervous.

"Where is Great Chief English?" demanded Klatassine.[4]

Cox did not reply.

"King George's men are great liars," spat Tellot in disgust.[5]

They had thought they would not be taken prisoner, but would be allowed to camp with their families until Governor Seymour arrived. Cox had foreseen possible difficulties and had planned his trap well. The eight men were bound and heavily guarded while a strong stockage was put up. Then they were placed inside it.

Cox's actions angered Alexis, who had been under the same impression as the captives. He had thought they were to camp with him.

Cox, said Alexis, "spoke with two tongues."[6]

The method used by the gold commissioner in capturing Klatassine was the subject of much controversy for a long time after. Clearly, Klatassine and his men had misinterpreted Cox's words, but the question was whether or not Cox had intended it that way. He had made it appear that Klatassine would not be harmed or even imprisoned if he came to Cox;

otherwise, he might expect death if caught by Brew. Cox had spoken of the "Big Chief," but he meant Begbie, who would try them, rather than Seymour, who would talk with them. Only Cox knew if he had meant for Klatassine to mistake the "Big Chief" for the "Great Chief English."

Alexis was not alone in his disgust with Cox. Some of the volunteers questioned the circumstances, and newspaper reports of the capture were critical.

"The account given by our informant of the means by which Mr. Cox obtained possession of the eight Indian prisoners… does not look very well,"[7] stated the Colonist, referring to information received from its correspondent on the Chilcotin expedition.

Cox, however, maintained in the following months that he had acted honestly. "There was no inducement whatever held out to the Indians to come in. It was entirely voluntary on their part."[8]

While Seymour had invested Brew with the power to conduct a court in the field, he had not trusted Cox with such authority. Cox decided that rather than hunt up Brew, it would be simpler to take the prisoners to Alexandria, where they could be tried by Begbie as he had stated to Klatassine. There were still a number of Siwashes at large. Let Brew chase them; Cox had the leaders.

He sent to Alexandria for 30 more men to accompany him across the Chilcotin plateau with the captives. Then he settled down to wait for a few days until the extra men arrived.

There were some tense times, since Klatassine's people stayed near the camp. Klatassine's son, Piell, swore that Cox would be killed for his lies. Klatassine and Tellot tried changing their stories, saying that none of the men with them were directly involved in the deaths of any white men and that they should be set free.

While there was no evidence against some of the prisoners, their guilt was up to the courts to decide.

Klatassine was miserable in the stockade. He had been tricked, and in so doing he had betrayed the cause of his people. He succumbed to a violent fit, beating his head on the log walls and clawing at himself, and had to be restrained and manacled. Later he offered Cox more money if he would let them go.

The good food provided to the prisoners and their families was meagre consolation, but it strengthened them after their recent diet of berries and tree roots.

Despite his methods and precautions, Cox allowed the

prisoners to have their wives and children with them in the stockade. Toowaewoot joined Klatassine with their small son and baby daughter.

At midnight each night, the guards would observe the Indian mothers rise, remove their infants from the baskets and unbind them. Then, sucking water into their mouths, they would squirt it back into the container to warm it. When each squaw had finished this, she would pour the water over the infant and dry it before putting it back in the cradle. This nightly bathing was done within a few minutes of midnight each night, the only timepieces of the Chilcotins being custom and habit.

* * *

It took Brew two more days to get back to his camp. The only food the men had was roots and berries provided by the resourceful Indian guides. On the morning of the 18th, he sent Elwyn with a scouting party down Tatlayoko Lake. From there he was to continue south to see if there were more Chilcotins camped on the Homathko or Memeya rivers.

The entire expedition was now short of food. On the 22nd, a rifle was pointed at the head of one of the horses. The boom echoed off the hills and the horse fell kicking. Its throat was cut and the volunteers fell on it with their knives.

William Byers came over and cut himself a slice, roasted and breakfasted on it. Then he, Charles Page and Malcolm McLeod rode north out of the camp. Brew had ordered them to Alexandria with letters and pleas for food.

When Elwyn returned the whole party left for Puntzi Lake to await the pack train.

Brew's determination and courage had gained him new respect from his men. He did not ask anyone to do what he himself wouldn't do. Over difficult country he had sometimes pushed them 30 to 40 miles, and they were now tough and bush-wise. But the anxiety and physical privations were having their effect on Brew. Normally portly, he had become lank and haggard. He was a physically weakened man, but he had not once condoned complaints about their poor situation. He would continue as long as necessary.

* * *

Cox grew impatient waiting for his reinforcements, and told his men to prepare to leave. They would meet the reinforcements on the way.

So, with their eight prisoners and Indian allies, and tailed by the relatives of the prisoners, the volunteers started back over the Chilcotin plain. It was a long ride, and it was as monotonous as ever, but it was the last one, the end of a dreary experience which they could all talk about for a long time.

They reached Alexandria on August 27, and from there Klatassine, Tellot, and their fellow captives were taken by the steamer *Enterprise* up to Quesnellemouth, where they were locked in the log jail. The building was heavily guarded and, inside, the prisoners were heavily shackled.

Byers, Page and McLeod had arrived in Alexandria ahead of Cox but, of course, so had word of the captures. The Upper Fraser was buzzing with the news. Brew's three men were organizing a pack train to send back to Puntzi. When that was done Byers would return to New Westminster to report on Brew's expedition, but news of Cox's success was already reaching there, also. The newspapers carried headlines proclaiming the glorious success of the expedition, and the residents of the two colonies breathed relief.

* * *

On Sept. 3 Charlie Page and Malcolm McLeod reached Brew at Puntzi Lake with the new provisions and the news of Klatassine's capture. Brew and his men received the news with mixed emotions. They had started off in June accompanied by the governor of the province, proud and confident that they would be the ones who would get the job done. They had maintained their discipline throughout, and they were the ones in whom Seymour had put the most trust. While they had been rushing around the mountains actively seeking the rebels, despite facing starvation, Cox had sat comfortably encamped at Fort Chilcotin waiting for the Indians to come to him. Now, he was back in civilization bathing in the glory, while they were left to clean up.

It might take many more weeks or months to capture the remaining fugitives, but it was Brew's job to make the attempt, at least until weather conditions prohibited, and he set about to do so. They had not much more time than to march to Bella Coola before cold weather set in, but Anahim's territory lay on the route, and it was believed the rest of the rebels would seek winter refuge there. The help of Anahim would have to be enlisted. When Brew had left Puntzi for Tatlayoko Lake, he had sent a messenger to Anahim asking for a meeting, but the message had been ignored.

One morning the men awoke at Puntzi to find their blankets covered with snow. It was the first snowfall of the year. On the same day Brew left Puntzi once more, heading northeast instead of south from Tatla Lake. Along the way they continued to destroy Indian fishing places and unoccupied lodges. He sent five men ahead under Morris Moss, a trader who had joined the expedition at Bella Coola, to Bentinck Arm to search out the area below the slide. The rest would go with Brew to Anahim's village.

Moss left the plains and made the return trip down the Great Slide and into the Bella Coola Valley. He and his five men were at Shtooiht or Stuie about 15 miles below the slide when they were visited by 18 Indians. Anahim was the leader of the group. He had heard of the continued harassment of Klatassine and that he, Anahim, was being sought. Now, the chief decided, was the time to offer help to the whites. He brought with him eight horses from McDonald's pack train.

Anahim's men were heavily armed, but Moss had to restrain one of the volunteers from trying to arrest them all. Moss invited Anahim to share his hospitality, and the Nancootlem Chilcotins stayed for two days.

Anahim said he was willing to help capture the murderers, if he received "cultus potlatch"—a handsome present—as a demonstration of the whites' good faith. Anahim, after all, had brought the horses and even if they were not his, an exchange was customary.

Moss responded by presenting the greedy old chief with some flour and other supplies, and advised him to go alone to talk with Brew. If the expedition was to be continued, Anahim would be a welcome guide.

There was skepticism on the part of many of the men in the field about enlisting Anahim's aid instead of arresting him, for there was evidence that he had at the least condoned the attacks on the whites. But Moss would leave the decision up to Brew, and he gave Anahim, at the chief's request, a "paper" explaining to Brew who he was and what had transpired at Shtooiht.

Brew at this time was at Nancootlem wondering where Anahim was. It was a touchy situation, for there was a lot of hearsay evidence that Anahim could have stopped the attack on McDonald, and though he didn't participate in it, had received plunder from it. He personally did not become directly involved in the rebellion but he might have persuaded or allowed some of his men to take part. Anahim might even have fully joined with Klatassine if not for the show of strength by the Bentinck Arm expedition, and there was conjecture that he was leading the group of Ansanies and Nancootlem Chilcotins who had planned to attack the expedition at the Great Slide. He certainly had done nothing so far to aid the whites against Klatassine, which was perhaps understandable since they were close relatives.

All this was not enough, in Brew's eyes, to risk apprehending Anahim. There was no positive proof, only second-hand information and speculation.

He was told that Anahim had gone off fishing and trading in the Bella Coola Valley, but would be back soon. While he was at Nancootlem, Brew took the opportunity to look around the territory, and fanned his men out once more in a by-now familiar and standard search for clues.

Brew's men turned up 30 caches belonging to Anahim and his people. Some were found on an island in one of the lakes, and more were discovered along the banks of the lake. All of them were searched, but nothing was found that might have belonged to McDonald or his party.

However, in one Indian lodge they found a carpet sack and part of a buckskin coat that was tentatively identified as belonging to McDonald. Again, the same story was given in explanation—they were gifts from those who had attacked McDonald. Brew realized that in addition to the few men who had actually fought McDonald, dozens more had watched and taken a share of the plunder. And many others who had not been present had received various items later on. There were perhaps hundreds of Chilcotins who would have to be arrested if that kind of evidence was to be the basis for action.

Anahim was said to have received seven horseloads of goods from the train plus several more horses, yet it was all but certain that he was in Bella Coola the day of the attack. Since his home village was only a few miles from where McDonald was attacked, he would almost naturally, as chief and relative of Klatassine, come into some of the booty. But that didn't make him guilty of murder.

There was another discovery which had nothing to do with evidence against the Indians, but it was an upsetting one. Re-examining the site of the attack, the volunteers found that wolves had dug up the bodies again. The bones were gathered up to be packed to Bella Coola with the expedition for burial.

Anahim stayed with Moss for two days and then left for home. He took with him a few of his men and left the others to fish. He met Brew half way between the Great Slide and Nancootlem. Brew called a halt to travel and invited Anahim to camp with him.

Brew examined the paper Moss had given the chief and they spent several hours talking. The expedition leader soon found out why this powerful Chilcotin, respected as peaceful and cooperative by some, was looked on as a greedy old rascal by others.

Anahim took a rather uncommunicative and stubborn stance at first.

What did he know of the attacks on the whites? Very little.

Who had led them? He didn't know.

Why did it happen? He didn't know.

Where were the rest of the murderers? Somewhere in the mountains, he supposed.

Would he help the whites? He was short of food, but if he had some flour, some powder, some caps and some whiskey, he might be able to look for Ahan and the rest.

Anahim was not exaggerating the need for food. Though he himself had some at the moment, his people were already starving, and had eaten several horses. Brew agreed to the request and Anahim went off for a couple of days.

He returned without any of the warring Chilcotins, but he brought in four horses which he said he had taken from other Indians. They, like the ones he had given Moss, were part of McDonald's pack train.

Anahim promised Brew that he would keep looking for the rest of the murderers and that he could certainly catch them in the winter.

Brew accepted his word and gave him some more ammunition and clothing. He also handed him a note which would be good for the purchase of more goods at Bella Coola.[9]

There was nothing left for Brew to do now, and he took his weary men the remaining miles to the Great Slide and down into the Bella Coola Valley. They encountered the rest of Anahim's men, who fled into the forest apparently because they were apprehensive about how Anahim had made out.

A few days later Brew reached Bella Coola. The *Victorian* correspondent captured the feeling of exhaustion and the deprivation endured by the volunteers with the last simple line of his report on the expedition:

"On Sept. 29 the expedition reached Bella Coola and the following day got on board the gunboat *Forward* and were conveyed to New Westminster, having been absent 107 days."

* * *

Judge Matthew Baillie Begbie was a gentleman of both refined and rough manner. He was tall and lean, with intense eyes, hair that he let grow just over his ears, full sideburns, moustache and goatee. A graduate of Cambridge, he had practised in the English Bar for 15 years before coming to Canada, and had been sworn in as the first judge for the Court of British Columbia in 1858. His private personality was gentle, modest and kindly, and he was a man of superior intelligence.

In the untamed Indian lands and brawling mining districts of the interior, Begbie was a purebred among mongrels, but it was his job to bring British law and justice to bear and he went about it with unflinching efficiency. The wild natives and American goldseekers feared and respected the "Hanging Judge" as honest and just—though sometimes a bit unorthodox—but autocratic and decisive. He took no foolishness or criticism in his court. Anyone who offended him by what he considered contempt of court landed in jail.

His efficiency did not prevent him from seeking out carefully all the facts of a case, and he was ever concerned that those who stood charged before him should receive the fullest consideration and fairest trial. But his knowledge of the law was not as good as it should have been, and his courtroom manner not always impartial, so his decisions were not always right.

Nevertheless, the mining districts were full of disruptions, murders, and cheating, and Begbie kept the lid on a potboiler that might have become not only totally lawless, but a threat to the British presence in the Pacific Northwest.

In regard to the native population, the judge was determined to give them the same benefits of British justice as the whites, and he tried to understand their ways, for he fully realized they did not understand those of the whites. Indians and Europeans held different sets of values, and while it was British law and not native law that must be upheld, Begbie never took crimes involving Indians at their face value. They could depend on him for humane treatment and a full hearing.

On Sept. 27, almost a month after the Chilcotin prisoners had been shut up in the improvised jail, Begbie arrived at Quesnellemouth from the Cariboo goldfields where he had been holding an assize.

Quesnellemouth, built around Indian villages on the low banks of the Quesnelle River, had gained superiority over Alexandria as a settlement of importance with the opening up of the goldfields of Williams Creek. Quesnellemouth was the head of navigation and therefore the supply centre, the gateway, of the diggings. Though its growth was recent and it was alive with miners, its commerce gave it a certain atmosphere of civilization compared to the gold towns.

The trial began the day after Begbie's arrival.

Sanstanki and his son Cheloot were not brought to trial, since there was no substantial evidence that could tie them to any crime, though Klatassine had named them as "murderers" the day he had come in to Cox's camp at Fort Chilcotin.

Acting in defence of the accused men was John G. Barnston, the lawyer who had an interest in the Bentinck Arm road company, whose route had been taken by Brew's expedition from Bella Coola. H.P. Walker acted as prosecutor in the absence of the Attorney-General.

William Fitzgerald, of Cox's expedition, and a French-Canadian named Baptiste, would interpret for the Chilcotins.

Begbie, in his opening remarks to the jury, cautioned them on the importance of their task, and of the importance of maintaining law and order in the new colony. The prisoners stood accused of charges involving the brutal murder of several citizens of British Columbia, who had been cut down with little opportunity to defend themselves. Yet the jury must not let emotion interfere with their judgement, and they must carefully consider all the evidence. They must be absolutely certain of their verdict. If the guilt of the prisoners was not established beyond any doubt, then they must be allowed to go free.

The first indictment entered was against Tellot for attempted murder in an attack on William Buckley on the Homathko. Klatassine, Piell, Chessus and Cheddeki were charged with aiding and abetting and inciting, or being accessories before the fact.

Buckley gave testimony recounting the attack on the workmen's camp and of the events that followed. Barnston cross-examined him on several details and he was allowed to step down.

Qwhittie described the second attack, on Brewster and his men, and Squinteye related being told of Smith's murder. Barnston brought out the point that the words of the Indians other than Klatassine were not more than hearsay.

Barnston continued to cross-examine the witnesses called by Walker, but there was little he could do to cast doubt on the testimony. Cox was the last witness called and at 5:30 p.m. the jury retired, taking a surprisingly long time to return with its verdict. Tellot was found guilty of attempted murder and Klatassine of aiding and abetting, but one member of the jury would not vote for a guilty verdict on the other three and they were acquitted.

The next day, the trial continued and the Grand Jury was summoned to enter another indictment against Chessus. Then a true bill was found against Tahpitt in the murder of William Manning and the case went to the petty jury.

Walker called Nancy, Manning's squaw; and Ilsedocknell,

her friend. As Nancy spoke, claiming to see Tahpitt kill Manning and describing the scene that followed, Tahpitt angrily leaped to his feet.

"These are lies!" he shouted.

The squaw retorted that she spoke the truth.

"Some words of the woman are true and some are lies," claimed Tahpitt. "I did not wish to kill but Anahim forced me by threats."[10]

Begbie did not order Tahpitt removed or bound, and the Indian settled down. Nancy finished her testimony and William Fitzgerald was then called to relate the finding of Manning's body in Puntzi Creek.

Cox was again called, and simply stated that Tahpitt was with Klatassine when he had entered the camp at Fort Chilcotin and had been identified as one of the rebels.

A guilty verdict was returned.

On testimony of Tom, Leslie Jones, Cox and Buckley, Klatassine and Piell were found guilty of murdering Alexander McDonald at Nancootlem.

Then came Chessus for the murder of the settler John Clark at Brewster's work camp. Buckley. Qwhittie and Jones took the witness stand and another guilty verdict was brought in. That left Chedekki, but he had been acquitted of the charge in regard to Buckley, and there were no witnesses who could testify further as to his part in the rebellion. Walker, however, asked that he be retained in custody and sent to New Westminister for trial, where Peterson could testify to having recognized him in the Homathko attack.

Begbie asked the other five if they had any statement to make on sentence being pronounced. The charges had been dealt with very quickly, and the proceedings of the court had not been fully understood by them. They knew the white men had decided they had done things that were wrong and that they must be punished for it. But they did not believe themselves to be wrong.

One by one, through their interpreters, they spoke their innocence.

Tahpitt told Begbie of the threats made against him by Anahim and by Quotamski, another old Indian, if he did not kill the white man.

Klatassine admitted to having killed whites, but said he was induced by others who told him of the threat made by the whites to kill his people with smallpox.

Piell claimed to have done nothing at the Homathko camp and that he fired at McDonald but missed, killing only his

180

horse. "This had nothing to do with Alex's safety."[11]

Tahpitt rose again, saying that Anahim had constantly urged him to kill a white man. "I never had any idea of it until Anahim came and at last one day I took my gun and went out and shot him. After I shot him I was sorry and went and sat down. It was the first time I have done so. I never killed even an Indian before."[12]

Chessus said Smith had not been killed by him, but he admitted firing a shot at Jim Gaudet and that Brewster and his men were killed by the group Chessus was with.

Klatassine then spoke to the witnesses and his fellow prisoners.

"Tell the truth. I have done so."

"What is your law against murderers?" Begbie asked them.

"Death," they replied.

"Our law is the same. You are guilty of death."[13]

The pronouncement of sentence of death by hanging was not an easy one for Begbie to make. Besides the fact that he deplored violence and never had liked pronouncing the ultimate penalty, he realized that the Chilcotins' concept of murder was different from that of the whites. They differentiated between war and murder just as whites did, but while they considered their fight an act of war, under British law it represented only the brutal murder of men who were, for the most part, unarmed and had not directly or deliberately given any provocation.

The Chilcotins lived by violence, and the brutality of the murders was not an act of insanity or particular fiendishness, but of custom inherited from many generations past. Yet, again, the Indians of the colony now lived under the protection and jurisdiction of the whites, and they must learn to obey a new set of laws. An example must be made, all five must die. No recommendation for mercy could be given.

Before he left Quesnellemouth, Begbie went to the jail with Baptiste and talked with the prisoners. Why, he asked Klatassine, had they given themselves up.

"We had no flour, no meat, no food," replied the condemned chief. "We could not hunt, or fish, we could not light a fire. We hoped their hearts would be towards us as to Alexis."[14]

Klatassine told Begbie of receiving the gift of tobacco from Cox and of having been assured of meeting the Great Chief Seymour. The tobacco meant peace.

"Then we thought ourselves safe."[15]

In their conversation, Begbie became much impressed by

the intelligence and noble bearing of Klatassine.

Together with his notes of the trial, the judge enclosed an explanation of the verdicts and sentencing for Governor Seymour. There was, he said, no doubt of the guilt of the five prisoners who had been condemned of murder. And their acts must be considered murder in the eyes of the law despite the "ignorance and habits" of the prisoners.

"The conviction of Tellot would not be followed, in England, by execution: at least where others suffered capitally for the same offence. Piell is young—very mild-looking, much under the influence of Klatassine. But he shot McDonald's horse, riding away. Klatassine is the finest savage I have met with yet, I think. But I believe also he has fired more shots than any of them. It seems horrible to hang five men at once—especially under the circumstances of the capitulation. Yet the blood of 21 whites calls for retribution. And these fellows are cruel, murdering pirates—taking life and making slaves in the same spirit in which you or I would go out after partridges or rabbit shooting.

"I do not envy you your task of coming to a decision."[16]

That decision was whether or not Seymour would exercise mercy and commute the sentences of any of the prisoners.

* * *

Rev. Robert Christopher Lundin Brown hurried toward the *Enterprise* as the riverboat gathered up steam at the quay at Quesnellemouth. The Anglican priest had been in the Barkerville mining district and was on his way south back to Lillooet, his parish. As he'd entered Quesnellemouth he had seen the boat and hastened to the dock to exchange news with those leaving for Alexandria.

Standing on the dock puffing on a pipe was Judge Matthew Begbie.

They exchanged some smalltalk and Begbie told him he was heading back to New Westminster. He mentioned the trials he had just presided over in Quesnellemouth, among them being those of five Indians upon whom he had had to pronounce the death sentence. They badly needed religious instruction.

Brown had not intended to stay long in Quesnellemouth. But he said he would do what he could.

The judge replied that he would try to insure sufficient time before the execution of the sentence.

The *Enterprise* blew her last whistle. Begbie boarded her and she moved out onto the river.

So Brown was left in Quesnellemouth with five Indians to instruct in the ways of the Lord, to attempt to prepare five criminals for death by hanging. Five criminals who spoke almost no English, whose Chilcotin tongue was as different from the Lillooet dialect the reverend knew "as French is from Spanish or Italian."[17]

These were not grubby American miners who could casually seek the forgiveness of God Almighty as they readied to meet him, but savages who little understood His ways. It was partly for that reason Brown felt compelled to put all his energies into saving the souls of these five Chilcotins.

There was another reason, though. Three years before, at about the same time of year, Rev. Brown had travelled by foot and by canoe up to Alexandria from his Fraser's Canyon mission. At that time, Alexandria was still nothing more than a log stockade surrounding the buildings of the Hudson's Bay Company.

The HBC agent in charge of the post had informed him of a tribe of powerful Indians encamped near the settlement and suggested they visit them. So, one night after dinner, the two white men went to the camp situated on a hillside near the fort. It was the first time the priest had seen the Nancootlem Chilcotins and they did not strike him at first appearance as being powerful or rich. In fact, they contrasted quite sharply with the beauty of the scenery in which they were encamped.

He had later written: "A set of men and women more squalid and repulsive I have rarely beheld. Dark faces with big mouths, high cheek bones, ferocious black eyes, narrow foreheads, long tangled hair black as night. Their thin and sinewy frames with little on them save dirt and a piece of blanket or a deerskin—no, their appearance was not prepossessing, and yet, wherever there is a human face, however disfigured by sin, is there not a human mind which can apprehend God's truth, and a human heart which is in need of it?"

The HBC man had explained who the priest was, and a few of them gathered around to hear an off-the-cuff sermon on salvation. The priest spoke in French, and this was first translated into Chinook, then into Chilcotin.

It was an attentive audience, and Brown noticed, sitting in front, a particularly powerful looking Indian, elbows resting on drawn-up knees. The savage's dark blue eyes bore into Brown as he spoke.

After the sermon was finished the Indian had gone up to the speaker and fumbled with the reverend's clothing. Attempting to appear unconcerned, the priest asked what it was that was wanted.

The "assailant" reached under his own buckskin shirt and

pulled out a crucifix which hung around his neck on a small chain. He held it out toward the priest.

Brown had understood immediately what was meant. Years before, as long as two decades ago, Roman Catholics had first entered these regions to preach to the Indians, to convert them and baptize them. They had managed to get the rudiments of Christianity to take hold among these heathens. And they had left many an Indian with a crucifix as the true sign of faith.

Since Brown wore no crucifix, his credentials for preaching were in doubt. He explained that he was a King George priest, different from the others, and that King George priests wore the cross within their hearts.

The big Indian seemed satisfied and they shook hands and parted. Brown had remembered that meeting for a long time afterward, for he had never seen an Indian as powerful and fearful looking as that one.

That man had been Klatassine, visiting Quesnellemouth with his Nancootlem relatives, and now they were to meet again under much different and sadder circumstances.

Through the local stipendiary magistrate, Brown was referred to the French Canadian breed Baptiste, who agreed to serve as interpreter for him.

Together they went to the jail. Brown was surprised to see how squalid it was. It immediately saddened him to see the prisoners squatting heavily shackled on the ground inside, not even able to exercise. The inside of the cell was unlighted, and there was nothing for the Indians to do but squat all day long in the dark. What a fate for men who had had thousands of miles as their homes in which to range freely all their lives.

Despite their confinement, they were still strong-looking men, far more impressive than the lower Fraser River Indians Brown was used to administering to.

He immediately recognized Klatassine as he entered the cell. The chief was sitting opposite him: he looked up calmly and with mild curiosity as Brown came in with Baptiste.

Klatassine did not remember Brown until he was reminded of that meeting three years ago at Alexandria.

"The King George priest."

"Yes."

Brown found Klatassine and his four comrades to be subdued but unrepentent. He told them that he was here to help them, that God was listening and wanted to receive them into Heaven. It was going to be a long and difficult task, but perhaps not as hard as Brown had first thought.

Listening to the low, quiet voice of Klatassine and observing his gentle manner and obvious intelligence, Brown found it difficult to think of him as a criminal. Indeed, all of them except Chessus were polite and attentive. Chessus, sitting at the opposite end of the wall from Klatassine, looked ferocious and deadly even though he made no move and spoke no threats.

Beside Klatassine was Tahpitt, a sincere and intense Indian, good-looking and strong like Klatassine, though somewhat smaller. He was in his thirties and obviously at the prime of his life.

Beside Tahpitt was Tellot, a moody but quiet individual who had exercised considerable power in his tribe and who felt depressed at the betrayal of the King George men.

Then came Piell, Klatassine's son, a mild-mannered lad of 18 who had a wife and child. Begbie had been impressed with Piell's look of innocence and found that the lad was entirely devoted to and trusting in his father.

Brown spoke in Chinook or French as it suited him and Baptiste interpreted expertly. The priest hoped to pick up some Chilcotin as they went along, but for now this awkward method would have to prevail. He gradually worked the conversation towards the questions at hand: law and sin.

The law, he said, must be upheld. Sin must be punished.

Brown did not apply this to the prisoners' own case until the next meeting, when he said they had sinned by murdering good white men and had incurred God's displeasure and had to be punished for it.

Klatssine rejected that idea, explaining why he had killed the whites, only to protect his people from extermination by them.

"We are all in one way or another sinners and need salvation," the priest assured him. "We have all broken one or another of God's commandments. Have you not sinned in other ways?

"If you acted in mere self defence in killing off the whites, what could justify falling upon them so treacherously and then brutally mangling their remains. And even if Brewster's murder was justified, was it right to eat his heart?

"But, indeed, it was not justified. God's law is 'thou shalt not kill'."

"We meant war, not murder," said Tellot.

"Was it war to attack men while they slept? The Great Father does not like that. And have you not acted poorly to your own countrymen, stolen from other tribes, killed other Indians, taken them as slaves?"

Klatassine listened carefully to Brown, but he could not understand the man's meaning. Was a way of life wrong because someone came with a different way? Was it wrong to protect one's own way of life, to protect one's wives and children from death?

But a mutual respect grew between the chief and the reverend. Brown was not a real priest like the Catholic fathers who had come before, but he spoke like they did; he told good stories about St. Paul and Jesus Christ and other men who had faced great odds. Klatassine listened to him day after day and felt his awe of this white god returning to him. This Great Father was not like the guardian spirits of the Chilcotins who watched over only one individual. Not everyone had a guardian spirit, but this white God watched and could do all things. He was like the Raven who could turn himself into anything he wanted, only more powerful. While the Chilcotins knew that everyone had a soul, the souls of the Chilcotins remained in the country after the body died. The whites said their souls went into the sky to live with the Great Father.

Lundin Brown knew that he was making slow progress with his students, and it made him work harder. He emphasized the need to be sorry for what they had done. God the Great Father had the power to do all things and He said the prisoners had done wrong. The whites were His children as much as the Indians were and He did not like His children to kill each other.

The prisoners did not want their souls to be condemned to wander in fire for eternity. They had thought they did right and they wanted to do right at this time, too. Gradually they became more believing, and began studying carefully what Brown was teaching them.

Even when he thought he was making progress, Brown left the jail each day with a feeling of exhaustion and sadness. "The image of this man used to haunt me night and day," he wrote of Klatassine. "I forgot his crimes and thought only of his inevitable doom...the tones of his voice as he repeated the Lord's Prayer in touching cadences, of his liquid and musical language ever present to my ear."

After several visits Brown came to the big question. Were they sorry for what they had done?

Klatassine answered that they were sorry, and Brown's heart soared for a moment at his accomplishment. The others, except Chessus, nodded in agreement with the war chief.

"If you were free would you do again what you did?"

Klatassine said he would not. "My heart is good for the King

186

George men."

"Do you see how they must punish you?"

Klatassine looked straight ahead, then replied, "Yes."

Brown continued to teach them more prayers, with Baptiste translating into their own tongue. "*Toujours, ils ne lachaient pas la priere,*" Baptiste remarked one day as they left the little log building.

"They will need much prayer," said the priest.

In the days that followed, the matter of baptism was brought up and Brown said if they truly wanted to be saved they would have to let him baptize them.

One night after visiting them he wrote in his diary:

"They are disposed to look on me with suspicion as being not a right priest but say nothing save thank me for my visits and for my promise to be with them to the last, but they seem to notice how little I say about the blessed virgin and from the omission they seem to suspect me. But all has gone well hitherto and I hope well to the end."

Klatassine and Tellot were much interested in the idea of baptism. If all their sins were to be forgiven with baptism, why did the whites baptize their children? Why not wait until they were old and had accumulated a large debt of sins which could be forgiven with this baptism ceremony? Since they were about to die, this seemed like a good time to be baptized.

They still felt they had acted out of unselfish motives, but now believed it when they were told it was wrong. Brown felt a deep sympathy for their predicament, yet he could not condone the actions of the prisoners no matter what their reasons. They deserved to die.

One Saturday after a long interview which included instruction in baptism, Klatassine and Tellot asked to be baptized. Piell and Tahpitt already had been baptized long ago. Cheddeki and Chessus, though, refused. Cheddeki was not yet condemned, awaiting removal to New Westminster for his own trial, and said he would wait to see what happened there. Chessus was his usual rebellious self, and Brown found him frightening. The day after he had harangued against self-conceit—a vice Brown considered all Indians to have—he received a message through the jailer that they didn't wish to see him anymore.

So Brown waited a day and then went to the jail again. They received him with pleasantness and told him the reason they didn't want to see him was that he didn't wear a crucifix. It was the same old problem, but he told his pupils that he thought the real reason was his preaching of the divine law of humility.

After discussing it some more, Klatassine asked him to stay, for the priest had baptized him and Klatassine was now a "King George Catholic." It was agreed that Brown should continue seeing them again to "make their hearts strong."

On Oct. 24 the jailer, an ex-navy officer, informed Lundin Brown of dispatches from New Westminster which had arrived that day on the *Enterprise* from Alexandria. They contained five death warrants. Governor Seymour had declined to exercise clemency in the case of any of the five prisoners. He had considered Begbie's trial notes In Council, but felt the example must be made of all of them.

Seymour did agree to one request made by Klatassine. The chief had asked that he be allowed to place the noose around his own neck and jump through the open trap door, thus dying at his own hand at the moment of his choosing.

Hanging day was set for Oct. 26.

The evening before, Brown went with Baptiste to the jail once again. Brown once more asked about the feelings of the prisoners, whether they were penitent and ready to meet the Great Father.

Klatassine spoke again of the smallpox threat made against his people, but the reverend reminded him that "it was God's visitation," that the white men were not at fault.

They talked at some length of the future, and the priest attempted to console the prisoners by assuring them that better things were in store for their people in the next generations.

"Indian children would be educated and taught to understand the mysteries of reading and writing. They would also learn trades, their people would be raised above the low and sensual life they now led and learn to find pleasure and useful work. They would no longer live an unsettled and roving life, a life in which virtue and religion were alike impossible. They would build good houses and till the soil and wear respectable clothing, each having his own separate dwelling, and being each the head of his own family, having but one wife as the Lord ordained."

But they would have to accept the presence of the white man, for the whites had been sent by the Great Father.

"The whites would not leave the land, no, they had been sent here by the Great Lord of all. Up till now that goodly land had been turned to small account." The whites had been sent "for the good of mankind and for the greater glory of the land itself. Above all, it was the will of the Highest."

The priest droned on about how the gold and silver never

would have been taken out of the land but for the whites, how the whites would develop the land as God willed it, putting steamboats on the rivers and criss-crossing it with roads and trails so that all could use it as they wished.

It was also the will of the Great Father that these five men not live to see all of these wonderful things; it was He who was punishing them, but who would receive them at His side.

To Klatassine and his comrades, the priest often spoke in riddles. If they were being punished, then how was it they were going to this Heaven? If they were being forgiven, why were they still being punished? If it was a glorious thing to go up into the sky and sit by the Great Father, why was this called punishment? But to the King George priest, it seemed to make perfect sense, and if they could not entirely follow his reasoning, they believed in his honesty.

* * *

On the morning of Oct. 26 Klatassine decided not to take his own life on the scaffold as he had requested. Instead, he would die at the same moment as the others.

He and his four companions were taken from the jail, pinioned and led up the stairs to the platform. Each was placed standing near a trap. Short prayers and recitations taught them by Brown were spoken almost inaudibly. "This my son was dead and is alive again, was lost and is found...." "I will arise..."

They were placed on the drops, and blindfolded, and the nooses were adjusted.

"Have courage!"

It was Tahpitt.

Then, to the Indians in the crowd, most of whom were Carrier, Tahpitt added, "Tell the Chilcotins to cease their anger against the whites, we are going to see the Great Father."

Then there was silence. The signal was given, the traps opened, the ropes jerked. The lives of Klatassine, Tellot, Tahpitt, Piell and Chessus were suddenly over at the same instant.

When the bodies had been allowed to hang for an adequate length of time, they were removed and buried in the forest near Quesnellemouth. Brown conducted Anglican rites and wooden crosses were erected over the graves.

* * *

Seymour made certain that the leaders of the Chilcotin expeditions were recognized for their service. He had been much impressed with Brew's leadership and perseverance in particular.

Brew was accordingly presented by Seymour on behalf of the government with a costly silver tea service, bearing the inscription:

"Presented on behalf of the Government and people of B.C. by the Governor and Executive Council to the Hon. Chartres Brew in gratitude for his services in the suppression of the insurrection of the Chilcoatin (sic) Indians."

Though Seymour had been as disappointed with Cox as he was pleased with Brew, the feisty gold commissioner was presented with an identical tea service similarly inscribed.

The gifts were more ornamental than practical—Brew was still a bachelor and would remain so for the rest of his life; Cox's Indian squaw for whom he had forsaken his first wife had little use for a silver tea service.

Donald McLean's widow, Sophia, was awarded a pension by the Legislative Council of 100 pounds a year for five years.

Seymour looked on his participation in the Chilcotin expeditions as quite a personal accomplishment. Referring to Brew, he said: "I shall always look back with satisfaction to the time when I had the honor to serve under him as one of the New Westminster Volunteers."[18]

Seymour retained his bitterness toward the admiralty for its initial lack of support, and he was warned by Edward Cardwell, the Duke of Newcastle's successor in the Colonial Office, to maintain good relations with Esquimalt. A complaint was laid over a statement by Seymour in regard to the rebellion that he had "despatched" ships. This, the admiralty claimed, was an assertion by Seymour of authority over the navy. But Cardwell wrote it off as a slip by Seymour and the Secretary of the Admiralty was assured that no interference with the authority of the naval officers had been intended.

Cardwell congratulated Seymour on his actions in quashing the rebellion:

"I have to express my very great satisfaction that you have safely returned to the duties of your Government, and that so much discipline and good order was maintained and so little loss of life incurred."[19]

However, he also saw it as a strictly colonial responsibility, for which the British government should not be expected to share in the cost:

"I am sensible of the expense which is thrown upon the Colony by the operations which you report, but I would observe that they are undertaken exclusively in the interest of the Colony, and that the expense is in a great measure due to the high rate of profit which the Colonists are realizing and therefore can hardly be viewed as any matter of complaint."[20]

But if the colony was not to be compensated for the expense of putting down an Indian rebellion, neither was the man whose enterprise had led to that rebellion.

Alfred Waddington's pleas fell on unsympathetic ears. Seymour did not feel Waddington's charter should be purchased by the colony or that he should otherwise be compensated, and Cardwell agreed, saying he could not sanction any payment or other encouragement to the road-builder.

Brew was outspoken in his utter disdain for the very idea. In the first place, he said, "...it is quite possible that the outbreak might have been averted if Mr. Waddington had visited the Homathco and arranged the intercourse between his men and the Indians."

Brew steadfastly rejected Waddington's claims regarding expenditures and even the possibility of success:

"From the time he explored the route himself he must have given up all idea of commencing the wagon road for he could but know that the whole colony could not supply the funds that would be required to complete it.... The Government has undertaken no obligations, neither, I conceive, has the Colonial Government. It may be a loss but no dishonour to Mr. Waddington if the Government will not buy his useless charter and trail from him. He was supplied with resources not his own. He has not opened the route, and he was very far from the eve of success. The enterprise was not a public one, it was a private speculation. While every one laments the murders which were perpetrated and pities Mr. Waddington for his losses, I believe there is scarcely a person in the Colony thinks him entitled to compensation and few will deny that he brought his misfortunes on himself."[21]

This last statement was denied by Waddington, who asserted that the government should have provided at least a show of force by the visit of a gunboat to Bute or some policing, but had not. The Indians had been tempted to their crimes by this failure, he stated.

But, again, his claims were rejected. Stated Brew:

"The Government felt no apprehension because nothing was known of the injudicious treatment of the Indians by Mr. Waddington's Foreman and men. I believe he did not know of it, but he ought to have known it and prevented it...."[22]

Waddington continued public controversy in other matters concerning the rebellion, engaging in letter to the editor exchanges with various individuals involved in it, defending his road-building enterprise and alleging mismanagement of the expeditions. He charged that Brew had freely given liquor to the Chilcotins, that Morris Moss had made personal profit from supplies that should have been used for his men, that Hamilton had supplied the Chilcotins with ammunition knowing how it might be used, that Anahim was wrongly allowed to retain his freedom despite conclusive evidence against him.

Such charges brought angry denials and Waddington refused to keep quiet.

But Waddington's Bute Inlet road-building venture was finished. He could not persuade the B.C. colonial government to take it over and he could not raise any money to continue it himself. The massacres were not alone to blame for the reluctance of potential investors. Much of the public discussion resulting from the Chilcotin war had been directed at the suitability of the route itself, and Brew was instrumental in substantiating the previous claims of New Westminster interests that the eventual widening of the incomplete Homathko trail into a wagon road was economically unfeasible.

On the 12th of December, Seymour laid before the opening of the Legislative Council in New Westminster the costs incurred by the colony.

"You will have anticipated my explanation that the great outlay on unforseen contingency was caused by the suppression of the Chilcoten (sic) insurrection of last summer. The expense incurred in this way was about 16,000 pounds."[23]

The governor took the opportunity to briefly explain the uprising and to praise those who had suppressed it:

"A party of roadmakers well provided with food, but unarmed, lay down to sleep among a number of armed Indians, who were almost in a state of starvation. Let me do justice to the dead. On the scaffold at Quesnellemouth it was stated that they gave no provocation. But so it was, the Indians were suffering all the pangs of hunger, while the white men slept unarmed. An attack was made on the sleepers at daybreak, and but three of them escaped...."

Seymour described the events that followed, the further attacks, and the actions that had been taken. He praised Donald McLean:

"The ruggedness of the coast range, aided by the absence of all means of transport, seemed to debar us from access to the Chilcoten country from the sea, but an expedition under a gentleman of great reputation for courage and skill in dealings with the native tribes of the colony had left the Upper Fraser for the interior."

He continued on about the various activities of the expeditions and the breakthrough when Alexis agreed to help. He concluded:

"It is well known to you how the New Westminster party then ransacked the remotest recesses of the Bute Inlet mountains; how the Indian chiefs, harassed by the bands of volunteers which had come upon them from the opposite points of the compass, found themselves without food or fire, reduced to the sole alternatives of suicide of surrender.

"It is my duty to speak with the utmost praise of the men who came forward from Cariboo and New Westminster to engage in a conflict formidable from the nature and extent of the country over which it raged, and one in which it appeared at one time as if famine were to fight on either side. I saw more of the party raised in this neighborhood, and can confidently say that, strengthened as it was by a large and admirable military element, the force numerically small, could scarcely have been surpassed in efficiency and good conduct in the mother country or any one of her colonies. The Alexandria volunteers presented an equally fine and formidable appearance."[24]

* * *

In May of 1865, Ahan and Lutas appeared at Nancootlem with their families and several other Chilcotins who had spent a particularly hard and long winter in and near the Cascade Mountains. Afraid to come down to the villages for fear of capture, they had eked out the cold winter months on the verge of starvation.

Anahim, true to his word to Brew despite the outrage caused by his not being imprisoned himself, persuaded Ahan to give himself up. Whites would come again and harass him until he and his family were either starved to death for sure this time or shot. If, however, Ahan offered enough presents to the Great Chief Seymour, they would probably forgive him.

When the small band of holdouts arrived at Nancootlem, Anahim sent a messenger down to John Ogilvy, now the constable and collector for the government at Bella Coola. Ogilvy dispatched Morris Moss, the trader, with 12 Bella Coola Indians up river. Ahan's group, meanwhile, had started down the Bella Coola River by canoe.

Moss rode into their camp and surprised Ahan before he could make any move. Thus, rather than presenting themselves voluntarily for surrender, Ahan and Lutas became immediate captives. Identified by Anahim, those who had come with Ahan and Lutas were also taken into custody.

Ahan and Lutas had with them several hundred dollars

worth of furs with which they had intended to buy their pardon.

Moss and his Bella Coolas took the captives down to the Arm, to be taken by ship to New Westminster.

Ahan made no attempt to hide the truth about his part in the attack on McDonald's pack train and his murder of McDougall. He was a chief and he would lie to save himself.

Those who had been arrested with him and Lutas were freed, but Ahan and Lutas were brought to trial in a Special Assize on July 3, 1865, in New Westminster before Henry Pering Pellew Crease.

Crease, like Begbie, was British and had practised law in England. He had become the first barrister in British Columbia, later a member of the Legislative Assembly of Vancouver Island and then Attorney-General under Seymour in B.C. He was appointed to try the two Chilcotins via a special commission from Seymour.

His coarse beard moving back and forth as he talked, Crease told the grand jury their job was to "unravel the last tangled skein"[25] of bloodshed and murder which had enveloped the Bute Inlet and Chilcotin territory the previous summer.

The entire story behind the causes of the uprising would probably never be known, he said, but the jury should realize the horror felt by the Indians for the smallpox, and their resulting fear and hatred of white men.

A true bill was returned against both Indians and they were placed on trial for the murder of McDougall. Chartres Brew acted as Queen's Prosecutor while T.L. Wood, the attorney-general for Vancouver Island, acted in defence of Ahan and Lutas.

A petty jury was empanelled and sworn and Brew opened the case for the prosecution. He reviewed the attack on the pack train and introduced a confession taken by Moss from Ahan which had been spoken in Chinook but taken in English.

Moss, Achpicermous, and Frederick Harris were called to testify. Wood put up a strong and vigorous defense, pointing out the differences in customs and values of the native Indians and the whites, attacking the evidence of Achpicermous, stating the fealty felt by Indians for their chiefs. He also questioned admissibility of the confession of Ahan, since it was placed before the jury in a language other than that which it was made.

The jury took one and a half hours to bring in a guilty

verdict. Ahan told Crease he had been persuaded to shoot McDougall by Klatassine and offered Crease many skins and presents if he would save his life. Before sentence was passed, Wood launched an attempt to have an arrest of judgement ruled on the basis of a technical deficiency in the indictments and on the English vs. Chinook question.

He claimed that a confession should be in the exact words used by the prisoner and that Chinook was a language of gestures as well as speech.

Crease ruled that the testimony of Moss, Brew, and Achpicermous as to verbal confessions made by Ahan was enough to support the verdict. He also pointed out that Wood's contention came a little too late, since Ahan had chosen to admit verbally to the court, as well, that he was guilty.

On July 4, Ahan and Lutas were sentenced to death.

Seymour chose to pardon Lutas, for "there has been enough life sacrificed already," but not too much not to execute Ahan, whose crimes were "too great for me to spare his life."[26] Seymour made those statements in a letter to Cardwell June 8, 1865, almost a month before Ahan and Lutas came to trial. He had already decided their fate.

Seymour immediately pardoned Lutas following the trial. Moss accompanied Lutas and Achpicermous across the Strait from New Westminster to Victoria on the steamer *Enterprise*, and from there by canoe to Bella Coola.

Early on the morning of July 15, 1865, Ahan was executed on gallows set up behind the New Westminster jail.

As far as Seymour was concerned, this marked the end of the whole affair, making "the assertion of the law complete over every Indian who shed the blood of the white men during the outbreak of 1864."[27]

This, of course, wasn't quite true. He was ignoring Anukatlk, who had killed McLean, and Cheddeki, who had escaped while being transported from Quesnellemouth to New Westminster. They and others who had taken part in the rebellion, including Cusshen, Yahooslas, and several more, were never apprehended.

Just what became of these people and of the families of the warring factions has not been recorded. They lived out their lives in the Chilcotin plateau and nearby mountains, spawning descendents who continue to live in the same area. There was some sporadic trouble with the few whites who still chose to settle and ranch on the plateau, but there was no more violence to compare with what had taken place. Gradually, white "civilization" invaded the Chilcotin, but today they live a comparatively primitive existence on land shrunk from hundreds of thousands of acres to a few small reserves. The rest has been split up into vast ranches; the many lakes are crowded with fishing and hunting resorts. From Williams Lake to Bella Coola, the 250 miles of road is unpaved, and the native population lives in relative isolation. Each July, the Chilcotins converge on the tiny village of Anahim, on Anahim Lake, for a wild rodeo.

The fates of the whites involved in the Chilcotin war are more clearly chronicled, many of them going on to etch their names prominently into B.C. history. Chartres Brew was transferred from New Westminster to the Cariboo as magistrate and gold commissioner, but the hard work and harsh climate took its toll on his health, and he died on May 31, 1870. He was buried near Barkerville, and Judge Begbie wrote his epitaph:

"A man imperturbable in courage and temper, endowed with a great and varied administrative capacity, a most ready wit, a most pure integrity, and a most humane heart."[28]

Cox's feud with Seymour continued, keeping him from rising up the ladder of the civil service. He was transferred about in his job as gold commissioner, retaining his independent nature till his death. He became a member of B.C.'s Legislative Council for a time, but was dismissed by Seymour in 1867 for impudence.

John Ogilvy, the man who had replaced Donald McLean as Cox's second in command on the expedition and been appointed constable at Bella Coola, was murdered by a whiskey peddler he tried to arrest on a ship there in 1865.

Thomas Elwyn, Brew's second in command, farmed for a time in the lower Fraser and rose to the position of Deputy Provincial Secretary after the union of Vancouver Island and B.C. into one colony. He died at 51, in 1888.

Judge Begbie later became Chief Justice for B.C., but he is best remembered for his part in law and order in the Cariboo during the gold rush.

Alfred Waddington, though his Bute Inlet road scheme died, never gave up his idea of a trans-continental link with Canada. Bute Inlet, of course, would be the western terminus. He pressed his idea for an east-west railroad in Ottawa and London, seeking financing and government support.

Ironically, as the idea which at first was branded premature was beginning to take hold, he caught smallpox in Ottawa and died.

The inscription on his tombstone read:

"Alfred Waddington, the original promoter of Canadian Pacific Railway, Born at Crescent House, Brompton, London, Oct. 2nd, 1801, Died at Ottawa Feb. 26th, 1872, His remains were deposited in this spot by his friends in Canada, and this stone was erected to his memory by his affectionate brother, Frederick."[29]

British Columbia did not progress as rapidly in the next few years after the suppression of the rebellion as Governor Frederick Seymour would have liked. In fact, as the production from the gold fields dwindled, the colony faced severe financial difficulties.

But he didn't have as many problems as his Vancouver Island counterpart, Governor Edward Kennedy, who was attempting to resist the continued demands for responsible government. Kennedy could not bring himself to trust the likes of Amor de Cosmos, and a widening rift appeared between the governor and the people of Vancouver Island.

The fight for responsible government was replaced for a time by calls for union of the island and mainland colonies, and, in November, 1866, union was proclaimed. Kennedy, by this time highly unpopular on the island, was recalled, and Seymour became governor of the united colony, with Victoria as the capital. And, he gave up bachelorhood for marriage.

Seymour took a great deal of pride in his ability to deal with Indian disputes, and he often went to the source of the trouble to smooth over relations between hostile tribes or mediate differences between natives and Europeans. He was, in fact, sometimes criticized for spending too much time on such matters.

Unfortunately, his willingness to devote time and energy to the B.C. Indian problem did not result in a clear or effective Indian policy. Although Seymour liked to say that his policy was one of dealing with the native tribes firmly and fairly, he did not believe there was any necessity of establishing a stated, organized Indian policy. Instead of embarking on a program such as that which had been started years before by James Douglas on Vancouver Island to obtain rights to Indian lands through purchase and treaty, Seymour met individual incidents of complaint one at a time. Instead of creating the basis for understanding and compromise between the two races, he unwittingly entrenched the foundation of hostility and injustice represented by the Chilcotin War.

In early June of 1869 Seymour visited Skidegate on the Queen Charlotte Islands to deal with a problem brought about by whiskey traders. He got things settled down, but while there he came down with dysentery.

He had not been physically strong since his tenure in the tropics before coming to New Westminster, and Seymour became very ill. However, he continued on to Bella Coola on the H.M.S. *Sparrowhawk* where there was more Indian trouble to be dealt with. He died on June 10 in Bella Coola.

Governor Seymour's greatest source of pride in regard to relations with the Indians had been his actions in the Chilcotin uprising, and perhaps it was fitting that his death should take place while he was engaged in settling an Indian dispute in the same village from which he had started five years earlier on the Chilcotin expedition.

Those expeditions, he felt, had insured that the native Indians would never again attempt to rise up in force against the white population and, indeed, they never did. Isolated incidents continued, but the supremacy of the whites over the native Indians was firmly established and unquestionable.

Seymour's pride and confidence in that fact was perhaps best summed up in one of his letters to Colonial Secretary Cardwell regarding the Chilcotin expeditions:

"That Europeans should thus run down wild Indians, and drive them to suicide or surrender in their own hunting grounds, in the fruit and fish season, appears to me, I confess, little short of marvellous."[30] ●

FOOTNOTES

ONE

1. George McDougall to John Stuart, Jan. 18, 1822.

2. R.C. Lundin Brown, *Klatassan and Other Reminiscences of Missionary Life in British Columbia*, London, 1873, p. 120. The footnoted conversation as well as much of the information on his relationship with the prisoners at Quesnellemouth is drawn from this source.

3. The exact meaning of the word 'Chilcotin' is uncertain, and is translated variously as "men of the warm water" (Chilco), "people of the young man's river" and "people of the blue water."

4. Alfred Waddington, *The Fraser Mines Vindicated, or, the History of Four Months*. Victoria, 1858.

5. Often spelled 'Homathco' in the 1800's. 'Homathko' was the other common spelling and is the one used today.

6. Distances according to Waddington's calculations, in his "On the Geography and Mountain Passes of British Columbia in connection with an Overland Route" and other writings.

7. Unsigned letter to the editor, *British Colonist*, Victoria, Oct. 3, 1862.

8. George M. Grant, *Ocean to Ocean, Sandford Fleming's Expedition through Canada in 1872*, London, 1873, p. 327.

9. Waddington to editor (May 23, 1863), *British Colonist*, June 2, 1863.

10. Modern-day name for the Memeya is Southgate River.

11. Descriptions drawn from those of Robert Brockstedt Lane, *Cultural Relations of the Chilcotin Indians of West Central British Columbia*, thesis for Doctor of Philosophy, University of Washington, Seattle, 1953, pp. 40-42, 47-48; Frederick Whymper, *Travel and Adventure in the Territory of Alaska*, New York, 1871, p. 37; R.C. Lundin Brown, *Klatsassan*, p. 4.

12. Also spelled Teloot, etc. The spelling of names of Indians involved in the Chilcotin War varies from source to source. Spellings used here are generally the most common.

13. Waddington to editor, *British Colonist*, May 28, 1863.

14. *British Colonist,* Aug. 30, 1862.

15. Waddington to editor (May 23, 1863), *British Colonist,* June 2, 1863.

16. Frederick John Saunders, " 'Homatcho,' or The Story of the Bute Inlet Expedition, and the Massacre by the Chilcoaten Indians," *Resources of British Columbia,* March-April 1885.

17. East branch is now called the Homathko River, while the west branch is now Mosley Creek.

18. Not the same one as the modern day Mt. Waddington, which is located 40 miles northwest of Bute Inlet and was renamed in this century from Mystery Mtn. or Mystery Peak.

19. Saunders, "Homatcho."

20. Deposition of Cheddeki given to Baptiste ('Battish'), 1864.

21. Brew to Seymour, May 23, 1864.

22. Quoted in Margaret A. Ormsby, *British Columbia: A History,* Vancouver, 1958, p. 224.

23. *British Colonist,* July 31, 1862.

24. *British Columbian,* New Westminster, March 7, 1863.

25. *British Colonist,* July 30, 1863.

26. Nancootlem and Anahim were, like other Indian place names, spelled in various ways by the Europeans, eg. 'Nicootlem,' 'Nancootloon,' 'Anaham,' 'Anachim.'

27. Henry Spencer Palmer, *Report of a Journey of Survey from Victoria to Fort Alexander via Bentinck Arm,* New Westminster, 1863, pp. 7-8.

28. Quoted in Cliff Kopas, *Bella Coola,* Vancouver, 1871. pp. 81-82.

29. Francis Poole, *Queen Charlotte Islands, A Narrative of Discovery and Adventure in the North Pacific,* London, 1872, p. 179.

30. Described by Lane, *Cultural Relations of the Chilcotin Indians,* p. 46.

31. William Brewster to sister, Jan. 13, 1864.

32. John G. Barnston and Ranald Macdonald to James Douglas, July 24, 1861.

33. Whymper, *Travel and Adventure,* p. 38.

TWO

1. Brewster to sister, Jan. 13, 1864.

2. Whymper, *Travel and Adventure,* p. 37.

3. Whymper, memorandum to *British Colonist,* May 9, 1864.

4. Whymper, *Travel and Adventure,* p. 38.

5. Cheddeki's deposition.

6. Based on Cheddeki's account. Other conversations involving Cheddeki which are recounted here are also based on his account of the deposition.

7. The white man referred to may have been Alex McDonald or his partner William Manning.

8. Whymper, *Travel and Adventure,* p. 38.

9. Lundin Brown, *Klatsassan,* p. 98.

10. *Ibid.,* p. 8.

11. Whymper, *Travel and Adventure,* p. 39.

12. Whymper, memorandum to *British Colonist,* May 9, 1864.

13. Whymper, *Travel and Adventure,* p. 42.

14. *Ibid.,* p. 42.

15. *Ibid.*, p. 45.

16. *Ibid.*, p. 46.

17. It is not known what became of Whymper's sketch of Tellot. The Provincial Archives of B.C. have several of Whymper's sketches, but not this one.

18. Account based on Squinteye's testimony, in "Trial Notes of Sir Matthew Baillie Begbie, Chief Justice of British Columbia," Sept. 28-29, 1864.

19. *British Colonist*, May 12, 1864.

20. *Inland Sentinel*, Kamloops, July 22, 1880.

21. According to Cheddeki, who wasn't involved in the attack on Brewster's camp but was told the details by participants.

22. Conversation related by Qwhittie, in "Begbie's Trial Notes."

23. *British Colonist*, May 12, 1864.

24. *Victoria Chronicle*, Victoria, May 6, 1864.

25. *Ibid.*, May 11, 1864.

26. *British Colonist*, May 12, 1864.

27. Frederick Seymour to Duke of Carlisle, May 20, 1864. 54.

28. Seymour to Edward Cardwell, March 21, 1865.

29. Quoted in Seymour to Arthur Edward Kennedy, June 4, 1864.

30. A.N. Birch to W.C. Cox, May 14, 1864.

31. *British Columbian*, May 17, 1864.

32. Seymour to Kennedy, June 4, 1864.

33. Waddington to Colonial Secretary, V.I., Oct. 8, 1864.

34. Based on Waddington's account, *Ibid.*

35. Brew's Report, mss, n.d., Provincial Archives of B.C.

36. Seymour to Duke of Carlisle, May 20, 1864.

37. Seymour to Duke of Carlisle, May 20, 1864. (Second letter of same day.)

38. Brew's Report.

39. E.A. Atkins, untitled mss., n.d., PABC.

40. Brew's Report.

41. Proceedings at inquest held at Bute Inlet, May 23, 1864 before C. Brew, JP and T. Elwyn, JP, verdict signed by Leslie Jones, Foreman, for self and fellow Jurors.

42. Chartres Brew to Seymour, May 23, 1864.

43. Nancy's testimony, Sept. 29, 1864, in Begbie's Trial Notes.

44. *Ibid.*

45. Quoted in Ilsedocknell's testimony, Sept. 29, 1864, in "Begbie's Trial Notes."

THREE

1. Seymour to Cardwell, Aug. 31, 1864.

2. *British Colonist*, May 30, 1864.

3. *Ibid.*

4. Seymour to Cardwell, Aug., 31, 1864.

5. Seymour to Cardwell, Sept. 23, 1864.

6. Brew to Seymour, May 23, 1864.

7. *British Columbian*, June 18, 1864.

8. *Ibid.*, June 8, 1864.

9. Waddington to editor (June 12, 1864), *British Colonist,* June 13, 1864.

10. Waddington to editor (May 28, 1864), *Chronicle*, May 29, 1864.

11. *Chronicle*, May 29, 1864.

12. Whymper, *Travel and Adventure*, pp. 56-57.

13. *Chronicle*, May 12, 1864.

14. *British Colonist*, May 12, 1864.

15. *Ibid.*, May 23, 1864.

16. *Ibid.*, June 1, 1864.

17. *British Columbian*, May 14, 1864.

18. *Ibid.*, May 18, 1864.

19. *Ibid.*, May 21, 1864.

20. Waddington to Colonial Secretary, May 28, 1864.

21. Brew's Report.

22. Seymour to Cardwell, July 7, 1865.

23. Cox to Birch, May 29, 1864.

24. Remains of these earthworks, through weather-worn and overgrown, can still be seen today. They are located only a few yards from the main Chilcotin road to Anahim Lake.

25. Conversation according to Achpicermous' testimony, Begbie's Trial Notes, Sept. 29, 1864.

26. According to testimony of Frederick Harrison, "Notes on Special Assiz holden at New Westminster", 3 & 4 July, 1865, before Henry P. Pellew Crease, Judge.

27. The Chilcotins had been believed by the whites to lack skill with firearms. In the May 12, 1864 edition of the *British Colonist,* a "former Bentinck Arm packer" described them as "cowardly and treacherous" and as well-armed but poor marksmen.

28. *British Colonist,* Oct. 14, 1864.

29. The story was rather typical of the many erroneous reports printed in the newspapers of the day, which in their apparent desire to "scoop" each other and to emphasize their viewpoints, published virtually every rumor they heard. It often took several editions for an event connected to the rebellion to be refined into a semblance of truth.

30. *British Colonist,* June 1, 1864.

31. *Ibid.*, June 3, 1864.

32. *Ibid.*, June 2, 1864.

33. Full account of this meeting was carried in *British Colonist,* June 2, 1864 and in its weekly edition June 7, 1864.

34. Account of this meeting based on that given by *British Colonist,* June 3, 1864.

35. Bute Inlet Massacre: Programs, Minutes & Volunteer roll of Public, mss. PABC.

36. Seymour to Kennedy, June 4, 1864.

37. Palmer, *Report of Journey of Survey*, p. 7.

38. *British Colonist,* June 28, 1864.

FOUR

1. Quoted in Mel Rothenburger, *We've Killed Johnny Ussher!,*

Vancouver, 1973, p. 7. p. 10.

2. *Ibid.*, p. 10.

3. The incident involving Tlhelh et al is told by A.D. Morice, *History of the Northern Interior of British Columbia,* Toronto, 1905.

4. *British Colonist,* March 25, 1865.

5. Seymour to Duke of Carlisle, May 20, 1864.

6. Cox to Birch, June 19, 1864.

7. *Ibid.*

8. *Ibid.*

9. *Ibid.*

10. *British Colonist,* June 6, 1864.

11. Incident and conversations according to E.A. Atkins, mss.

12. *Ibid.*

13. *British Colonist,* June 28, 1864 (report written June 20, 1864).

14. Palmer, *Report of Journey of Survey,* p. 9.

15. *British Colonist,* July 15, 1864.

16. Mt. Deluge is now called Nusatsum Mtn.

17. *British Colonist,* Oct. 14, 1864.

18. Seymour to Cardwell, Sept. 9, 1864.

19. *British Colonist,* Oct. 14, 1864.

20. Atkins, mss.

21. Palmer, *Report of Journey of Survey,* p. 18.

22. Seymour to Cardwell, Sept. 9, 1864.

23. *Ibid.*

24. Based on account in 'Diary of a Volunteer,' *British Colonist,* Oct. 15, 1864.

25. Lundin Brown, *Klatsassan,* p. 72.

26. Seymour to Cardwell, Sept. 9, 1864.

27. *Ibid.*

28. *Ibid.*

29. Cardwell to Seymour, July 16, 1864.

30. Seymour to Cardwell, Oct. 4, 1864.

31. Cardwell to Seymour, Oct. 19, 1864.

32. Conversation recounted by Seymour in letter to Cardwell, Sept. 9, 1864.

33. *Ibid.*

34. *British Colonist,* Oct. 17, 1864.

35. Seymour to Cardwell, Sept. 9, 1864.

36. Cox's testimony, "Begbie's Trial Notes," Sept. 29, 1864.

37. *Ibid.*

38. Recounted by William Byers in *British Columbian,* Sept. 7, 1864.

FIVE

1. Lundin Brown, *Klatsassan,* p. 42.

2. Conversation according to Cox in statement taken Aug. 15, 1864 and published in the *British Columbian,* Aug. 14, 1864. It seems unlikely that Klatassine actually referred to his own men as 'murderers' since he regarded the conflict as war.

3. According to William Byers, a former corporal in the Royal Engineers

who was with Brew's expedition and heard the account of the surrender second hand. In *British Columbian*, Sept. 7, 1864.

4. *Ibid.* The difference of meaning between Big Chief and Great Chief is important to note in that it helped lead to Klatassine's surrender. When Cox stated the Indian would be allowed to talk to the Big Chief, he meant Begbie, while Klatassine took it to mean Great Chief Seymour. Whether or not Cox intended the misunderstanding is open to speculation.

5. According to Byers in *British Columbian*, Sept. 7, 1864: "All with the exception of Tellot complied (in laying down arms), but he grasped his musket by the muzzle (sic) and smashed it to atoms against a tree, and drawing his knife dashed it to the ground and coolly folding his arms across his breast invited them to shoot him, remarking, with scorn depicted on his countenance, that the 'King George men were great liars'." The part about smashing the rifle and throwing the knife away was denied by others in the party. J.D.B. Ogilvy, in an undated letter published in the *British Columbian* Sept. 17, 1864, called Byers' account of Tellot's actions "simply untrue."

6. According to Begbie in letter to Seymour, Sept. 30, 1864.

7. *British Colonist*, Sept. 7, 1864.

8. Cox's testimony in "Begbie's Trial Notes", Sept. 29, 1864.

9. Brew and Waddington disagreed violently on the question of Anahim's involvement and guilt in the uprising. Waddington claimed that "this rascal (Anahim) was strongly suspected . . . of having taken an active part in the murders, and that with the greatest reason; and he was still more strongly suspected of having taken an indirect part in them. He certainly did nothing, as Chief of his tribe, to hinder them, though the murder of Mcdonald's party took place in his territory, and he undoubtedly had the greatest share of the spoils . . ." [letter to editor (Oct. 26, 1864), *Weekly British Colonist*, Nov. 1, 1864]. Brew stated that "I know it was alleged that Anaheim got a large share of the property of which Alick McDonald and his party were robbed. I cannot say that such is not the case . . . I am satisfied that Anaheim knew nothing of the plunder and murder of Mr. Waddington's men till several days afterwards, and all the Indians I have examined agree in saying that if Anaheim had been at home Alick McDonald would not have been attacked." (Brew's Report.)

10. In "Begbie's Trial Notes", Sept. 29, 1864.

11. *Ibid.*

12. *Ibid.*

13. Begbie to Seymour, Sept. 30, 1864.

14. Seymour to Cardwell, Nov. 23, 1864.

15. Begbie to Seymour, Sept. 30, 1864.

16. *Ibid.*

17. Lundin Brown, *Klatsassan*, p. 97. Lundin Brown's later comments and conversations with the prisoners are also taken from this source.

18. Seymour to Cardwell, Sept. 9, 1864.

19. Cardwell to Seymour, Oct. 29, 1864.

20. *Ibid.*

21. Brew's Report.

22. *Ibid.*

23. According to Edgar George Shankel in his University of Washington Ph.D. thesis (1945), the cost of the expedition "would have been sufficient to

extinguish the Indian title to all the land in British Columbia" (p 74). In other words, had the colony not been trying to save money by not paying the Indians for the land being taken by the Whites, it could have resolved the situation justly and avoided bloodshed much more cheaply than it ended up.

24. *British Columbian*, December 14, 1864.
25. *British Columbian*, July 4, 1865.
26. Seymour to Cardwell, June 8, 1865.
27. *Ibid*.
28. Chartres Brew File, PABC.
29. *Victoria Daily Times*, Dec. 7, 1926.
30. Seymour to Cardwell, Sept. 9, 1864.

SELECT BIBLIOGRAPHY

ATKINS, E.A. "History of the Chilcotin War," transcript Provincial Archives of British Columbia, n.d.

BANCROFT, HUBERT HOWE (et al). *History of British Columbia 1792-1887 (The Works of Hubert Howe Bancroft)*, Vol. XXXII, History Company, San Francisco, 1887.

BEGBIE, MATTHEW BAILLIE. "Notes on Proceedings, British Columbia Supreme Court," Quesnellemouth, Sept. 28-29, 1864.

BREW, CHARTRES. "Remarks on Mr. Waddington's Petition," mss PABC, 1864.

BRITISH COLUMBIA, GOVERNOR. "Despatches from Governor Seymour and Administrator Birch to the Colonial Office, April 26, 1864 to Dec. 20, 1865," Can. Archives, photostat UBC Special Collections.

BROCK, PATRICK WILLET. "Dossiers of Ships of the Royal Navy who Served in the Pacific Station," mss papers, PABC.

"Bute Inlet Massacre: Programs, Minutes and Volunteer Roll of Public," mss, PABC, 1864.

"Chartres Brew." File, PABC.

CREASE, HENRY P. PELLEW. "Notes on Special Assize holden at New Westminster on 3 & 4 July, 1864."

Deposition of Achpicermous ('Alpicmush'), taken by Morris Moss, Oct. 8, 1864.

Deposition of Cheddeki, taken by Baptiste ('Battish'), 1864.

DUFF, WILSON. "The impact of the White Man." *The Indian History of British Columbia* (Vol. 1), Anthropology in British Columbia Memoir No. 5, Victoria, 1964.

DUFF, WILSON. *Thoughts on the Nootka Canoe*, Queen's Printer, 1965.

FAWCETT, EDGAR. "The Bute Inlet Massacre — The Adventures of a Surveyer's Rodman in the Wilds of British Columbia," typescript PABC, n.d.

FERRAND, LIVINGSTON. "The Chilcotin." *Reports on the North-Western Tribes, 1892-98*, British Association for the Advancement of Science (12th and Final Report), London, Bristol Meeting, 1898.

GOUGH, BARRY M. *The Royal Navy and the Northwest Coast of North America, 1810-1914: A Study of British Maritime Ascendancy*, University of British Columbia Press, Vancouver, 1971.

GRANT, GEORGE M. *Ocean to Ocean, Sandford Fleming's Expedition through Canada in 1872*, Sampson, Low, Marston, Low & Searle, London, 1873.

HAWTHORN, H.B.: BELSHAW, C.S.: JAMIESON, S.M. *The Indians of British Columbia,* University of Toronto Press, 1958.

"Henry Spencer Palmer." File, PABC.

HEWLETT, EDWARD SLEIGH. "The Chilcotin Uprising: A Study of Indian-White Relations in Nineteenth Century British Columbia," Thesis for Master of Arts Degree, University of British Columbia, 1972.

HOWAY, F.W. "The Bute Inlet Massacre and the Chilcotin War 1864-1866," *British Columbia from Earliest Times to Present* (Vol. II), S.J. Clarke Publishing Company, Vancouver, Winnipeg, Montreal, Chicago, 1914.

HOWAY, F.W. *The Work of the Royal Engineers in British Columbia 1858 to 1865,* Victoria, 1910.

KOPAS, CLIFF. *Bella Coola,* Mitchell Press Ltd., Vancouver, 1970.

LANE, ROBERT BROCKSTEDT. "Cultural Relations of the Chilcotin Indians of West Central British Columbia," Ph.D. thesis, University of Washington, 1953.

LUNDIN BROWN, R.C. *Klatsassan and other Reminiscences of Missionary Life in British Columbia,* Published under the direction of the Tract Committee, Society for Promoting Christian Knowledge, London, 1873.

McFEAT, TOM, ed. *Indians of the North Pacific Coast.* McClelland & Stewart Ltd., Toronto, 1969.

McKELVIE, B. *Tales of Conflict.* The *Vancouver Province,* Vancouver, 1949.

MATHER, BARRY; McDONALD, MARGARET. *New Westminster, The Royal City,* J.M. Dent & Sons (Canada) Ltd. and The Corporation of the City of New Westminster, 1958.

MORICE, ADRIAN GABRIEL. *History of the Northern Interior of British Columbia,* William Briggs, Toronto, 1905 (3rd edition).

ORMSBY, MARGARET A. *British Columbia: A History,* The MacMillan Company of Canada Ltd., Vancouver, 1958.

PALMER, HENRY SPENCER. *Report of a Journey of Survey from Victoria to Fort Alexander via Bentinck Arm,* Royal Engineer Press, New Westminster, 1863.

PARKER, ANN FITZGEORGE. *Gold Rush Justice,* Burns & MacEachern Ltd., 1968.

PETHICK, DEREK. *Victoria: The Fort,* Mitchell Press Ltd., Vancouver, 1968.

PETTIT, SYDNEY G. "Matthew Baillie Begbie." *British Columbia Historical Quarterly,* January, April, July and October, 1947.

POOLE, C.E. *Queen Charlotte Islands, A Narrative of Discovery and Adventure in the North Pacific,* (first published by Hurst and Blackett, Publishers, London, 1872), J.J. Douglas Ltd., West Vancouver, 1972.

"Proceedings at an Inquest held at Murder Camp before C. Brew and T. Elwyn on the 25th of May, 1864 on the bodies of William Brewster, John Clark and Jem Gawley," typescript UBC Special Collections.

Prospectus of the Bentinck Arm and Fraser River Road Company Ltd., Victoria, V.I., 1862.

REID, R.L. "Alfred Waddington," *Proceedings and Transactions,* The Royal Society of Canada, Ottawa, 1932.

REID, R.L. "Pathfinders and Road-builders," *Journal of the Dept. of Public*

Works, Victoria, October, 1938.

ROBINSON, LEIGH BURPEE. *Esquimalt, 'Place of Shoaling Water'*, Quality Press, Victoria, 1947.

ROTHENBURGER, MEL. *We've Killed Johnny Ussher!*, Mitchell Press Ltd., Vancouver, 1973.

SAUNDERS, FREDERICK JOHN. "Homatcho, or The Story of the Bute Inlet Expedition and the Massacre by the Chilcoaten Indians," *Resources of British Columbia* III, No. 1 (March 1885) and No. 2 (April 1885).

SEYMOUR, FREDERICK. "Speech of His Excellency the Governor, At The Opening of The Legislative Council, 12th December, 1864," *The British Columbian*, Dec. 14, 1864.

SHANKEL, GEORGE EDGAR. "The Development of Indian Policy in British Columbia." Ph.D. thesis, University of Washington, 1945.

SHANNON, WILLIAM. "Chilcotin Massacre of 1863," typescript, PABC, n.d.

TEIT, JAMES ALEXANDER. "Appendix: Notes on the Chilcotin Indians," in *The Shuswap*, Edited by Franz Boaz, Memoirs of the American Museum of Natural History, Vol. IV, Part III (Reprint from Vol. II, Part VII of the Jessup North Pacific Expedition), E.J. Brill Ltd., 1909.

The Royal Engineers. A Record of Their Part in the Building of British Columbia, Published by Royal Engineers' Old Comrades Association, Vancouver, 1939.

"The Waddington Massacre," *Inland Sentinel*, Yale, July 22, 1880.

"Thomas Elwyn." File, PABC.

VANCOUVER ISLAND. "Extracts from the depositions respecting the Bute Inlet Massacre made before J.L. Wood, Esq., Acting Stipendiary Magistrate for Vancouver Island, which may lead to the identification of the murderers," *Government Gazette*, June 25, 1864.

WADDINGTON, ALFRED. "On the Geography and Mountain Passes of British Columbia in connection with an Overland Route," *Journal of Royal Geographic Society*, 1868.

WADDINGTON, ALFRED. *Overland Communication by Land and Water Through British North America*, Higgins, Long & Co., Victoria, V.I., 1867.

WADDINGTON, ALFRED. *Sketch of the Proposed Line of Overland Railroad through British North America*, Ottawa, 1876.

WADDINGTON, ALFRED. *The Fraser Mines Vindicated, or, the History of Four Months*. Victoria, 1858.

WADDINGTON, JOHN. *Who's Who in the Family of Waddington*, Wada Ltd., London, 1934.

WATTS, ALFRED, Q.C. "The Honorable Sir Matthew Baillie Begbie," *The Advocate*, Sept.-Oct. 1966.

WOOLACOTT, ARTHUR P. *Mackenzie and His Voyageurs*. J.M. Dent & Sons Ltd., London & Toronto, 1927.

WHYMPER, FREDERICK. "The Inlet," memorandum in *The Colonist*, May 9, 1864.

WHYMPER, FREDERICK. *Travel and Adventure in the Territory of Alaska*, Harper & Brothers, New York, 1871.

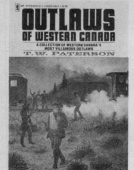